BEAMAN'S COMMENTARY
ON THE
GOSPEL OF JOHN

ROY OLIVER BEAMAN, ThD
EDITED AND REVISED BY MICHAEL R. SPRADLIN, PhD

[handwritten inscription: To Mary My dear friend in Christ, Michael Spradlin John 3:16]

innovo
PUBLISHING

Published by Innovo Publishing, LLC
www.innovopublishing.com
1-888-546-2111

Providing Full-Service Publishing Services for Christian Authors, Artists & Ministries:
Books, eBooks, Audiobooks, Music & Film

BEAMAN'S COMMENTARY ON THE GOSPEL OF JOHN

Scripture taken from the NEW AMERICAN STANDARD BIBLE®, Copyright © 1960,1962,1963,1968,1971,1 972,1973,1975,1977,1995 by The Lockman Foundation. Used by permission.

American Standard Version, Thomas Nelson and Sons, 1901. Public domain.

King James Version. Public domain.

THE HOLY BIBLE, NEW INTERNATIONAL VERSION®, NIV® Copyright © 1973, 1978, 1984, 2011 by Biblica, Inc.® Used by permission. All rights reserved worldwide.

New English Bible. Oxford University Press, 1970.

Charles B. Williams, The New Testament: A Translation in the Language of the People. Boston: Bruce Humphries Inc., 1937. Slightly revised in 1950 (Chicago: Moody Press).

The Revised Standard Version of the Bible, copyright © 1946, 1952, and 1971 the Division of Christian Education of the National Council of the Churches of Christ in the United States of America. Used by permission. All rights reserved.

In order to preserve the author's voice, the editing process has allowed deviations from *Chicago Manual of Style*.

Library of Congress Control Number: 2017955866
ISBN: 978-1-61314-410-7

Cover Design & Interior Layout: Innovo Publishing, LLC

Printed in the United States of America
U.S. Printing History
First Edition: 1935
Fourth Edition: 1977
Fifth Edition (Revised): December 2017

By Roy Oliver Beaman, ThD
Professor Emeritus of Mid-America Baptist Theological Seminary
Professor Emeritus of the New Orleans Baptist Theological Seminary

Edited and Revised by Michael R. Spradlin, PhD
President of Mid-America Baptist Theological Seminary

Roy Oliver Beaman, ThD (1904-1996)

Professor Emeritus of Mid-America Baptist Theological Seminary
Professor Emeritus of the New Orleans Baptist Theological Seminary

ENDORSEMENTS

"The linguistic and exegetical skills of Dr. Roy Beaman are legendary at Mid-America Baptist Theological Seminary. Through meticulously editing and updating Dr. Beaman's commentary on the Gospel of John, Dr. Michael Spradlin shows us why. Dr. Spradlin is to be commended for giving us a volume that is crisply written, well organized, exegetically insightful, personally edifying, and even quite quotable. Pastors and church leaders will refer to it again and again."

—Christopher W. Morgan, Dean and Professor of Theology, California Baptist University, and author/editor of sixteen books, including *The Love of God*, *The Glory of God*, the *Systematic Theology Study Bible* (ESV), the *Theology in Community* series, and the *Theology for the People of God* series.

"I remember well the several years of classes and seminars spent under the tutelage of Dr. Roy Beaman. Throughout my graduate and doctoral studies, my classmates and I stood in awe of the kind and gracious gentleman before us. His scholarship was undeniable; his love for his Savior supreme; his love for God's Word flowed without restraint. He was kind enough to grant a few of us permission to look through some of his many file cabinets overflowing with his writings. Those of us who knew him best were most amazed that he rarely published. This volume is long overdue. Many thanks to my friend and president, Dr. Spradlin, for its arrival."

—David Shackelford, PhD, Chairman and Professor of New Testament and Greek, Mid-America Baptist Theological Seminary

"Beaman's commentary is a breath of fresh air for anyone who loves God's Word and John in particular. Here we have a rare thing: a commentary on text instead of a commentary on the commentaries of John. A scholar's mind, a pastor's clarity, and a disciple's heart shine through in this exposition. Professors, pastors, and the average person in the pew will benefit from reading Dr. Beaman's commentary."

—Wayne Cornett, PhD, Assistant Professor of New Testament and Greek, Mid-America Baptist Theological Seminary

"Dr. Roy Beaman left a strong legacy of spiritual richness and scholastic rigor that still resonates through the ranks of Mid-America Baptist Theological Seminary. Although I had not the privilege to meet Dr. Beaman or sit under his tutelage, this book allows me and others to glean from his historical, exegetical, and devotional insights from the Gospel of John. This work will provide Bible students with a treasured resource on the fourth Gospel from a scholar uniquely gifted to investigate the text deeply and exposit it accessibly. I am so grateful that Dr. Michael Spradlin undertook this project to publish a very unique commentary on the glorious Gospel of John."

—**Kenneth R. Lewis, PhD, Director of Information Services, Assistant Professor of Biblical Studies, Mid-America Baptist Theological Seminary**

CONTENTS

SECTION I: EDITOR'S PREFACE, BACKGROUND & COMMENTARY

SECTION II: BEAMAN'S COMMENTARY ON THE GOSPEL OF JOHN: 1935–1977

PART I: PROLOGUE

4: THE RESULTS IN BOTH FAITH AND UNBELIEF: CONCLUSION, CHAPTER 12

PART III: HIS SELF-REVELATION TO HIS DISCIPLES, CHAPTERS 13-17

SECTION I:
EDITOR'S PREFACE, BACKGROUND & COMMENTARY

EDITOR'S PREFACE

Upon discovery of the unpublished manuscript of Roy Beaman's *Commentary on the Gospel of John*, I was reminded of the biblical depth and brilliance of my former Greek and theology professor. I remembered that Dr. Beaman rarely published his materials because of his passion for perfection and his sense that the job was never done. I have edited the document for clarity but have tried to let the voice of Dr. Beaman shine through. Some technical references are left unexplained in the text, but the reader should be able to understand them in the context of the passage.

As a practical aid in using this commentary, Dr. Beaman included several items. For the pastor, he added sections entitled "Sermon Suggestions." The intent of this is to guide someone in initiating their sermon preparation. Beaman also ended his major sections with a list of questions that could be used when teaching the material in a church or classroom setting.

At various times, Dr. Beaman refers to his own translation of the Greek New Testament. Alas, no copy of this exists. Therefore, the King James Version (KJV) of the Gospel of John has been supplied to aid the reader. Dr. Beaman was also fond of—and frequently cited—the 1901 American Standard Version (ASV) for its literal approach to translation. This version is no longer in print but is sometimes included in various software packages as an alternative translation for study. Dr. Beaman also had his own translation of John (BV for Beaman Version). He makes reference to his translation, but no copy of it exists.

No bibliography was left as a part of this manuscript on the Gospel of John. Dr. Beaman was meticulous in citing sources and has left a number of authors' names and a few references to other works. The bibliography has been recreated, but since the development of the work spanned forty years, it is impossible to know which edition was cited. If any improper citations are present, they are unintentional and due to the lack of a full manuscript with notes at our disposal. Since the author stated that the work spanned revisions from 1935 until 1977, it can be assumed that no works after this time period were used.

A very special thank you goes to the wonderful members of the staff of Mid-America Baptist Theological Seminary who lovingly restored the manuscript: Betty Bailey, Christy Cole, Deanna Coscia, Teri DeGeorge,

Doris Foster, Karen Nelson, Glenda Norville, Hayden Perry, Cathy Rech, Dana Sneed, Kelsey Verdell, and Carol Wilson.

I could not have completed the work without the yeoman's service of our editor, Rachael Carrington. Rachael organized the material and helped to locate numerous obscure references. Others who made significant contributions were Terrence Brown, director of the library at Mid-America Baptist Theological Seminary, Maria Wooten, executive assistant to the president, and Aaron Ducksworth, research assistant.

—*Michael R. Spradlin*

A Biographical Sketch of Roy Beaman, ThD

In February 1942, when Pastor Roy Beaman registered for the draft after the outbreak of World War II, he stood five feet, five inches tall and weighed 145 pounds. Few knew at that time the great shadow he would cast as a New Testament scholar (for over fifty years). Living in Tampa, Florida, at the time with his wife, Mary, he was pastoring Calvary Baptist Church.

The Beaman family had long resided in the Murray, Kentucky, area since the early 1800s. Of his people, Roy Beaman was reputed to have written the following about his grandmother in the 1930s:

Mary Russell Beaman
(1834–1897)

> *Mary Russell Beaman, Charles's wife, was at first a Presbyterian. Her people came probably from the Carolinas, to near Nashville, more nearly Columbia. Around 1850, probably earlier, they moved near Hickory, Graves County, Kentucky. There are several Russell burials in the cemetery at [the] Baptist Church. These data I got from Lillian on one of my trips to Paducah around the time I married in 1933. Her memory was particularly sharp, nearly comparable to mother's on general data, not dates.*
>
> *I think that grandmother had sandy hair. Uncle Albert had rather red hair, and father's hair was more sandy when he was younger. Lillian and Matt Russell had rather red hair[,] though their brother's hair was less red.*
>
> *Father and mother moved back to live with grandmother between the births of Jesse and Letie (I think, though Jesse may have been born at the Beaman place). She took typhoid about 1896 and died after lingering several days.*

Charles and Mary's sixth child was a son they named Theophilus Alonzo Beaman, born in 1866. Sometimes called "Alonzo," he grew up and married Theodocia "Docie" Barton Beaman, and they carried on the family tradition of farming.

Alonzo and Docie added a son to their family, Roy Oliver Beaman, born January 25, 1904, in Murray, Kentucky. The sixth child born into his family, Roy Beaman grew up on a farm but must have surrendered to the Lord's call on his life at an early age.

Roy was listed as a Bible teacher in the 1930 census when he was twenty-six years old because he had begun a decade-long association with West Kentucky Bible School (WKBS) in Murray, Kentucky. A 1936 edition of *The WKBS Voice* lists Roy Beaman as president of the school and editor of *The Voice*. In addition to these

Theophilus Alonzo Beaman (1866–1938)

duties, he taught Greek, Bible, Spanish, and Hebrew. Showing his passion for linguistics from an early age, Beaman also tutored in the languages of Sanskrit and Latin. He married Mary Thompson in 1933. They had one daughter, Mary Anne (Beaman) Gwin.

Ending his association with WKBS, Beaman moved to Florida to pastor Calvary Baptist Church in Tampa. He also attended Florida Southern College, graduating from there in 1942. He then

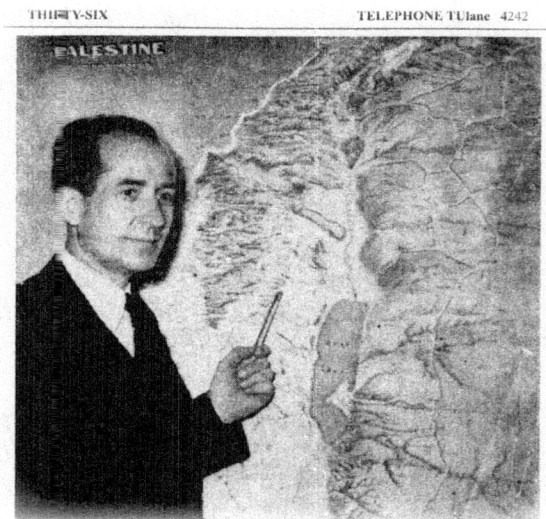

Roy Beaman, 1951

moved to Louisville, Kentucky, to study at Southern Baptist Theological Seminary. Beaman earned his master of theology in 1944 and his doctor of theology degree in 1946. He did post-doctoral study at both the University of Louisville and the University of London.

Beaman taught at Central College in Arkansas from 1946–47 and then joined the faculty of New Orleans Baptist Theological Seminary in New Orleans, Louisiana, in 1947. After decades as a faculty member in New Orleans, he joined the faculty of a new seminary started in 1972, Mid-America Baptist Theological Seminary. His many years of personal and professional study made him proficient in thirty-eight languages other than English.

Beaman preached, taught, and wrote voluminously during a long and impressive ministry. He was gathered to his people on August 4, 1996.

FOREWORD

Dr. Roy O. Beaman was a most unusual man. My own fellowship with him began in 1949, when I began my studies at New Orleans Baptist Theological Seminary (NOBTS). I studied beginner's Greek, archaeology, and Latin with him. I also taught with him for eight years at NOBTS. It seemed that he knew everything! He was gifted with a photographic memory and a deep hunger for knowledge. One could hardly enter his office because of the stacks of books, periodicals, and clipped articles. The amazing thing was that he seemed to know what was there and where it was located. One day in his office, I asked a question. He said, "Gray, I have an article on that subject from the *New York Times* from September 27, 1925." He walked to a chair, on which was a large stack of books, periodicals, and various articles. He reached into the stacks and pulled out that article.

Dr. Beaman worked to some extent in thirty-nine languages and was proficient in German and a master of Greek, Hebrew, and Latin. Another amazing thing is that he was humble, approachable, and spoke so that small children loved him and could talk with him. My son and eldest granddaughter were especially blessed by association with him.

When we began Mid-America Baptist Theological Seminary in 1972, I asked Dr. Beaman to come and teach with us. In addition to serving as a Baptist pastor, Dr. Beaman taught for twenty years in a Bible school in Kentucky and taught at New Orleans Baptist Theological Seminary for twenty years. Though he was sixty-eight years of age in 1972, he came to teach with us and taught another twenty years! Much of his teaching occurred around the coffee tables.

As you read and study this commentary on the Gospel of John, you will be blessed. Dr. Beaman's knowledge of the original language and his ability to communicate are unusual. You will be encouraged to continue studies in the Word of God, you will have a good knowledge of the Gospel of John, and you will have a deeper knowledge of God, of His blessed Son, and of what we should be. I commend this book to you. Enjoy!

—*B. Gray Allison, President Emeritus, MABTS*

SECTION II:
BEAMAN'S COMMENTARY ON THE GOSPEL OF JOHN:
1935–1977

Author's Preface

July 13, 1977

I wrote this study first as outlines for Sunday school teachers in 1935. I next enlarged it as a series of popular evening lectures to a group of high school and college students, several ministers, and the general working class of Christian men and women. Slightly revised, it next became the basis of Sunday school lessons; then guidance sheets for a class of young ladies in college in 1946; and then (almost without revision) the exposition for an intensive exegesis for a seminary class without knowledge of Greek in 1948 or 1949.

In the present (1977) revision, only minor changes were made on chapters one through twelve. More additions reached intensity on chapter seventeen. Even yet, certain paragraphs of the Gospel have been treated more thoroughly than others. In specific areas, more commentaries have been consulted than in others. The stencils have been cut by more than one typist and reveal certain irregularities. These I regret.

Small allotments were prepared until 1948. This mimeographing exceeded 200. March 1952 saw a reissuance of 1,000 copies, half of which sold in one year.

This June–July 1977 revision adds an introduction for beginners, for seasoned researchers, and for the specialist. I have wanted the bibliographical references to help guide all to the many rich works on this inimitable Gospel.

When it seemed best to me, I have translated the Greek. Somewhat do I wish that I had inserted in full my translation of John, made quite some years ago.

Incidentally, I may say that I have longed for time to prepare a thorough work on John, embodying the critical, the archaeological, the expository, the homiletical, and the devotional. A work in progress, this teaching of John in July 1977 has advanced the work appreciably.

I doubt that any of you are familiar enough with the Scriptures not to need to read each verse as it is mentioned in the notes. How can you get the discussion if you do not know the passage being treated? Fix in mind the analysis of the Gospel before seriously reading these notes.

Let me adapt the 1871 conclusion of Schaff (1889) after he enlarged Lange's (1870) work: "Our best efforts to interpret the unfathomable depths of the words of the eternal Son of God, as recorded by His favorite disciple, are but the stammerings of a child."[1]

Roy Beaman

---

1. Special introduction to the *Gospel of John* in Lange, p. xiv.

BEAMAN'S COMMENTARY NOTES

As later manuscripts and earlier writers show, the word *euangelion* (good news, evangel, gospel) was implied. It assumed or developed a technical reference to a book purporting to tell the "good news" of redemption through the Lord Jesus Christ.

The question of authorship inheres in the shortest titles. Since one needs to judge the question of authorship only in the light of full data, I treat this point later. Those who reject John the apostle as the author must, if objective, survey all relative data before forming an opinion.

The number of the Greek manuscripts of John was never few enough to excite suspicion. Then and now the number exceeds that of classical writings.

As to the criterion of age, recent discoveries of manuscripts of John have been spectacular and assuring. What can we say of textual data behind the Geek manuscripts named *Codex Vaticanus* and the *Codex Sinaiticus* of the fourth century? The Beatty papyrus of the Gospels and Acts (identified as "p45"), dating to the third century and purchased in 1930–31, pushed our evidence back a century. Manuscript p52 of John 18, dated to about 135 AD and identified by C.H. Roberts in 1935, is our oldest known New Testament manuscript. It goes back to approximately a generation after the death of John. Scholars have claimed that about such a period would be required for the Gospel of John to have gotten from Ephesus in Asia Minor into a scriptorium in Egypt. This can be difficult to assess, for the manuscript was not in a private hand. Manuscripts p66 and p75 of the Bodmer collection at Geneva, Switzerland, significantly date around 200 AD., several scholars preferring 175 AD.

As to the condition of the text, none is better attested than John. Some of us urged that p45 and p52 allowed no loose copying in the second and third centuries. Quite a few argued that the wildest copying came then. When p66 and p75 were put to rigid examination, all saw that these demonstrate faithful, not careless, copying. All along, I urged that as a rule, each copyist copied according to his ability.

He who persists to claim large variants or displacements or interpolations in John has not kept abreast of discoveries. Nothing disturbing has come to light. Very much of an assuring nature is available to all who wish to learn!

Burney of Oxford, in *The Aramaic Origin of the Fourth Gospel*, 1922, and scholar C.C. Torrey sought to show that John was written in Aramaic. Just before his death, Torrey admitted that 95 percent of the scholars differed from him. He subjectively clung to his view.

The reasons on the other side have multiplied. Discoveries of the Koine dialect of Greek have been shown to illustrate what were claimed as Aramaisms and Hebraisms. That is, they were current in ordinary Greek.

The present swing away from Gustav Adolf Deissmann (1866–1937), James Hope Moulton (1863–1917), Archibald Thomas Robertson (1863–1934), and others is subjective. Scant data no longer leaves us in doubt. Yohanan Aharoni (1919- 1976) of the museum in the new city told me in 1957 that discoveries in Israel since 1948 left no doubt about the use of Greek in first-century Palestine.[2]

One may draw firm conclusions. (1) Data shows that Jesus may as easily have spoken Greek as Aramaic and Hebrew. (2) No Aramaic portion of a New Testament manuscript has yet come to light. (3) In the light of available data, no one can assume that Jesus spoke only Aramaic. In any case, if the New Testament is inspired, our task is to interpret the Greek New Testament. Besides, as of now, we have no Aramaic New Testament.

---

2.   Editor's Note: Yohanan Aharoni taught at the Hebrew University of Jerusalem from 1954 to 1968.

INTRODUCTION

THE PURPOSE OF JOHN

John 20:30-31 shows that John wrote to show or teach sinners how to be saved. This is the only book of the Bible written to sinners on how to be saved. Use John in winning souls. The threefold design is as follows: (1) that they might believe the Messiahship of Jesus; (2) that they might believe His Divine Sonship or deity; and (3) that they might have eternal life by believing. The Greek participle for believing is a bit clearer if it is translated, "by believing" or "by means of believing."

THE TEXT OF JOHN

John 1:10-13 may be regarded as the key text of the entire book. Numerous illustrations are given in the whole story to teach three major truths: (1) The teachings and signs (a better translation than "miracle" for the Greek of John) of Jesus reveal Him as the Bread, the Life, the Truth, the Way, the Door, the Good Shepherd, etc.; (2) The unbelief of the people is set forth; and (3) The faith of the disciples is recorded in vivid contrast to the unbelief of sinners. Charles R. Erdman, in his *The Gospel of John: An Exposition* (1916), takes this development of contrasting faith and unbelief as the guiding principle of his exposition.

THE SUMMARY OF JOHN

The prologue (John 1:1-18) summarizes all that is given in the book. The rest of the story illustrates and explains these great truths to incline sinners to believe. Nothing short of mastery of these verses is adequate. A good start is half the race.

THE KEY VERSE OF JOHN

John 1:18 is the climax of the introduction and the text and summary of the whole that follows. This verse outlines itself, and its three truths glimpse the entire inimitable Gospel.

1. Human sin and need: "No man has seen God at any time." Moses saw only a manifestation of God, not God in all His glory. No sinful creature can do more and live.

2. The all-sufficiency of Jesus: "The only begotten Son Who is in the bosom of the Father." His closeness and fellowship qualify Him for the task of meeting the need; perfect intimacy was His.

3. His full revelation of the Father: "That One [emphatic in the Greek] declared Him." The word *declared* means interpreted, revealed, explained, made known. It is the key word and the characteristic note of the book of John, as our outline shows. It makes vivid the idea expressed by John when referring to Jesus by His title, "Word.' Memorize this verse. In dramatic fashion, each actor or witness steps upon the scene with some new testimony. These testimonies either develop faith or deepen unbelief. When Thomas cries, "My Lord and my God," the demonstration is complete. With this climax, John looks back over the book as a whole and concludes with a clear statement of his purpose.[3]

A BRIEF OUTLINE OF JOHN

1. Introduction: Jesus the Word and revealer of the Father, 1:1-18

2. His self-revelation to the world, 1:19–12:50

3. His self-revelation to His disciples, chapters 13–17

4. His self-revelation in the Cross and resurrection, chapters 18–21

---

3. "Truly" in the King James Version becomes "therefore" in the 1901 American Standard Version.

Part I:

Prologue

1: JESUS THE WORD AND REVEALER OF THE FATHER, 1:1-18

(1) In the beginning was the Word, and the Word was with God, and the Word was God. (2) The same was in the beginning with God. (3) All things were made by him; and without him was not any thing made that was made. (4) In him was life; and the life was the light of men.

(5) And the light shineth in darkness; and the darkness comprehended it not. (6) There was a man sent from God, whose name was John. (7) The same came for a witness, to bear witness of the Light, that all men through him might believe. (8) He was not that Light, but was sent to bear witness of that Light. (9) That was the true Light, which lighteth every man that cometh into the world. (10) He was in the world, and the world was made by him, and the world knew him not. (11) He came unto his own, and his own received him not. (12) But as many as received him, to them gave he power to become the sons of God, even to them that believe on his name: (13) Which were born, not of blood, nor of the will of the flesh, nor of the will of man, but of God. (14) And the Word was made flesh, and dwelt among us, (and we beheld his glory, the glory as of the only begotten of the Father,) full of grace and truth.

(15) John bare witness of him, and cried, saying, This was he of whom I spake, He that cometh after me is preferred before me: for he was before me. (16) And of his fulness have all we received, and grace for grace. (17) For the law was given by Moses, but grace and truth came by Jesus Christ. (18) No man hath seen God at any time; the only begotten Son, which is in the bosom of the Father, he hath declared him. (John 1:1-18)

The theme of the beginning of John is that the eternal and incarnate Word is the revealer of the Father. We use words to make known to others our thoughts. Christ is the Word of the Father in making Him known. That is why He is called the Word, the Logos (the transliteration of the Greek word). Make a list of the other titles of Jesus in this chapter.

1.1 THE PERSON AND WORK OF CHRIST AS THE WORD, 1:1-5

Note the stretch of John's thought in John 1:1-5. He gives the pedigree of Jesus Christ and points out His relation to God, to creation, and to man.

1.1.1 THE DEITY OF THE WORD, 1:1-2

Three great truths appear in 1:1-2, the second being repeated for emphasis (1:2):

1. His eternity and preexistence: "In the beginning was the Word." Christ had no beginning on His divine side, yet we are all creatures of time. The verb *was* means to exist; the verb for *made* in 1:3 and for *was* in 1:6 means to become or to come into being. The force of the statement is this: since He was in the beginning, He must have been before the beginning; therefore, He is eternal.

2. His personality and communion with the Father: "With God"—The Father and the Son are not the same person. This assertion of plurality of persons in the Godhead lays a firm basis for the doctrine of the Trinity.

3. His deity or Godhood: "The Word was God." He is the same in nature, essence, and being, though different in person. The article with the Greek for *Word* and its absence with *God*, which is true to the Greek language, shows that the statement is not convertible, so as to read and identify them, "God was the Word." He is more than a manifestation of God; He is God. *Deity* is a stronger term than *divinity*. One can use the term *divinity* of Jesus and deny His Godhood or deity. The Unitarian can accommodate his mind to using *divinity* since he may affirm that Jesus is divine as all men are divine. It is, therefore, preferable to speak of the *deity* of Jesus rather than merely of His *divinity*.

1.1.2 THE CREATORHOOD OF THE WORD, 1:3[4]

Jesus is not a creature; He is the Creator. It is stated positively and negatively that He was the active agent in creating or bringing into being all things.

1.1.3 THE WORD AS THE SOURCE OF LIFE AND LIGHT, 1:4-5

Was or *existed* are better translations than *became*; He had life spontaneously and underivedly. Plant and animal, human and angelic life all come from Jesus, especially eternal life for sinners who are all dead in trespasses and sins. Darkness pictures ignorance, misery, and wrong; light speaks of knowledge, happiness, right. Life and light are correlative terms with John.

1.2 THE RECEPTION OF THE WORD IN THE WORLD, 1:6-13

1.2.1 JOHN THE BAPTIST WAS A WITNESS OF THE LIGHT, 1:6-7

Only blind men need to be told of the light; it is self-evidencing to those who have eyes to see. God takes special pains to get man's attention. Ponder the evangelistic note: "believe." "Through him" refers to the person of John the Baptist (John 5:35). *Witness* is one of the key words in John. It refers to what is felt with the heart and seen with the eyes; it is the opposite of hearsay. In the court room, we easily recognize the difference.

1.2.2 JESUS HIMSELF IS THE GENUINE LIGHT, 1:8-9

There are two adjectives in the Greek for *true*. One means true in the sense of not being false; the one used here means true in the sense of genuine, real, and the fulfillment of typical light. Jesus lights every man

---

4. See also Colossians 1:16.

with the light of conscience and reason. This statement does not favor Universalism.

1.2.3 THREE ATTITUDES OF MEN TOWARD THE WORD, 1:10-13

1. The world did not recognize Him (1:10). For two reasons, the world should have recognized Him—His presence here and His Creatorhood. His being in the world may include both His omnipresence and His incarnation. The fact that it is mentioned first makes the one lean a bit toward the first.

2. "His own" of the Jewish people did not receive Him (1:11). That is a way of saying that they rejected Him. The first "own" is gender neutral in the Greek and means "His own things": His people, His city, His and, His nation. The second "own" is masculine and refers to rejecting by the people themselves: "His own people."

3. An elect few received Him (1:12-13). "But" introduces a gracious contrast. "As many as" has a twofold significance: (1) only those that believed; (2) all those that believed. Believing on Him and receiving Him picture the same act of saving faith from two angles. (On a separate sheet of paper, gradually collect all the pictures, figures, or illustrations of faith found in this Gospel.) Saving faith is faith in a person, and that person is the Lord Jesus. The object of faith is more than getting religion; it is getting a person, even Jesus, in the soul. At the moment of faith, He bestows two blessings: adoption and the New Birth.

1.2.4 ADOPTION, 1:12

Two words for power need to be distinguished: one means the energy to do something (*dunamis*, from which comes our "dynamo" and "dynamite"); the other means the right or privilege. It is not the regular word for power in this place. This gives the right or privilege of children. Being His child is a bestowal, not a natural inheritance. Men become children in the act of the bestowal of the privilege. "His name" stands for what He is, for His person and work.

1.2.5 The New Birth, 1:13

This gives the nature of children—the natural order for regeneration to come after adoption. The word *were* does not place the birth before the act of faith; it merely stresses, as the auxiliary of the passive voice in English, the fact that we do not birth ourselves, but God does it. The sinner is active in faith in response to divine impulses but passive or acted upon in the New Birth itself. This may be a fine point but an important one. It involves the divineness of the work of regeneration and the responsibility of the sinner to trust Jesus.

The Greek is plural in its use of "not of bloods," because there are many lines of inheritance in each one. The New Birth is not inherited; one is not a Christian because his parents are. Spirituality does not flow in the blood stream, nor does it pass with the genes.

"The will of the flesh" means that works done by the individual cannot save him. That cuts out baptism and all works that men do to save themselves. The act of baptism is subject to the will of the man submitting and to the will of the man doing the baptizing, but the New Birth is subject to none other than God Himself.

"Of God"—the true source of the New Birth. After three negative statements, John introduces the positive. That is a fine way of stating vital truth.

1.3 The Word, Through Incarnation, Reveals the Father, 1:14-18

1.3.1 The Glory of His Incarnation, 1:14

"Was made" is a better translation than "became." His incarnation means that Jesus, as God, became a man. He did more than assume a human body; He became a man, sin excepted. He became what He had not been: a man. He remained what He had always been: God. Christ incarnate is, therefore, the God-Man. Never did a hyphen mean so much as here.

His incarnation means His "in-flesh-ment." This is the specific meaning of incarnation. In a broader sense, His incarnation covers His entire earthly life. He dwelt, or tabernacled, here for thirty-three years, "full of grace and truth." *Grace* means favor. In the salvation in Christ Jesus, grace means God's unmerited favor bestowed on undeserving, ill-deserving, and hell-deserving sinners. Law demands everything and receives nothing worthy from the sinner. Grace demands nothing but gives everything sinful man needs. His incarnation was real, not a mere appearance, as the ancient Docetics taught.

1.3.2 THE LAW THROUGH MOSES: GRACE AND TRUTH THROUGH JESUS CHRIST, 1:15-17

"Grace for grace" is a better understanding than "grace instead of grace." That means that He gives more grace to take the place of what we use. His supply never runs out. The law was given through Moses; he did not originate it. Grace and truth came into being (the full meaning of the word *came*) through the personal agency of Jesus Christ. The feeling of grace was in God's heart but became a manifested reality only through Jesus Christ. There could have been no grace and saving truth for men except through Jesus Christ. They are exclusively His.

1.3.3 THE SON IS THE PERFECT REVEALER OF THE FATHER, 1:18

See the notes above in sections 1.1 and 1.2. Do our theories retire God or put Him on the throne? Is God real to you? Jesus came to make God real to you.

1.4 QUESTIONS ON JOHN 1:1-18

1. Where does one find the purpose of John's Gospel?
2. What is that threefold purpose?
3. What may be regarded as the key text of the Gospel?
4. What is the relation of 1:1-18 to the entire Gospel?
5. What is the relation of 1:18 to the prologue and to the Gospel?
6. What is the key word to the Gospel?

7. How does the three-point outline relate to this key word?

8. What is the significance of the title, "Word"?

9. What three great truths does 1:1 teach? Show what part of the verse relates to each one.

10. What is the difference in the deity and the divinity of Jesus?

11. What is the relation of Jesus to creation?

12. Who else in the New Testament teaches this same truth?

13. What is meant by "true light"?

14. Distinguish the two uses of "his own" in 1:11.

15. According to 1:12-13, what two blessings come at faith?

16. What does His incarnation mean? Give its two meanings—the narrower and the broader.

17. Explain "grace for grace."

1.5 SERMON SUGGESTIONS

Often I have preached through John in a revival. The twenty-five double-verilys were compressed into twelve radio sermons. In one radio series, I preached more than forty minutes on John 1.

Give a running exposition of 1:1-18. Three focal points are suggested in paragraphs at the beginning of this work.

I now use "Is God Real to You?" on 1:18.

Try this:

- Jesus as the Word and the Genuine Light

- John as a Witness

- Three Attitudes Toward Jesus (1:10-13)

- The Incarnation

- The Stewardship of Grace

- Contrasts Between Law and Grace

PART II:

HIS SELF-REVELATION TO THE WORLD, 1:19-12:50

2: The Testimony of John and of Jesus' First Disciples, 1:19-51

(19) And this is the record of John, when the Jews sent priests and Levites from Jerusalem to ask him, Who art thou? (20) And he confessed, and denied not; but confessed, I am not the Christ. (21) And they asked him, What then? Art thou Elias? And he saith, I am not. Art thou that prophet? And he answered, No. (22) Then said they unto him, Who art thou? that we may give an answer to them that sent us. What sayest thou of thyself? (23) He said, I am the voice of one crying in the wilderness, Make straight the way of the Lord, as said the prophet Esaias. (24) And they which were sent were of the Pharisees. (25) And they asked him, and said unto him, Why baptizest thou then, if thou be not that Christ, nor Elias, neither that prophet? (26) John answered them, saying, I baptize with water: but there standeth one among you, whom ye know not; (27) He it is, who coming after me is preferred before me, whose shoe's latchet I am not worthy to unloose. (28) These things were done in Bethabara beyond Jordan, where John was baptizing.

(29) The next day John seeth Jesus coming unto him, and saith, Behold the Lamb of God, which taketh away the sin of the world. (30) This is he of whom I said, After me cometh a man which is preferred before me: for he was before me. (31) And I knew him not: but that he should be made manifest to Israel, therefore am I come baptizing with water. (32) And John bare record, saying, I saw the Spirit descending from heaven like a dove, and it abode upon him. (33) And I knew him not: but he that sent me to baptize with water, the same said unto me, Upon whom thou shalt see the Spirit descending, and remaining on him, the same is he which baptizeth with the Holy Ghost. (34) And I saw, and bare record that this is the Son of God. (35) Again the next day after John stood, and two of his disciples; (36) And looking upon Jesus as he walked, he saith, Behold the Lamb of God!

(37) And the two disciples heard him speak, and they followed Jesus. (38) Then Jesus turned, and saw them following, and saith unto them, What seek ye? They said unto him, Rabbi, (which is to say, being interpreted, Master,) where dwellest thou? (38) He saith unto them, Come and see. They came and saw where he dwelt, and abode with him that day: for it was about the tenth

hour. (40) One of the two which heard John speak, and followed him, was Andrew, Simon Peter's brother. (41) He first findeth his own brother Simon, and saith unto him, We have found the Messias, which is, being interpreted, the Christ. (42) And he brought him to Jesus. And when Jesus beheld him, he said, Thou art Simon the son of Jona: thou shalt be called Cephas, which is by interpretation, A stone.

(43)The day following Jesus would go forth into Galilee, and findeth Philip, and saith unto him, Follow me. (44) Now Philip was of Bethsaida, the city of Andrew and Peter. (45) Philip findeth Nathanael, and saith unto him, We have found him, of whom Moses in the law, and the prophets, did write, Jesus of Nazareth, the son of Joseph. (46) And Nathanael said unto him, Can there any good thing come out of Nazareth? Philip saith unto him, Come and see. (47) Jesus saw Nathanael coming to him, and saith of him, Behold an Israelite indeed, in whom is no guile! (48) Nathanael saith unto him, Whence knowest thou me? Jesus answered and said unto him, Before that Philip called thee, when thou wast under the fig tree, I saw thee. (49) Nathanael answered and saith unto him, Rabbi, thou art the Son of God; thou art the King of Israel. (50) Jesus answered and said unto him, Because I said unto thee, I saw thee under the fig tree, believest thou? thou shalt see greater things than these. (51) And he saith unto him, Verily, verily, I say unto you, Hereafter ye shall see heaven open, and the angels of God ascending and descending upon the Son of man. (John 1:19-51)

2.1 THE TESTIMONY OF JOHN TO JESUS, 1:19-28

2.1.1 JOHN'S TESTIMONY TO THE COMMITTEE FROM THE JERUSALEM SANHEDRIN, 1:19-28

Note how John answered their two questions. This is realistic and dramatic.

2.1.2 "YOU, WHO ARE YOU?" 1:19-24

John did not quiver before this august body—"he confessed and denied not." He refused the opportunity to be, for a period, very popular.

Negatively, John told them that he was not the Christ nor Elijah nor the prophet mentioned by Moses in Deuteronomy 18:15. John's righteous impatience comes out in shortening his answer each time: "I am not the Christ ... I am not ... No."

Positively, John said he was a voice through which Jesus was crying or giving aloud His message. How would you answer if you were asked, "What do you say concerning yourself?"

John's description aptly describes the work of a preacher and of all Christian witnesses—a voice for Jesus to use. The voice is true to its purpose only when it is an instrument for the delivery of the message committed, without changing it anywise. A voice does not originate its message but conveys it.

What a stirring message he gave! "Make straight the way of Jehovah." The great evangelist Isaiah had so spoken. These words call for thorough repentance. All the rocks, bushes, and other hindrances have to be moved out of the way. The ground has to be leveled. That is the work of repentance.

2.1.3 "WHAT IS YOUR WORK OR MISSION?" 1:25-28

John's answer was twofold, concerning his witnessing and his baptizing: (1) He was sent to witness concerning Jesus (see also 1:6-8). "There is standing One among you Whom you know not." How close and yet how far away they were! John felt wholly unworthy to be His servant to do the lowest job, even to loosing the thong of Jesus' sandal. (2) John was sent to baptize in water. "With water" is a faulty rendering. It is a possible rendering except that the context, the meaning of the Greek for *baptize*, and the symbolic import of the ordinance favor "in water." There is here no justification whatsoever for sprinkling as New Testament baptism. The original word *baptize* signifies to immerse, to plunge, to overwhelm, to cover up, to dip. Baptism is a burial (see Romans 6:4). Sprinkling and pouring fall short of a burial. Modern scholarship has voted thus for the meaning of the Greek. I can name only one dissenting scholar.

2.2 JOHN'S TESTIMONY TO THE PEOPLE, 1:29-34

On three successive days (1:29, 35, 43), we have "the Messiah announced, then pointed out, then followed" (Godet 1886).

John points out Jesus as the Lamb of God Who takes away the sin of the world. Jesus is the only One Who is able to take the burden of sin and bear it away from the guilty heart. Whatever "the sin of the world" means, He is abundantly able for all who come to Him. That means hope for every sin-sick soul.

Jesus as the Lamb of God is meek, submissive, gentle, and sacrificial. As the Lamb of God, He died on the cruel cross to pay our sin-debt.

John preached the deity of Jesus, calling Him "the Son of God" in 1:34. "I knew Him not" in 1:31 and in 1:33 probably means that John did not know the official position of Jesus as Messiah. He most probably knew Jesus as an individual. John was therefore given the sign of the Holy Spirit to make him know Jesus as the Messiah.

The coming of the Holy Spirit on Jesus is said to be "like a dove." A dove suggests peace; the Holy Spirit brings to our souls the peace that Jesus alone gives. Have you His peace?

2.3 JOHN'S TESTIMONY TO TWO OF HIS DISCIPLES, 1:35-36

John continues to preach Jesus as the Lamb of God. Read Isaiah 53, which John most likely had in mind.

2.4 THE TESTIMONY OF JESUS' FIRST DISCIPLES, 1:37-51

2.4.1 ANDREW AND SIMON PETER, AND PROBABLY JAMES AND JOHN, 1:37-42

That is good speaking when it influences men to turn to Jesus (1:37). Jesus is still asking, "What are you seeking?" in 1:38. Is it money, pleasure, or fame that you are seeking? Seek them not; they are in vain if sought for their sake alone. Let us answer with these disciples that we seek to know where Jesus dwells and seek to have fellowship with Him.

The name "Simon," shortened form of Simeon, means a simple hearer; Jesus promised that He Himself would make Simon like a stone for strength and firmness. That is what the name Peter means. Jesus and His fellowship transform character.

"We have found the Messiah." Every saved person can join in with Andrew in that. Finding Jesus as one's Savior is the greatest discovery in the world. Both Moses and the prophets told of Jesus. The Old Testament is full of Jesus.

"He brought him to Jesus." What an accomplishment! What an employment! What an objective! What an encomium! What an epitaph! Let us join the Andrew band in doing personal soul winning. Thrice in John we meet Andrew, and in each instance he is introducing someone to Jesus.

2.4.2 Philip and Nathanael, 1:43-51

Nathanael is the same as Bartholomew. As Philip found Nathanael, so we need to be finding lost souls. "We have found Him." That is our testimony. Do not argue with sinners; testify to them instead. "Guile" in 1:47 means deceit, pretense, insincerity. Our word to the faultfinder is simply this challenge: "Come and see" (1:46). "Believest thou?" What a challenging question that is! Jesus saw Nathanael underneath the fig tree; this searching fact touched the heart of Nathanael. You cannot get beyond His all-seeing eyes.

Nathanael made a very noble confession, in many ways comparable to that of Peter, of which we make so much. The divine insight of Jesus into Nathanael's soul removed any difficulty. He probably knew that Bethlehem was to be the birthplace of the Messiah. His coming from Nazareth would present, therefore, a real difficulty.

In 1:45, Philip calls Jesus the son of Joseph. The populace did not know the inner truth of the virgin birth. This popular statement in no wise contradicts the virgin birth stories.

"Greater things than these thou shalt see." Great vistas ever await the soul that comes to Jesus: enlarging spiritual vision is natural for Christians.

Here is the first instance of the double-verily in John's Gospel: "verily, verily." It is not used doubly in the Synoptic Gospels (Matthew, Mark, Luke). It is John's way of pointing with the index finger to the importance of the saying recorded. There are twenty-five instances

(1:51; 3:3, 5, 11; 5:19, 24, 25; 6:26, 32, 47, 53; 8:34, 51, 58; 10:1, 7; 12:24; 13:16, 20, 21, 38; 14:12; 16:20, 23; 21:18). Study to preach a series on these verses.

This statement was addressed to Nathanael, but the use of the plural shows that it is for all (1:51).

Heaven is opened in Jesus (1:51). All the barriers are removed; the doors swing wide open. The new and living way to God is open. He, no doubt, refers to Jacob's dream of the ladder that reached across the mighty chasm between God and man—a chasm of sinful man's formation (Genesis 28). Jesus fulfills the place of the ladder in Genesis 28. As the God-Man, He is the only link connecting earth and heaven and heaven and earth. See also Jesus' calling Himself the Door (John 10:9). The "ascending" of human need precedes the "descending" of God's merciful provision. It is the primacy of human need. God's mercy moves to meet the felt need of humanity. Sin is more than a mere incident to magnify God's mercy; it is the appalling cry of man's helplessness and hopelessness that God, in Christ, designs to meet.

Many testimonies about Jesus appear in this rich chapter, and many expressive titles are bestowed on Jesus. Erdman (1916) is right in saying, however, that "the greatest of all the witnesses is Christ Himself." The testimony reaches its climax when He calls Himself "the Son of Man." The title, which Jesus used of Himself more than any other, emphasizes His humanity, but it does not stop there. He is the One Who understands us; He is a real member of the human race, but He is the ideal, the perfect Man. The term applies to the Messiah and indicates His uniqueness as well as His humanity. When the article appears with the title, as it does usually, it means about the same as we mean by the God-Man.

2.5   QUESTIONS ON JOHN 1:19-51

1. Comment on John's two designations of himself: "I am a voice" and "I must decrease."

2. What were the two major questions of the committee from Jerusalem?

3. State three arguments for translating, "in water."

4.   What is suggested by the title "Lamb of God?"

5.   Explain John's "I knew Him not."

6.   Explain the play on the name of Peter.

7.   What does guile mean?

8.   The winning of what six men is most likely recorded in John 1?

9.   How many times does John use the double-verily?

10. Why does "ascending" come before "descending" in John 1:51?

2.6   Sermon Suggestions

Three of the radio sermons I preached summarized the Old Testament picture of the Messiah.

- John's Call to Repentance

- For Preachers

- John's Description of Himself (1:23, 27; 3:30)

- The Lamb of God

- Changed from Simon to Peter

- Life's Greatest Discovery

- Examples of Soul Winning

- Bringing Men to Jesus

- The Testimony of Nathaniel

- The Opened Heaven (see the note on 1:51)

3: His Public Revelation Through Teachings and Signs, chapters 2–11

3.1 Beginning Signs and Teachings, chapters 2-4

3.1.1 Jesus' First Sign: Water to Wine, 2:1-12

(1) And the third day there was a marriage in Cana of Galilee; and the mother of Jesus was there: (2) And both Jesus was called, and his disciples, to the marriage. (3) And when they wanted wine, the mother of Jesus saith unto him, They have no wine. (4) Jesus saith unto her, Woman, what have I to do with thee? mine hour is not yet come. (5) His mother saith unto the servants, Whatsoever he saith unto you, do it. (6) And there were set there six waterpots of stone, after the manner of the purifying of the Jews, containing two or three firkins apiece. (7) Jesus saith unto them, Fill the waterpots with water. And they filled them up to the brim. (8) And he saith unto them, Draw out now, and bear unto the governor of the feast. And they bare it. (9) When the ruler of the feast had tasted the water that was made wine, and knew not whence it was: (but the servants which drew the water knew;) the governor of the feast called the bridegroom, (10) And saith unto him, Every man at the beginning doth set forth good wine; and when men have well drunk, then that which is worse: but thou hast kept the good wine until now. (11) This beginning of miracles did Jesus in Cana of Galilee, and manifested forth his glory; and his disciples believed on him. (12) After this he went down to Capernaum, he, and his mother, and his brethren, and his disciples: and they continued there not many days. (John 2:1-12)

The Occasion: The Social Life of Jesus, 2:1-5

In this, there are two pictures:

1. Jesus and the feast (2:1-2): Cana was a town in Galilee about eight miles northeast of Nazareth and on the way to the Sea of Galilee, just twelve miles away. Jesus and His disciples were invited ("bidden") to the wedding feast and accepted the invitation. "His disciples" included the six in chapter one—Andrew and Simon Peter, John and James, Philip and Nathanael. The word disciple means learner, one taught. How we need to sit at Jesus' blessed feet and learn from Him (Luke 10:39; Matthew 11:29).

    His attendance at a marriage feast shows two things about His social life: First, marriage is honorable. The ordinance comes from God and here receives the approval of Jesus. "Genesis begins with a marriage sanctified by God the Creator, and John begins with a marriage sanctified by Jesus, the Redeemer" (Norris 1871). Second, merriment is lawful. God wants us to be happy but not sinful in gaining the merriment. This is a sound principle for all our social behavior.

2. Jesus and His mother (2:3-5): Mary had in her heart a confidence that Jesus could do something about the embarrassing situation. The wine had given out. No situation is too hard for Him; take every problem to Him and let Him solve it as He wills.

    Jesus' reply to Mary is the death knell to the Mariolatry of Catholics. They worship Mary but not with the sanction of Jesus. He called her "woman," which rebukes calling her "the Mother of God." She was mother of only His human nature and that not without a special miracle to preserve from contamination the seed that impregnated her womb. The Holy Spirit took the place of the father; but there was a double miracle—His being born without a human father and His being born of a sinful woman and yet without the taint of sin.

    Here is the first hint of the cross, from the lips of Jesus. She probably meant that this would be a good time for His public manifestation of His Messiahship. By studying "mine hour" throughout the Gospel, one seems driven to the conclusion that His supreme hour was the Cross, by which He glorified God. He surely knew that the Cross would be the culmination of His earthly mission.

"What have I to do with you?" most likely means "What do we have in common?" Compare with Mark 1:24. There is here a hint of His Messiahship. Mary gave good advice for us and shows her confidence in Her Son: "Whatever He says to you, do it." Compare also to 2 Samuel 16:10.

The Sign: The Omnipotence of Jesus, 2:6-10

A *firkin* is an English measure of about nine gallons. Each pot held eighteen to twenty-seven gallons, making from 108 to 162 gallons in all. Jesus is the Lord or Ruler of all nature. It was an act of creation. By His own all-powerful will and without spoken word, Jesus carried forward to completion in a moment processes of nature that usually occupied at least a year (see also Morgan 1960).

Do not miss the humor in this passage. The ruler of the feast twits (declares to be silly) the bridegroom with having kept the better wine until the last. Usually, he meant to say, a man gives his guests the better wine first, then when they get drunk, they will drink any old "slop." The humor fades only when we remember how like beasts men are to get drunk.

The Results of the Sign: The Glory of Jesus, 2:11

Tradition has Jesus doing childish things to gratify curiosity. One story tells of His making birds of clay and then making them fly, but Jesus never miracled without reason for it. How different this Scripture account from those childish stories! Here we have a criterion for judging much of the later accretions to the story of Jesus.

Furthermore, this story definitely marks this as the first of His miracles or signs. The Greek pointedly says, "Jesus did this as a beginning of signs."

The word for *miracle* John uses in His Gospel means *sign*. It stresses the purpose for the manifestation. A sign is a miracle or a manifestation of supernatural power (*dunamis*, power), but this word emphasizes that the deed is intended to teach a lesson. It is more than a prodigy to stir the minds of spectators; its intent is not sensational nor merely to get attention.

Two lessons were intended, and two results follow: First, the glory of Jesus was openly proved or demonstrated. The same word for "glory" appears in 1:14. The purpose of the sign was to accredit Jesus as the Messiah or Redeemer. No case is too hard for Him; the turning of the water into wine proves that; now He is the same all-sufficient One in His work as Redeemer. His motive in the story was love and sympathy in removing an embarrassment; His glory is as the Savior of redeeming love for sinners.

Second, this new proof of His Majesty strengthened the faith of the disciples. They had previously believed in the saving of their souls. They now believed without reserve; this established and developed their faith or confidence in Him.

These two form the purposes of the sign. The social lessons drawn above come from the texture of the story without being definite designs of the story, but these two are the heart of His miracling power. The fact that He attended the feast shows that exuberance of spirit is consistent with godliness, but the sign was not wrought to teach such. It came for the expressed purposes of 2:11.

John 2:12 is somewhat transitional. He tarried in nearby Capernaum a few days before going to Jerusalem. It marks a step in the transition from His private to His public life. "[N]ot many days" is a forceful figure (*litotes*) for increasing the effect of the statement; the moderation of the understatement means a few or several days.

The Greek has, "The mother of Him and the brothers and the disciples of Him." I like to think that John's leaving of "of Him" with Jesus' brothers indicates that they were not yet as close to Him as His mother and His disciples because they had not yet believed on Him (John 7:5). Now in John 7:5, the force of the "of Him" in the Greek is this: Though they were His brothers in the flesh and had many opportunities to see His power, they did not yet believe on Him. The question for us is whether we ourselves have believed on Him.

3.1.2 JESUS' CLEANSING THE TEMPLE, 2:13-25

(13) And the Jews' passover was at hand, and Jesus went up to Jerusalem, (14) And found in the temple those that sold oxen and sheep and doves, and the changers of money sitting: (15) And when he had made a scourge of small cords, he drove them all out of the temple, and the sheep, and the oxen; and poured out the changers' money, and overthrew the tables; (16) And said unto them that sold doves, Take these things hence; make not my Father's house an house of merchandise. (17) And his disciples remembered that it was written, The zeal of thine house hath eaten me up. (18) Then answered

the Jews and said unto him, What sign shewest thou unto us, seeing that thou doest these things? (19) Jesus answered and said unto them, Destroy this temple, and in three days I will raise it up. (20) Then said the Jews, Forty and six years was this temple in building, and wilt thou rear it up in three days? (21) But he spake of the temple of his body. (22) When therefore he was risen from the dead, his disciples remembered that he had said this unto them; and they believed the scripture, and the word which Jesus had said. (23) Now when he was in Jerusalem at the passover, in the feast day, many believed in his name, when they saw the miracles which he did. (24) But Jesus did not commit himself unto them, because he knew all men, (25) And needed not that any should testify of man: for he knew what was in man. (John 2:13-25)

The Passover, 2:13

The Passover, the first of the three great annual feasts of the Jews, occurred in the spring and commemorated the passing over of the death angel in Exodus 12. That is its retrospective aspect; prospectively, it pointed to Christ, our Passover (1 Corinthians 5:7). This was the first Passover during the public ministry of our Lord (2:13). He had attended the feast when He was twelve (Luke 2:42) and probably many other times. It was fitting that He should make His ministry more public in the capital city at a time when multitudes of pilgrims to the feast thronged the city from every quarter of the known world.

The Cleansing, 2:14-17

Jesus disapproves of all irreverent and mercenary behavior in God's house.

Their sin: We must begin here if we would understand His action. These traders thought to accommodate worshippers who came a long distance, by having animals for sacrifice there for sale and by offering to exchange the coin of foreign lands into Jewish coins, the only ones acceptable in the temple offerings. God provided that those who lived far away might turn into money what they had to bring and then buy anew upon arrival at the place of worship (Deuteronomy 14:24-25). What had started as a mere convenience had become disorder, greed, dishonesty, and extortion. This innocent beginning did not justify their turning the house of God into a selfish marketplace. Their motive was not only to make money. His house had become a place of trading, or an emporium (so the Greek).

His rebuke: He took the whip of cords as a badge of authority and tacitly claimed to be the Messiah. His attitude and rebuke flowed from His zeal for God's house. The original word for zeal comes from a root that means to be hot, to boil. His was a burning and flaming zeal. That speaks of its intensity and of His earnestness. Furthermore, He was fully conscious that it was His Father's house.

Would to God that we had the same glowing zeal for God's house, attendance upon its services, maintaining its worship, and praying in its courts. His action disapproves of all suppers, bazaars, etc. in the house of God for the raising of money. Money for the work of the Lord should come from voluntary tithes and offerings.

His actions made His disciples think of Psalm 69:9. His disciples, despite the misunderstanding of the Jews, appreciated His spirit and work. Do your actions and mine remind others that we follow the blueprint of His Word for us? Too much of our time is devoted to things that impede worship in the house of God. We all need a revival that will give us a hot desire for His sanctuary every time the door is opened for worship.

Their Challenge, 2:18-22

Jewish unbelief required a sign to prove a sign. Unlike His disciples, the Jewish rulers sullenly expressed their dissatisfaction. "Their demand was a stupid impertinence. It was like asking proof of a proof. His act was itself a sign which they should have interpreted" (Erdman 1916).

Jesus pointed to both His death (the destruction of the temple of His body) and His resurrection (the raising of the temple of His body) as sufficient signs, as an unanswerable argument or proof. This shows that His death did not come as an afterthought to Him. Others enter the world to live; He came to die for the sins of men and then to rise triumphantly. His resurrection is the keystone and the sealing of all His work.

With contemptuous incredulity, they referred to the material temple that Herod the Great had beautified. Sin blinded their minds to His meaning, and they failed to see that He foretold that they would be the destroyers and He the builder. He used the word that refers properly to the temple itself; the word used in 2:14 includes the temple buildings and grounds or courts He most likely pointed to His body when He spoke. Would that translators would keep *naos* (sanctuary) and *hieron* (temple area or sacred area) distinct!

The revelations of time clear up many passages of Scripture that were once misunderstood (2:22). The great event of the resurrection enlightened the dull understanding of His disciples. Compare the same power in His death (John 8:28) Their faith was again strengthened (compare 2:22 with 2:11).

The word of Jesus and the Old Testament Scriptures are of equal authority. You cannot deny nor believe one without denying or believing the other. Acceptance of the Lordship of Jesus accepts His word just because He said it; faith in Him needs no extra bolstering up. Do you truly believe?

The Result, 2:23-25

The omniscient Christ detects spurious believers.

His signs: This is the first of those general statements about Jesus' miracles. One must expand his imagination to take in the many things Jesus did. These may have occurred on several days out of the seven required for the feast of Passover.

Their faith: Because they saw these outward evidences, many believed. The participle *beholding* has a causal force here. The ground of their faith was what they saw with their physical sight and no more. Seeing and accepting signs is not conversion. Their faith grew out of sight without personal heart trust in Him.

His attitude: Jesus saw through their hearts and would not commit Himself to them. He would not believe or trust (so is the Greek word) that they were genuine. Jesus makes no errors in distinguishing the true from the false. We must be cautious in our evangelistic efforts but cannot know for sure who is genuine.

His attitude resulted from His omniscience, His knowing all things. He knows thoroughly, fully, and finally all men. No one can add to His knowledge by even firsthand and eye-witness testimony concerning man because He knows it all already. The word for *need* refers to a need that grows out of conditions and circumstances. Nothing can arise to throw Jesus off His track; already He knew perfectly every conceivable circumstance. Jesus is the greatest psychologist of all time. Jeremiah 17:9-10 declares that no man can know the deceitful human heart. Only the Lord can know its depths. No stronger proof could be given of the deity of the Lord Jesus. He knows what is in man. That is why He told of the brood of sins that come out of the depraved heart (Mark 7:21-23). You cannot put anything over on Him. Open fully your heart now.

3.1.3 THE NEW BIRTH: OR JESUS' CONVERSATION WITH NICODEMUS, 3:1-21

(1) There was a man of the Pharisees, named Nicodemus, a ruler of the Jews: (2) The same came to Jesus by night, and said unto him, Rabbi, we know that thou art a teacher come from God: for no man can do these miracles that thou doest, except God be with him. (3) Jesus answered and said unto

him, Verily, verily, I say unto thee, Except a man be born again, he cannot see the kingdom of God. (4) Nicodemus saith unto him, How can a man be born when he is old? can he enter the second time into his mother's womb, and be born? (5) Jesus answered, Verily, verily, I say unto thee, Except a man be born of water and of the Spirit, he cannot enter into the kingdom of God. (6) That which is born of the flesh is flesh; and that which is born of the Spirit is spirit. (7) Marvel not that I said unto thee, Ye must be born again. (8) The wind bloweth where it listeth, and thou hearest the sound thereof, but canst not tell whence it cometh, and whither it goeth: so is every one that is born of the Spirit. (9) Nicodemus answered and said unto him, How can these things be? (10) Jesus answered and said unto him, Art thou a master of Israel, and knowest not these things? (11) Verily, verily, I say unto thee, We speak that we do know, and testify that we have seen; and ye receive not our witness. (12) If I have told you earthly things, and ye believe not, how shall ye believe, if I tell you of heavenly things? (13) And no man hath ascended up to heaven, but he that came down from heaven, even the Son of man which is in heaven. (14) And as Moses lifted up the serpent in the wilderness, even so must the Son of man be lifted up: (15) That whosoever believeth in him should not perish, but have eternal life. (16) For God so loved the world, that he gave his only begotten Son, that whosoever believeth in him should not perish, but have everlasting life. (17) For God sent not his Son into the world to condemn the world; but that the world through him might be saved. (18) He that believeth on him is not condemned: but he that believeth not is condemned already, because he hath not believed in the name of the only begotten Son of God. (19) And this is the condemnation, that light is come into the world, and men loved darkness rather than light, because their deeds were evil. (20) For every one that doeth evil hateth the light, neither cometh to the light, lest his deeds should be reproved. (21) But he that doeth truth cometh to the light, that his deeds may be made manifest, that they are wrought in God. (John 3:1-21)

Nicodemus was a sincere seeker investigating for himself, wisely choosing a time of quietness. If he had not been disposed to believe, Jesus would not have revealed Himself to the man as He did. Nicodemus, the man whom Jesus trusted, is thrown into definite contrast with those whom He did not trust (John 2:24). John 3:1 begins with the word *but*, which brings out this contrast. Whatever one makes of his coming "by night," he came; that is good.

"The conversation fell into three movements" (Morgan 1960, 47) and was in the form of a dialogue. Nicodemus talks, and then Jesus answers him. Erdman (1916) says of Nicodemus, "His character is sketched in three scenes; in the first, he appears as a cautious inquirer, in the second, as a timid defender, in the third, as a secret disciple of Christ" (35).

The First Movement or The First Dialogue, 3:1-3

The admission of Nicodemus (3:1-2): He did not deny the miracles or signs of Jesus. He rather regarded them as proof that Jesus was a divine teacher, having God's presence with Him.

His being a "ruler" of the Jews means that he was a member of the Sanhedrin court and a man of high learning, influence, and reputation. He was very religious and a great teacher of the Bible and had a passing reverence for Jesus, but he was not saved.

The revelation of Jesus (3:3): Jesus answered the inmost thoughts of Nicodemus rather than his spoken words. That shows His ability as a great Teacher. The double and emphatic "verily, verily," the second instance, was calculated to arouse interest. It is the birthmark of truth as imprinted there by Jesus. "I say to you" emphasizes the authority of Jesus. He taught, but not as the scribes taught. His teaching was with authority and with power. No mere man can take these words on his lips without sacrilege.

The word *see* refers to spiritual vision or perception. This is because man is naturally blinded to spiritual things (1 Corinthians 2:14).

"Again" means stressing the heavenly source and nature of the New Birth. See also the note in the margin[5] of the American Standard Version (1901).

A birth was chosen to picture the change needed because the chief idea of a birth is that a new life has come into the world. The Bible does not warrant our drawing full parallels between the natural and spiritual birth, such as conception before birth or a regular time for the period of gestation. Figures do not walk on all fours, nor does any simple metaphor express the whole picture.

Nothing short of a miracle will save, namely, the miracle of the New Birth. It is not a process but an instantaneous miracle. The use of the aorist tense clinches this.

This great blessing is called elsewhere a resurrection (John 5:25), a creation (2 Corinthians 5:17), a regeneration (Titus 3:5), and a partaking of the divine nature (2 Peter 1:4). The total effect of these pointed figures tells us the whole story; no single one of them does. What God does for the soul in salvation is so everlastingly rich that one figure cannot tell it all.

The "kingdom of God" is spiritual in nature. It is the reign of God in the human heart. "See" is about the same as our "experience."

---

5. The American Standard Version (ASV), 1901, was a single column Bible that had a wide margin in which various comments were made to help understand the text being referenced. When Beaman references the "margin," he is referring to the references in the margin of the ASV 1901 version.

The Second Dialogue, 3:4-8

The difficulty of Nicodemus (3:4): It is hard to get sinners to think about spiritual things instead of physical things. He missed the force of Jesus' "from above," as many today miss it.

The Answer of Jesus, 3:5-8

The absolute necessity of the New Birth (3:5-7): George Whitfield, helper of the Wesley brothers, preached over three hundred times from the words, "Ye must be born again." Someone asked him why he preached so often on the New Birth. Whitfield answered in the words of the text: "Because ye must be born again." You can go to heaven without several things, but you cannot possibly go without being born from above. You can go to heaven without baptism, church membership, and many other things that are right in their place, but the birth from above is absolutely necessary. The word *must* indicates moral and not environmental necessity only. Men *need* to be born again; but more, they *must* be born again.

The metaphor is altered to entering the kingdom as a realm; it is just the same as seeing the kingdom, only that the illustration is varied somewhat.

A Special Study, 3:5

Many have been troubled over what "born of water" means. Let us investigate the facts.

First, note that the whole expression is "born of water and *of* the Spirit." The second "of" is printed in our Bible in italics to show that it is not in the Greek. Only one preposition with the two nouns shows that it is one birth, not two. If "water" refers to baptism, then you have two births. Literally, it is "out of water and Spirit." This gives the source of the one birth as twofold. Whatever these mean, they are the two parents of the New Birth.

Second, one of these parents is declared to be spiritual. The other must be likewise spiritual. The water has spiritual significance and, therefore, cannot refer to material water in baptism. Jesus would keep us from a material interpretation of "water" by adding that mere human nature, however beautiful or cultured or sincere or religious it may be, cannot rise above itself, cannot produce anything different from or better than itself. The flesh or depraved nature cannot produce the spiritual life. John 3:6 expresses the necessity of the birth and is not intended to explain "water" as referring to what is called a "wet" birth.

Third, the simple fact is that both "water and Spirit" are figurative expressions declaring spiritual truths. The Greek for "Spirit" is *wind* and is so translated in 3:8. The verb *bloweth* in 3:8 has the same root. Now the wind is taken throughout the Scriptures as a type or figure of the Holy Spirit. The "water" is likewise figurative. Throughout the Bible, "water" is figurative of cleansing. I give a few of these instances.

Nicodemus would be familiar with Ezekiel 36:35. This "clean water" refers to the ceremonial water that had the ashes of a red heifer sprinkled in it. See Numbers 19. It typifies the blood of Jesus Christ. In Ephesians 5:26 we have cleansing with the washing of water by the Word. Jesus declared in 15:3, "Now ye are clean through the word that I have spoken to you." Nicodemus could think of Psalm 119:9: "Wherewithal shall a young man cleanse his way? By taking heed thereto according to Thy word." We must be born out of water or cleansing power of the Word that applies the cleansing blood of Jesus Christ. "The blood of Jesus Christ His Son cleanseth us from all sin" (1 John 1:7).

If the blood cleanses from all sin, there is none left for baptism really to cleanse away. Baptism can, therefore, cleanse away only figuratively or symbolically.

Furthermore, sin is a disease of the heart. Outward and material water cannot cleanse away the inner and spiritual malady of sin. We must have a spiritual power to do the cleansing, and no other cleansing power meets the requirements except the merit of the blood of Jesus Christ applied through the word of the gospel.

Fourth, Jesus blamed Nicodemus for not knowing this truth (3:10). Nicodemus was blameworthy because it was taught in the Old Testament; as an example, take Ezekiel 36:25. But, since baptism is not taught in the Old Testament, this "water" in John 3:5 cannot possibly refer to baptism.

If Jesus had only said "born of baptism and the Spirit," there would be no room for disagreement. If He meant baptism, why did He not say so? And if He did not say so, what clear reason do we have for saying so?

Fifth, after all, baptism is a burial (Romans 6:4) and not a birth. We bury dead men; we do not bury to kill. Men must first be killed in their hearts to sin before they are ready for the burial of baptism. No man is ready for baptism until he is born from above. The Scripture order is as follows: the New Birth, then baptism. It is never the New Birth through baptism.

The following is a sermon excerpt:

Jesus answered, Verily, verily, I say unto thee, Except a man be born of water and of the Spirit, he cannot enter into the kingdom of God.

Consistent interpretation will explain this expression in the light of the context. How would Nicodemus understand it? He had the Old Testament and could be blamed for not knowing it. Jesus used words that would be intelligible to Nicodemus. Nicodemus could not be blamed for not knowing about baptism. The Jewish mind would not think He referred to literal water. Again all admit that it is a figure. Never once in the New Testament is baptism called "water." The whole matter turns upon this question: Of what is "water" a figure?

If Jesus referred to baptism, He was merely substituting a ceremony for the many ceremonies of Judaism. Other expressions in this conversation emphasize the intensely spiritual nature of the New Birth. It is "out of the Spirit" and "from above" (Greek for "again").

Whatever "water" means, it is necessary to salvation. Note the words, "except," "must" and "cannot." Why therefore, did Jesus not emphasize it on other occasions if He referred to baptism? The truth is that He always chose a representation of grace that would be understood by His hearers. Note the different figures in John: the water of Salvation in John 6, etc.

To what Old Testament passages would the mind of Nicodemus turn? He would think of Psalm 119:9 which shows the cleansing power of the word. He would recall the wells of Salvation in Isaiah 12:3. He would think of the ceremonial water of Ezekiel 36:25 that tells of the blood of the Lamb. Compare John 15:3 and Ephesians 5:26.

"Water" therefore, pictures the word of the gospel or the blood which is revealed to us in the word of the gospel.

End of Sermon[6]

---

6. This Beaman sermon excerpt from 1936 was not a part of the original Beaman commentary but comes from the West Kentucky Baptist School, *The Voice*, Murray, Kentucky, February, 1936, p. 3. This document can be found in the Digital Library Online, Southern Baptist Theological Seminary Archives, Louisville, KY. Scanned and formatted by Jim Duvall.

The Illustration of the Wind Picturing in New Birth, 3:8

Note three points:

1. Both the wind and the New Birth are sovereign: "where it listeth, or pleases."

2. Both are mysterious: "canst not tell." You cannot explain all about the New Birth any more than you can the direction and source of the wind. The New Birth is a mystery, even to the admiring heart of the saint; how much more a puzzle and an enigma to men of the world.

3. Both may be known: "thou hearest." We can see, hear, and feel the effects of the wind. One knows when he is born again. Such a great and gracious transaction cannot take place in the soul without one's knowing it. Even the world may test its genuineness by the way we live.

The Third Dialogue, 3:9-21

The inquiry of Nicodemus (3:9): Surprised and bewildered, Nicodemus does not deny but asks how these things can be. Though he was very religious, he openly acknowledged that this high experience was foreign to him. Even in his doubt there was an element of hope; he was not altogether closed to improvement. Men may know much about the Bible and yet not know the Savior revealed in the very heart of the Bible. Do you know Him?

The Answer of Christ, 3:10-21

John 3:10-12 is introductory. In 3:10 Jesus expressed astonishment at the ignorance of Nicodemus, "the teacher of Israel"— the article "the" indicating his prominence in his profession. This outstanding teacher should have known about the New Birth from such passages as Ezekiel 36:26-28 and Jeremiah 31:33. John 3:11 shows that Jesus' teaching rests on firsthand knowledge of the truth. His message is not just hearsay. In two ways Jesus points out the unbelief of Nicodemus: "ye receive not our witness" and "ye believe not." First, John 5:9-11 stresses the greatness of the sin of unbelief. Second, in 3:12 Jesus invites Nicodemus to faith. He rebuked unbelief only that He might lead to faith. We may well search our rebuke of sin to see if that is our intent.

"Earthly" things mean things done on earth, as the New Birth. The word does not imply that Jesus referred to things of an earthly nature. "Heavenly" things likewise mean things done in heaven, such as the "how" of the New Birth, the secret purpose of God, the unfathomableness of the nature of God, etcetera. Jesus had set the simpler things before this learned man. "How manifest and glaring," remarks Jesus, "would your surprise and unbelief be if I told you the deeper things?"

After the introduction, Jesus declares three things:

1. Jesus declares what He is (3:13): He is the incarnate and omnipresent Son. He came down from or out of heaven that He might lift men up to heaven. "Even the Son of man Who is in heaven." In His deity, Jesus was present in heaven at the same time that he was speaking to Nicodemus. Only God is present everywhere. Jesus claimed deity; let us believe Him without wavering. Thomas said, "My Lord and my God."

2. Jesus declares what He came to do (3:14-17). Everyone ought to memorize these verses.

   Redemption illustrated (3:14-15): Jesus referred to an Old Testament story familiar to Nicodemus and found an analogy in the Old Testament to the gospel. It is the story of the brazen serpent in the wilderness (Numbers 21:1-9). Jesus was crucified or lifted up in this wilderness of sin that we might be healed from the serpent bite of sin. Sin is like the poison of a serpent—it gets into the blood stream, it affects the entire system, it is deadly. "Must" indicates that the sacrifice of Jesus was necessary if anyone was to be saved. This is the same "must" as in 3:7. Study the "musts" in Jesus' words and life.

   Their looking to the serpent of brass pictures one's believing on Jesus. One must feel that help cannot come from himself nor from those around him. He must look away to another; it is a look of trust, of dependence. This is another one of the many rich metaphors of faith in the Bible.

   The blessing is stated both negatively and positively: "not perish but have eternal life." To perish is to go to hell, and the believer will never go there. "Eternal" translates the same word as "everlasting" in 3:16 and means that which has neither beginning nor ending. The Greek word is a compound "ever-being, ever-existing." It has no beginning because Christ, Who is our life, is eternal. It has no ending because, as Jesus said in John 14:19, "because I live, ye also shall live." Eternal life is more than eternal existence; it indicates a quality of life. It is a blessed existence in contrast with the miserable existence of the wicked. See especially Romans 6:23.

In John 3:16, we have the source and method of our redemption—God's love and Christ's sacrifice. There is no good reason for limiting the word *world*. His love was divine, worldwide, and sacrificial. His love prompted the giving, and the giving opened the way, the only way, for God's love to become active toward man. He gave His best: "His only begotten Son." It means inner likeness, intimate fellowship, and unparalleled honor. Sonship does not imply precedence for the Father and subsequence for the Son. The metaphor should not be pressed too far. "Whosoever" includes you unless, by unbelief, you shut yourself out from eternal life.

Faith is the means that puts us into (Greek) Him. It is more than faith finding its resting place in Him; it is the means or, to personify, the agent that takes by the hand and leads the sinner out of the region or realm of danger and destruction into the shelter in Jesus Christ. Have you believed into Him? It is more than believing about Him; that is good, a good start in the right direction, but not enough. It must lead on to believing *into* Him.

3. Jesus declares the results to humanity from His coming (3:18-21): Justification on the believer and judgment on the unbeliever (3:18). Judgment and all danger of judgment are passed forever from the believer (John 5:24 and Romans 8:1). His sins being removed by Christ, the sinner cannot be condemned again, for there is nothing to condemn him; sin is the only condemning factor. Faith in Jesus Christ makes the difference. Where do you stand?

Men do not wait until they get to hell to be condemned or declared guilty; they are already condemned. The reason is, "for they have not believed." "Because" would suggest cause; the word here suggests only evidence or reason and would be better rendered by "for." All sin condemns.

The sin of rejecting Christ keeps one under the curse and proves that he is already judged as deserving the wrath of God. The only way to get from under this curse is to trust all into the hands of the Son of God. Rejecting the remedy does not kill; it keeps one from being healed. The disease in all its manifoldness kills, and unbelief kills or condemns in that it is a part of this manifold disease. The point is that condemnation or the fact of guilt is already a reality before the sinner takes the attitude of unbelief. Unbelief in Christ as Savior is the one sin that keeps one out of heaven.

Some reject the light (3:19-21); some seek Him and are blessed (3:21).

By the position men take in regard to Jesus, they class themselves as either reproved or saved (Godet 1886). Men "loved" darkness rather than light. Men still set their affection on the things of the darkness of sin rather than the Light of Life. The one cause is, "because their deeds are evil." One who practices evil things does not want the light to shine on him lest he become convicted of his crime. That is why some flee from the light while others seek it. He who loves and does the truth wants his deeds manifested that they have been wrought in God. Righteous deeds prove that God is working through man. The saint never wants the glory but gives it all to the Lord. "Reprove" can mean "convince" here (see also 16:8; 8:46).

His last word may have been an encouragement to Nicodemus.

Have you been born from above? Have you believed on Jesus? If you answer "yes" to the second question, you can be sure of the "yes" answer to the first. But that is the only route by which you can reach surety on the fact of your being born again. Of course, the proper fruits in your life strengthen the conviction. Furthermore, faith in Jesus does not meritoriously, but only instrumentally, save. The power is in the Savior; faith is the attitude of the heart in man that allows God, consistently with His own nature and purpose, to release this redeeming power to the human heart.

3.1.4 The Parallel Ministries of John and Jesus, 3:22-36

(22) After these things came Jesus and his disciples into the land of Judaea; and there he tarried with them, and baptized. (23) And John also was baptizing in Aenon near to Salim, because there was much water there: and they came, and were baptized. (24) For John was not yet cast into prison. (25) Then there arose a question between some of John's disciples and the Jews about purifying. (26) And they came unto John, and said unto him, Rabbi, he that was with thee beyond Jordan, to whom thou barest witness, behold, the same baptizeth, and all men come to him. (27) John answered and said, A man can receive nothing, except it be given him from heaven. (28) Ye yourselves bear me witness, that I said, I am not the Christ, but that I am sent before him. (29) He that hath the bride is the bridegroom: but the friend of the bridegroom, which standeth and heareth him, rejoiceth greatly because of the bridegroom's voice: this my joy therefore is fulfilled. (30) He must increase, but I must decrease. (31) He that cometh from above is above all: he that is of the earth is earthly, and speaketh of the earth: he that cometh from heaven is above all. (32) And what he hath seen and heard, that he testifieth; and no man receiveth his testimony. (33) He that hath received his testimony hath set to his seal that God is true (34) For he whom God hath sent speaketh the words of God: for God giveth not the Spirit by measure unto him. (35) The Father loveth the Son, and hath given all things into his hand. (36) He that believeth on the Son hath everlasting life: and he that believeth not the Son shall not see life; but the wrath of God abideth on him. (John 3:22-36)

This is the last testimony of John the Baptist before he was beheaded. It would be most profitable to collect and analyze the testimony or teachings of John. Such will surprise you.

John and Jesus Working Together, 3:22-24

Being received with coldness and unbelief in the capital city, Jesus withdrew from Jerusalem for a period of ministry in Judea in the vicinity where John was. The continuous tense of the Greek favors the idea of Hovey (1885): that this ministry covered about seven months.

The place was Aenon, which means a fountain, and was near Salim, a place not altogether located satisfactorily (see Hovey 1885). We are told that the reason for selecting this place was "because many waters were there," and "even in summer baptism by immersion could be continued" (Dods 1908). There is no ground whatsoever here for pouring or sprinkling as New Testament baptism. John 4:2 more exactly defines Jesus' baptizing as done by His disciples under His superintendence. This again gives Jesus' sanction to the baptism of John (see also Matthew 3).

The Relation of John and Jesus; or, Jesus Superior to John, 3:25-36

A SAD CONTENTION, 3:25-26

The word *then* in 3:25 has the force of "therefore"; that is, the joint work gave rise to the misunderstanding, but neither Jesus nor John was responsible for it, and they did not take part in it. Certain ones claimed that Jesus was opposing John. Nothing could have been further from the truth. "All" is here an exaggeration from spite and jealousy, and they wished to stir John to jealousy. The following words show that they could not at all do that.

A SPLENDID EXAMPLE, 3:27-30

John nobly declares that all opposition, even all comparison between Jesus and him, is entirely out of place. He was one preacher who could not be caught in the trap of jealousy. He was too much in love with the Lord Jesus. Would that all preachers were like him!

John 3:30 is the key to 3:27-36. "I," John, is the center of 3:27-30. "He," Jesus, is the center of 3:31-36. Or, "the friend of the Bridegroom," Jesus, is the center of 3:31-36.

Note three things in these noble words from John the Baptist:

1. A divine principle (3:27): "God gave Jesus this success; I rejoice." Heaven is the source of all good (James 1:17). It would be silly to be jealous because God gave something to another and not to you. "Beggars must not be choosers."

2. John's former declaration (3:28): His hearers were witnesses to what he had said. He could prove his point by their own testimony. John had not changed his message. Happy is the preacher (and all Christians) who sticks always to the truth, who will not be pulled away from the truth for cheap public favor. Praise to the preacher who is not afraid of what he has preached to men. John held that he was merely Christ's forerunner.

3. A tribute and prophecy (3:29-30): John so loved the Bridegroom that his noble soul rejoiced at any honor that came to Him. Does knowledge that Jesus is honored fill us with joy?

    "I must be decreasing"—self must fade before Christ. John would have nothing to do with pushing himself. Self and Jesus cannot both be honored in your life at the same time. Which will it be?

"He must be increasing"—may that be the ambition of all of us, all the time, everywhere! What are you doing to increase the honor of Jesus in the hearts of men? John, the morning star, fades in the presence of the glory of the Rising Sun, the Lord Jesus.

Two great personalities met. There was an immeasurable distance between the two. Would they clash? One deserved all the glory; the other delighted to give it. Sin is the unwillingness on our part to submerge our own personalities in His and His glory. Pride and self will push ourselves, but the most glorious personality is the Christ-mastered one. If we knew nothing more of John than this noble tribute, we would heartily accord him a prominent place in the divine record. See notes in section 2.1.2 regarding John's comment, "I am a voice . . ."

A Great Message, 3:31-36

Jesus is superior in origin (3:31). Jesus came from heaven, an honor that He shares with no one; therefore, He is truly above all. "Earthly" is here a different expression from that in 3:12. Here it does signify what has an earthly nature because of its source.

Jesus' teaching is superior (3:32-34; see also 3:11). He knows firsthand all He says (3:32). Both seeing and hearing are mentioned for emphasis. That tragic note so prominent in John, therefore, sounds in the failure of men to receive His witness. Every believer certifies this (3:33). John sadly added the note, "No man receives His testimony." That is relatively true today. The world cannot know the truth of God unless we set our seal to it in living testimony. For this work, God has chosen to use His redeemed ones. Do you do it gladly? How strong is your testimony for Him? God is true whether we certify it or not. Our certification brings good both to men about us and to our own souls.

The utterances of Jesus are the words of God Himself (3:34). There is a reason—God gave Jesus the Spirit without measure. "Unto Him," though it is not in the original, is implied by the genius of Greek usage. If Jesus needed the Spirit without measure, how much more do we!

The Father's love gave the Son universal sovereignty (3:35). On each one's attitude toward the Son depends his eternal destiny (3:36). The committal to Jesus of this sovereignty stemmed from the Father's love. This refers to Jesus in His mediatorial work; as deity, He had all sovereignty. For the rescue of man from sin, Jesus emptied Himself of the exercise of the rights of sovereignty, not the prerogative of sovereignty itself. The right inheres in His nature as an inalienable trait; without it He could not be God. The use of the right, however, He could voluntarily lay aside (Philippians 2:5-11). Yet to no mere man did God give this universal sovereignty!

John 3:36—application and warning: Memorize this verse. The themes of the contrary attitudes of faith and unbelief with their effects stand in vivid contrast.

1. The blessing on faith: "He that believeth on the Son hath everlasting life."

2. The simple condition: "believeth." No other condition is mentioned. We must not strive to correct the Word of God by adding others. To believe on Him is to trust Him, to roll the burden on Him, to rely with the heart on the Savior. A participle in the original for "he that believeth" characterizes the one who has this blessing; the present tense emphasizes that the very moment one believes, he has.

3. The precious object: "on the Son." He alone is safe. Trust your soul to nothing else nor to anyone else. The original puts it, "into the Son." That does not sound very smooth in English, but the picture is very beautiful. Faith is the means that puts one into the Son, into Him as the only "Soul Shelter" from God's wrath. It cannot be said too emphatically: "Right faith is faith in the right object." It is more a question of whom you believe rather than of how much or how strongly you believe.

4. The present blessing: "hath." Eternal life is received here and now at faith. One does not have to wait to get to heaven to receive eternal life. "Hath" (old form for has): not ought to have but does have in actual possession. It is much more than only a promise. Eternal life is possessed at faith and will be realized in fullness later (Mark 10:30). Eternal life and the New Birth confer the same blessing, the expression being varied for richness.

5. The rich gift: "everlasting life." That means that the believer's blessedness cannot end. When one is saved, he is saved forever.

6. The curse on unbelief—the sin: "believeth not the Son." Some prefer "obeyeth not." Broadus' translation (1886)

has "disbelieves." If we choose to render "obeyeth not," to be consistent, we must remember that the one point of disobedience warranted by the text is in not believing into the Son. It is untrue to the text to bring in other things, and if we do not remain true to the text, why use it anyway? No greater sin can be named than not to believe on the Son. If I chose to render it, I would translate it, "he who is not persuaded with respect to the Son." The point is that the intellect is not reached; it dissents from the truth that Jesus is the only Savior. The emotions are not reached; the sinner still feels wrongly toward the Son as the only Savior. The will is not reached; it still refuses to bend to Him as the only Savior. The entire personality of the individual—in all three aspects—must be reached. An analysis of the negative side of faith helps one to understand the content of genuine and positive faith.

The curse is twofold. Negatively: "shall not see life." This means shall not have or experience life, blessed life, neither here nor hereafter. It does not mean non-existence any more than eternal life means eternal existence. Life does not signify mere existence or duration but gives quality to that existence. It is the quality of life that counts. Soul-sleeping, second-change, and annihilation contradict these statements. How dark!

Positively: "The wrath of God abides on him." The wrath of God is His holy displeasure at man's sin, "the fixed and necessary hostility of the Divine nature to sin." It is not a passing whim; it is a requirement of the holy nature of God. He must be just and holy or not be God. This necessity does not arise from any external requirement—God is free from that—but stems from the inner perfection of His nature. A god that would not oppose sin would indicate a similar nature with sin. This Word speaks of His retributive justice, how He treats others. Only here does John use the word in his Gospel; in Revelation he uses it in 6:26, "the wrath of the Lamb"; 16:19, "the wine of the fury of His wrath"; also 14:10; 11:18; 19:15. Two words appear in the Greek for wrath; Revelation 16:19 has both of them, "the fury of His wrath." The latter is the more settled, the more abiding emotion; the former emphasizes the intensity of the wrath. The term for the more settled phase of wrath suits the word that follows in John 3:36—that is, abides.

Abides, instead of removing or ending. The only removal is that affected at or through personal faith in Jesus Christ. Hell will be eternal for everyone, though a difference in the degree of the torment will persist. God's holy displeasure is already on the lost. It will break as a dark cloud unless one repents.

3.1.5 THE CONVERSATION WITH THE SAMARITAN WOMAN, 4:1-42

(1) When therefore the Lord knew how the Pharisees had heard that Jesus made and baptized more disciples than John, (2) (Though Jesus himself baptized not, but his disciples,) (3) He left Judaea, and departed again into Galilee.

(4) And he must needs go through Samaria. (5) Then cometh he to a city of Samaria, which is called Sychar, near to the parcel of ground that Jacob gave to his son Joseph. (6) Now Jacob's well was there. Jesus therefore, being wearied with his journey, sat thus on the well: and it was about the sixth hour. (7) There cometh a woman of Samaria to draw water: Jesus saith unto her, Give me to drink. (8) (For his disciples were gone away unto the city to buy meat.) (9) Then saith the woman of Samaria unto him, How is it that thou, being a Jew, askest drink of me, which am a woman of Samaria? for the Jews have no dealings with the Samaritans. (10) Jesus answered and said unto her, If thou knewest the gift of God, and who it is that saith to thee, Give me to drink; thou wouldest have asked of him, and he would have given thee living water. (11) The woman saith unto him, Sir, thou hast nothing to draw with, and the well is deep: from whence then hast thou that living water? (12) Art thou greater than our father Jacob, which gave us the well, and drank thereof himself, and his children, and his cattle? (13) Jesus answered and said unto her, Whosoever drinketh of this water shall thirst again: (14) But whosoever drinketh of the water that I shall give him shall never thirst; but the water that I shall give him shall be in him a well of water springing up into everlasting life. (15) The woman saith unto him, Sir, give me this water, that I thirst not, neither come hither to draw. (16) Jesus saith unto her, Go, call thy husband, and come hither. (17) The woman answered and said, I have no husband. Jesus said unto her, Thou hast well said, I have no husband: (18) For thou hast had five husbands; and he whom thou now hast is not thy husband: in that saidst thou truly. (19) The woman saith unto him, Sir, I perceive that thou art a prophet. (20) Our fathers worshipped in this mountain; and ye say, that in Jerusalem is the place where men ought to worship. (21) Jesus saith unto her, Woman, believe me, the hour cometh, when ye shall neither in this mountain, nor yet at Jerusalem, worship the Father. (22) Ye worship ye know not what: we know what we worship: for salvation is of the Jews. (23) But the hour cometh, and now is, when the true worshippers shall worship the Father in spirit and in truth: for the Father seeketh such to worship him. (24) God is

a Spirit: and they that worship him must worship him in spirit and in truth. (25) The woman saith unto him, I know that Messias cometh, which is called Christ: when he is come, he will tell us all things. (26) Jesus saith unto her, I that speak unto thee am he.

(27) And upon this came his disciples, and marvelled that he talked with the woman: yet no man said, What seekest thou? or, Why talkest thou with her? (28) The woman then left her waterpot, and went her way into the city, and saith to the men, (29) Come, see a man, which told me all things that ever I did: is not this the Christ? (30) Then they went out of the city, and came unto him. (31) In the mean while his disciples prayed him, saying, Master, eat. (32) But he said unto them, I have meat to eat that ye know not of. (33) Therefore said the disciples one to another, Hath any man brought him ought to eat? (34) Jesus saith unto them, My meat is to do the will of him that sent me, and to finish his work. (35) Say not ye, There are yet four months, and then cometh harvest? behold, I say unto you, Lift up your eyes, and look on the fields; for they are white already to harvest. (36) And he that reapeth receiveth wages, and gathereth fruit unto life eternal: that both he that soweth and he that reapeth may rejoice together. (37) And herein is that saying true, One soweth, and another reapeth. (38) I sent you to reap that whereon ye bestowed no labour: other men laboured, and ye are entered into their labours. (39) And many of the Samaritans of that city believed on him for the saying of the woman, which testified, He told me all that ever I did. (40) So when the Samaritans were come unto him, they besought him that he would tarry with them: and he abode there two days. (41) And many more believed because of his own word; (42) And said unto the woman, Now we believe, not because of thy saying: for we have heard him ourselves, and know that this is indeed the Christ, the Saviour of the world. (John 4:1-42)

Jesus' Change of Fields, 4:1-6

Jesus' Reasons for Moving from Judea to Galilee: A rumor that Jesus opposed John, 4:1-3

That could never be, but things do not have to be true for dame rumor to scatter them abroad. Even if Jesus won more disciples than John, that would not mean opposition to John. Jesus' sense of ministerial ethics, however, was one of the points in His changing fields. These verses could have easily been placed in the former section under this thought—Jesus retires in respect for John.

The Divine Plan for Jesus' Life, 4:4

The word *must* indicates that it was necessary for Jesus to go through Samaria because the blueprint of His Father led that way. Ordinarily, people making that trip did not pass through Samaria; they rather crossed the Jordan into Perea, went up beyond Samaria, and then recrossed into Galilee. Grace, however, does the extraordinary. The Greek language has two words for must—one indicates a necessity arising out of needs, circumstances, surroundings; the one used here indicates a moral necessity arising from the divine appointment.

No honor in His own country (John 4:44).

The imprisonment of John (Matthew 4:12): His imprisonment is not mentioned by John; but the other writers do mention it, and this is the chronological place for it.

Both John and Jesus made disciples before baptizing them, not by baptizing them (4:1). This is the Baptist way. Jesus did not personally baptize anyone. That proves that it does not take baptism to save. Jesus is the Savior; yet if it takes baptism to save, then He would not be the full Savior.

JESUS' BEING TRIED PROVES HIS HUMANITY, 4:6

Jesus had the weaknesses incident to humanity yet without sin itself. Adam in Eden did not get weary. That shows that Jesus was made in the likeness of sinful flesh (Romans 8:3), but that does not affirm sameness, only likeness. He came down as near to us as He possibly could without taking the actual taint of sin. Oh, the marvels of the sympathizing Savior Who understands!

Yet he was never too tired to win a soul! Let Him be your example.

Jesus' Conversation with the Woman, 4:7-38

JESUS OFFERS SALVATION TO A GENTILE, 4:7-9

The gospel is for all, Jew or Gentile, moral or immoral, Nicodemus or this woman.

Note how apparently abruptly Jesus introduces the matter of salvation. Yet that is the glory of the Savior as a personal soul winner. He began with what she was thinking to lead her to think what He wanted her to think. He began with her where she was to lift her up to His level. Jesus used the material to lead her to the spiritual. She wanted to bring up the differences or prejudices between the two nations. Learn from Jesus not to allow the sinner to draw you away from the main topic of salvation into a discussion of prejudices and secondary matters. He was the master soul winner, and we may sit at His feel and learn from Him.

JESUS LEADS HER TO KNOW HER SINS AND TO KNOW HIM AS THE MESSIAH, 4:10-26

How Jesus produced conviction of sin in 4:10-20. Jesus saw perfectly what she needed and proceeded to awaken in her soul a sense of spiritual things. Her ignorance was twofold: she did not know the "free-gift" (the Greek is a bit stronger than merely "gift") of God, and she did not know Who was talking with her (4:10). If sinners only ask for it, He freely gives.

He directs her to "living water"; she was thinking of material water. She thought He was talking of water from the well and wondered how He would draw it. She could not conceive that He was greater than Jacob who dug the well. She would have enjoyed not having to make the long and tiresome trips there for water.

Because of this, Jesus proceeds to contrast the two kinds of water. Material water does not satisfy for long. Spiritual water does satisfy, and that, forever. He offered to give her the water of life; He would not have to draw such water from a well. He Himself is the water of life. Living water is not stagnant water but running water—well, spring, and artesian well. What He would give her would be artesian in its supply, bubbling up into everlasting life.

Still thinking of material water, the woman asked for what Christ had to give (4:15). It would make life easier for her; she would not have to trudge along the dry, sandy, and wearisome road to draw water. Many follow this woman in thinking of salvation from the material standpoint; they think of the material blessings. We must, however, regard the honor of the Lord as first of all.

What a strange answer Jesus gave her (4:16)! She had not even mentioned her husband. Jesus did this to arouse in her soul a sense of sin and a need of the spiritual. Jesus agreed with her that she then had no husband but referred to her past five husbands. This showed His knowledge of her inner life. He is reading the inmost thoughts of her soul. Neither can we hide anything from Him. His eye sees through veneer and hypocrisy. Others may not know us aright or may persist in misunderstanding us, but Jesus always knows, loves, and cares. Nothing this truth can dim; He gives His very best to those who leave the choice with Him.

Jesus' knowledge of her inner life convinced her that He was a prophet (4:19). First, she saw Him as a weary traveler; then she regarded Jesus as a despised Jew. Next, she showed Him the respect due a gentleman; that is the meaning of "sir" in 4:15. Now, she acknowledges that He is a prophet, used perhaps here more in the sense of a man of God or one who speaks for God than one who foretells future events. She is yet to own Him as the Messiah (4:26 with 4:29). Her townsmen will see Him as the Savior of the world (4:42).

WHAT JESUS DECLARED TRUE WORSHIP TO BE, 4:20-24

The false standard of worship (4:20): Some feel that she was shrewdly seeking to change the subject. If that had been so, Jesus would not have told her so much. His revelation of her hidden life made her conscious that she was in the presence of a divine messenger; she had long wanted to ask someone this knotty question of the rightness or wrongness of the claims of the Jews and Samaritans. She had been taught that worship was limited to a certain place, such as Mount Gerizim, the holy mountain of the Samaritans. She thinks of worship as formal and ceremonial.

The true nature of worship (4:21-23): The place does not limit it; it is spiritual (4:21). Though 4:22 is not the main concern of Jesus, He does answer her question. Jerusalem has been the divinely appointed place relative to the revelation of salvation made through the Jews.

It is a two-fold worship—in spirit and truth. In the heart, not in symbols of either Jewish or Samaritan stamp, Les the real worship. Dods (1908) said, "Two defects of all previous worship are aimed at; all that was local and all that was symbolic is to be left behind." Truth is reality. Note that the "in" is not repeated; one does not engage in worship in spirit, in a heart experience or in an emotional way, and another in truth. The two things inhere in worship, or the true nature of it is missed. Enthusiasm and sincerity are not enough, however essential they are; dry knowledge of the highest spiritual form is not enough.

He represents the Father as having a heart of love and longing for such worship. God does not delight in the solitariness of His own person as He does in the fellowship of men. A little word is omitted from the King James Version. Broadus (1885) renders thus, "For such the Father also seeks to be His worshipers." The American Standard Version of 1901 [hereafter referred to as the ASV] margin recognizes this little word *also*. Dods (1908) renders it "for of a truth." That would be the same as "indeed," "truly." A third view sees the truth more clearly—"the Father also" means the Father in addition to Jesus. It is a tacit suggestion of the Savior that He and the Father join in this seeking. This more spiritual economy springs from the heart, plan, and action of both the Father and the Son. Godet (1886) so construes the word *also*.

The divine ground of worship (4:24) is grounded on the nature of God. Better, "God is spirit." See also the phrases "God is Light" and "God is Love." These three expressions go together if we would fully understand God's nature and activity. "Spirit" stands first to emphasize it. The Greek article *the* with "God" shows that "God" is the subject. See also John 1:1, clause three.

God's spirituality demands a corresponding spiritual worship. "God is spirit" means that He is not material. Hovey (1885) says, "Immaterial, imperceptible to sense, He is everywhere in the fullness of His being; and that being is personal, knowing, feeling, and willing, with a knowledge that is infinite, a love that is perfect, and a power that is boundless." Dods (1908) remarks, "The prediction involves much; that God is personal, and much else. But primarily it here indicates that God is not corporeal, and therefore needs no temple."

This great truth must not be taken to the extreme of being used to discount public assembly for the worship of God. Jesus was exposing formalism and sacred places as abiding or being necessary to worship; positively expressed, He was stressing the true standard, nature, ground, and object of worship. One must take into consideration the context in which a certain statement was made; that is the historical principle of interpretation. Then, too, one must regard the spiritual intent Jesus had in mind; that is the spiritual principle in interpretation. That is not all there is to interpretation, but such does go a long way in the right direction.

How Jesus Revealed Himself as the Messiah, 4:25-38

Jesus was and is just what she was expecting the Messiah to be: the One Who knows all the future (4:25). To the Samaritans, the Messiah (meaning "Anointed One") was known as *Hashab* or *Hathab*, meaning the Converter, or as *El Muhdy*, meaning the Guide.

Jesus graciously met her despairing bewilderment with the announcement, "I that speak to thee am He." He had not so plainly declared Himself even to His disciples. This shows His tender mercies toward this darkened-minded and sin-stained woman. Besides, such a declaration to the Jews would have brought undesirable political involvements. Our Lord never ran from trouble when running would mean cowardice, nor did He foolishly precipitate such conflicts as would have brought His death earlier than allowable for the fulfillment of the many phases of His gracious work.

The ideas of this woman grew gradually. He was a man, a Jew, a gentleman, a prophet, but now the Messiah. Jesus made Himself known to her in fullness. He waits to make Himself known to any who have faith to receive Him!

While the woman witnesses, Jesus teaches His disciples (4:27-28). His disciples were full of Jewish prejudice about the need of the woman (4:27). They shared the Jewish notion that a man should not talk openly or publicly with any woman. "The woman"—better, "a woman." That means just any woman. This prejudice finds no justification in the Old Testament. They were wondering at His strange conduct but had learned enough about Him by now not to question His action. Silence often becomes us when speech is our desire.

She was full of joy in the new-found Savior (4:28-30). The word *then* in 4:28 has the force of *therefore*, as it often does, and points to two things: more immediately and only as the occasion, she left because of the coming of the disciples; remotely and yet strongly, she left because of this new hope in her heart, having found the Messiah.

The woman was wise in her witnessing. She invited them to come because of what she had experienced. She simply testified that He revealed her entire past to her. "Is not this the Christ?" Perhaps more accurately, "Can it be that this is the Messiah?" She did not argue that this One was the Christ; she said that the facts pointed that way. She invited them to come and investigate for themselves. Friend, that is the Christian method: "I have found it so; just test it out for yourself!"

The woman gave a private testimony, not a public preaching. Women should not speak in mixed public assemblies (1 Corinthians 14:34-35). One is hard run for an argument that thinks this testimony of the woman justifies women in preaching publicly.

Do you suppose she testified to the very men with whom she had lived in sin? Why not?

Their response was to investigate the matter. It ill becomes anyone to dismiss the issue of Christianity with a wave of the hand in indifference or supposed superior intelligence. The tense John used makes the picture very vivid, thus, "They went out of the city and were coming toward Him." That is, part of the next verses occurred while they were making the journey to Him.

He was full of doing the will of His Father in seeking the lost—the example (4:31-34). They had brought the food ("meat," not limited to flesh food, but food in general), which they went to the city to buy (4:8). It was the natural thing that He would eat and that they would urge Him to do it. He wanted to teach them a lesson in the spiritual. How slow they were to catch His meaning. Eating food is not always the most important. "Man shall not live by bread alone, but by every word that proceedeth out of the mouth of God." Jesus teaches them that one must often forego the satisfaction of natural desires out of preference for the spiritual, the work of winning lost souls. His deeper satisfaction was in revealing Himself to fainting souls. This is perhaps the greatest missionary message Jesus ever preached.

They were ignorant, said Jesus, of the food He had to eat. They were saying repeatedly to one another (force of the imperfect tense), "It isn't possible that someone brought Him something to eat, is it?" They could see that no natural explanation sufficed to explain Jesus' words. That gave their minds a readiness for His startling announcement in 4:34. Doing the Father's will to perfection or completion was His food. That was as natural and as necessary a part of His life as eating food for the body. His will must come first; if ours has to be bent to His, yet His comes first. That is not an autocratic imposition but a gracious implication of His undying love for us. It is not outward compulsion but an inner impulsion that leads the loving heart to give him the priority.

He declared that He was the One sent. A most delightful study in John is to note the many instances in which Jesus uses this title for Himself. The circumstances vary the important emphases given to it and enrich the picture greatly.

In studying the names and titles of Jesus, three things are to be noted: first, what the word itself denotes; second, what the word in its general usage connotes; third, what the word in the passage being studied connotes. In studying this particular passage, one must guard against fitting the passage into the exact mold of its general significance while guarding, on the other hand, against setting the passage against the general teaching of many passages.

"Christ" denotes the anointed One; its general usage refers it to the promised Messiah of the Old Testament. Its use by the woman here stresses His ability to show her to herself in completeness.

Therefore, He teaches His disciples to be soul winners and missionaries (4:35-38). Review the situation. Their unspoken prejudice, which He saw thoroughly, hindered their winning other disciples; His own example ought to have impressed them to put saving souls first.

"Say not ye, there are yet four months, and then cometh harvest?" Note that this is a question, not a command. The force is, "Surely you are not going to say this, are you?" He saw it in their faces; He saw that they wanted to work in the natural way. There is correspondence between natural and spiritual harvests, but the correspondence is not exact. He wanted them to see a ripe harvest all about them, and that illustrated by the woman whom He had won.

Jesus' Authority: "I say to you."

Christian Vision: "Look on the fields."

A World's Need: "White to harvest already."

A world steeped in sin is white to harvest. All that a Christian needs, provided he has the love of Christ in his heart, to call him to soul winning and mission work is the fact that men are lost. He needs no special impression. The standing need urges constant effort to win them. Let us be busy.

"Lift up your eyes." They are down on the natural level and seeing only the material things of life. Lift them up. "Look calmly, constantly on these dead ripe fields," for so is the force of the word *look*, which is the same as that translated "behold" in 1 14. Grasp every opportunity to hear or read about the needs in mission fields. Read missionary biographies.

They would reap rich results (4:36). These are a wage or reward in the fruit of souls saved and joy in their hearts.

No one worker can do all: "One soweth, and another reapeth." But the "another" must be of the same kind (so is the Greek synonym); he too must teach and preach the simple gospel of Jesus. A believer cannot sow and a modernist reap, and vice versa. It must be partnership in activity; but more, it must be partnership in intent and message as well.

"I sent you to reap" (4:38). For long I read this without seeing it. If we do not reap some, we are not fulfilling our commission. An adjustment needs to be made; life is too short, and precious souls are going to hell. Let us take up our task of reaping for the Lord.

The word *labor* implies toil. It is more than mere work or activity. Not all of the reaping will be free of burdens. Toil on until the close of your day of opportunity whether you see the joy of reaping as you desire it or not.

We must not forget our benefactors. We enter into the labor of others. Avoid, therefore, jealousies of all sorts and the taking of too much honor to yourself from results.

A Two-Day Revival in Samaria, 4:39-42

- Her work was the *basis* (4:39): "Because of the word of the woman." Just one soul on fire can prepare the way for a revival. Will you be that soul?

- Their request was the *occasion* (4:40): Contrast this with His cold reception elsewhere. Both their city and their hearts swung open to Him.

- Many saved was the *result* (4:41): One conversion led to many. Once the ice is broken, the water is more inviting. Note "many more"—many by much, many expanded to the degree of much.

- Personal experience was their *testimony* (4:42): This confession is full, broad, and noteworthy. I doubt that His disciples, later made His apostles, could have then reached this depth of truth.

These became types or the firstfruits of that great ingathering of the Gentiles that has come from the ever-widening influence of Jesus on the hearts of men.

There are in this story (4:1-42) three main pictures of Jesus: first, as the Water of Life; second, as the One whose bread is to seek the lost; third, as the Savior of the world. The message and the need fit together. Jesus fills every need of the human heart.

Let the Christian study Jesus as the model of personal work. He would not let her pull Him off to secondary questions but kept her on the main point of the need of her soul. Good things of Christian activity often crowd out the best thing in Christian living, namely, that of winning souls to the Savior. She was thinking of literal water; He spoke of it as a symbol of the spiritual water and life that he was longing to give her. Jesus' assessment is that His work equals His food.

3.1.6 JESUS' HEALING OF THE NOBLEMAN'S SON, 4:43-54

(43) Now after two days he departed thence, and went into Galilee. (44) For Jesus himself testified, that a prophet hath no honour in his own country. (45) Then when he was come into Galilee, the Galilaeans received him, having seen all the things that he did at Jerusalem at the feast: for they also went unto the feast. (46) So Jesus came again into Cana of Galilee, where he made the water wine. And there was a certain nobleman, whose son was sick at Capernaum. (47) When he heard that Jesus was come out of Judaea into Galilee, he went unto him, and besought him that he would come down, and heal his son: for he was at the point of death. (48) Then said Jesus unto him, Except ye see signs and wonders, ye will not believe. (49) The nobleman saith unto him, Sir, come down ere my child die. (50) Jesus saith unto him, Go thy way; thy son liveth. And the man believed the word that Jesus had spoken unto him, and he went his way. (51) And as he was now going down, his servants met him, and told him, saying, Thy son liveth. (52) Then enquired he of them the hour when he began to amend. And they said unto him, Yesterday at the seventh hour the fever left him. (53) So the father knew that it was at the same hour, in the which Jesus said unto him, Thy son liveth: and himself believed, and his whole house. (54) This is again the second miracle that Jesus did, when he was come out of Judaea into Galilee. (John 4:43-54)

Introduction to the Story, 4:43-45

Jesus goes again to Galilee, to Cana, and then toward Capernaum (see also John 2:1-12).

Our Lord sets an example to us to be busy always. This opens the Great Galilean Ministry (Matthew 4:12; Mark 1:14; Luke 4:14). Jesus spent much of His time in Capernaum for the next two years or thereabout.

The words *the two days* in the ASV are the same two mentioned in 4:40. "Into Galilee" fulfills the intention expressed in 4:3.

John Wesley is likely right in placing 4:44 in parentheses.[7] John cites this, kind of a proverb, only on the authority of Jesus. The statement must be studied from the viewpoint of its general truth and from its application here.

It indicates the tendency of people to be prejudiced against those from their own country. Clark and Pendleton, in their *Brief Notes on the New Testament* (1884, 53), say, "To judge of persons by their outward circumstances, and not by their character and conduct, is a mark of pride, prejudice, and littleness of mind." Dods (1908, 164) remarks, "The man that has grown up among us, whom we have seen struggling up through the ignorance, and weakness, and folly of boyhood, whom we have had to help and to protect and scarcely receive the same respect as one who presents himself a mature man, with already developed faculties, no longer a learner, but prepared to teach."

Montaigne complained that in his own country he had to purchase publishers, whereas elsewhere, publishers were anxious to purchase him. "The farther off I am read from my own home," he says, "the better I am esteemed." The men of Anathoth sought Jeremiah's life when he began to prophesy among them.[8]

What is the application of the statement? He uses it subsequently on two other occasions—Luke 4:54 and Matthew 13:57. It is phrased somewhat differently on different occasions. "His own country" may refer to Judea and Jerusalem. One would naturally see here a resumption of the story of 4:1-3, which had been interrupted by the account of the Lord's experience in Samaria.

The Galileans "received" (4:45) Him, which means that they tendered Him a respectful reception. I doubt that it refers to their faith; certainly it does not refer to their receiving Him into their hearts by faith. If it does refer to their faith, it is of a low type motivated by what they had seen and heard without its catching in their hearts. John often distinguishes different kinds or levels of faith.

"Having seen"—better, "because they saw." His miracles in Jerusalem (2:23) had sent His fame ahead to Galilee, and they were in

---

7. Editor's Note: No citation is given for Wesley.
8. Editor's Note: No citation is given for the quote by Montaigne.

expectancy for His coming. Jerusalem, the metropolis, set the fashion in their estimate of men and things (Alford 1859).

John identifies Cana as the place "where He made the water wine." This identifies the place, prepares for 4:54, and reminds us that Jesus had friends in that place (Dods 1908).

A Picture of the All-Sufficient Savior, 4:46-53

I point out three major pictures in this story:

1. A picture of need (4:46-47): A "nobleman" means a courtier, as indicating one's rank; a king's officer, as indicating he was in royal service; a royal person, as indicating his royal blood. We do not know which applies here. Some have suggested, however, that he may have been Chuza, the steward of Herod (Luke 8:3). The characteristic description for this story lies, however, in the clause, "whose son was sick at Capernaum."

    "Come down" (4:49): For Cana stood much higher than Capernaum (Wesley). It was some twenty miles from Capernaum to Cana, but that distance mattered not because this man was burdened.

    I take these lessons from J.C. Ryle (1860): (1) The rich and honorable have afflictions as well as the poor and lowly. Afflictions do not respect persons. (2) Disease and death attach the young as well as the old. If afflictions have not come to you yet, do not be proud, for they may come soon enough. (3) Afflictions may be a benefit. They led this man to come to Jesus. Many people never think seriously about Jesus until they or some of their family get into trouble. Do not complain about troubles if they bring you closer to Jesus. The direction in which afflictions turn you is the main thing.

    The objects of mercy come from all classes. Look around you and see someone in need. Study John 1:4—fishermen, a Rabbi, a sinful woman, this royal person. Note the variety.

2. A picture of growing faith (4:47-53): Jesus performed two miracles in one—He formed faith in this man, and He drove away the fever. Jesus is master of both the spiritual and material realms. The forming of faith was the greater miracle.

    There were three stages in the man's faith. G. Campbell Morgan (1960) names them thus: the act of obedient faith;

the appeal of venturesome faith; the assurance of vindicated faith. The Venerable Bede in the eighth century calls them the beginning of faith, the increase of faith, and the perfection of faith. "The father's faith passes through three stages, the belief that comes to ask for help, the deeper belief that rests upon Jesus' word to him and starts back home, and the yet deeper faith that gets confirmation of Jesus' word and power in the recovery of his son from the very time Jesus spoke the assuring word" (Gordon 1915, 143).

I suggest the following: Seeking or praying faith (4:46), tested or trusting faith (4:47-50), and strengthened or assured faith (4:51-53).

Seeking or praying faith (4:46)—family needs led him, the fame of Jesus directed him where to go, and love for his son worded his request.

Tested or trusting faith (4:47-50)—Jesus perceived that the faith of this man was not strong enough. He saw that the man was looking too much to outward signs, as has ever been true but is very evident today in the signs movement. Through this test, He perfected the man's faith into deeper trust in Himself. The wind causes the tree's roots to cling more tenaciously.

There was danger that he would regard Jesus as a mere worker of miracles. Does our faith rest on the physical senses, merely? Signs and wonders—the first naming the purpose of the miracle, the second the effect on the people. This man's slow faith is in ready contrast to the faith of the Samaritans who believed without any sign. The statement of Jesus designed a test for the man's faith, and the man stood the test. In 4:48 "Jesus therefore said," that is, in view of the imperfect faith He saw in the man. Jesus spoke to the deeper need first, and His statement awakened the man to wholehearted trust.

The courtier (royal official) considered the presence of Jesus at his own home necessary to his power to help. After Jesus spoke to the man, he went away without Jesus' bodily presence, in faith. Jesus did two things to develop faith: He spoke with apparent harshness, and He sent the man home with nothing but His word as a ground of faith (and whatever else He may have conveyed by His look of understanding tenderness). Jesus' command meant that Jesus claimed more power than the man had supposed; distance is no barrier to Jesus.

Strengthened or assured faith (4:51-53). You can always check on the words of Jesus and find them true and that they stand the severest test. His Word never fails. It will always do to trust. His Word and the facts always agree. "The more exactly the works of God are considered, the more faith is increased" (Wesley). "To believe because of a great benefit is blessed. It is even more blessed to believe through and over and in spite of a great sorrow" (Speer 1915).

Jesus never promises a sinner salvation at faith and then goes back on His promise. Have you trusted His promise or what you saw or what you felt or something else as a substitute for faith in Him and His Word? "Where is your faith?" His promise is worthy of your fullest trust. The actual healing of his son gave this man visual proof that Jesus tells the truth, and it was written to assure our faith. With this extra evidence, the courtier entrusted himself fully to Jesus.

"His whole house"—someone has called this "the first converted family" (4:53).

3. A picture of the all-sufficient Savior (4:47-53): I point out four phases:

His knowledge (4:48)—He knew that the heart of this man needed a deeper faith. He sees beyond the surface. He knows just what is in every heart (John 2:24-25). Why not let Him search the deep of your heart and fill your deepest need?

His ability not limited to place—He is both omnipotent and omnipresent. He has all power and is everywhere. His Word was as good as His presence (4:49-50). He is as truly able to save the sinner or aid the Christian as if He were bodily present.

His Word came true (4:52-53)—We need never fear any checking up on His Word or works, provided it is honestly done. They evermore stand the severest test. The coincidence of time was of divine superintendence. "The cure brings into prominence this distinctive peculiarity of a miracle that it consists of a marvel which is coincident with an express announcement of it" (Dods 1908).

His graciousness—He answered more than the man asked. He asked for the healing of his son; Jesus saved the courtier and his entire house.

Conclusion of the Story, 4:54

This is Jesus' second Galilean miracle. Again, the Scripture denies those childish miracles that tradition says He performed as a child in making birds of clay and making them to fly. He never performed miracles without purpose.

Many others had as deep physical needs. He did not heal all. "He came to remove their cause. He dealt only with illustrative cases. What He did in such cases, He did as a sign of what He would do in all cases" (Speer 1915).

The "again the second sign" connects 4:54 with 4:46 and then more remotely with 2:11. "Again a second" is a pleonasm, a figure in which for emphasis one puts a fullness not demanded for grammatical clearness.

Each of these two first miracles marked a crisis in His life. They furnish a strange contrast of circumstances: "the home of gladness and marriage festivity, and the darkened home of anxiety and pain and the shadow of death!" The one in John 2 "brought to a close the private career of our Lord"; the one in John 4 "ends the opening scenes of his public career" (Erdman 1916, 50ff).

It is certainly false to seek as some modern scholars do to suppose that John 4:46-54 is just another recording of Matthew 8:5-13. There was a difference in their condition—paralyzed versus fever; one was a centurion and a Gentile, the other a courtier and likely a Jew; one insists that Jesus not come under his roof, the other supplicant begs Him to do just that; the half-faith of the father is blamed, the extraordinary faith of the centurion is lauded (Dods 1908).

3.2 His Formal Manifestation in Signs and Teachings, Chapters 5-10

3.2.1 Jesus' Healing of the Infirm Man and His Sermon on His Deity, chapter 5

Jesus heals the man with thirty-eight years infirmity and preaches the Oneness of the Father and the Son.

> *(1) After this there was a feast of the Jews; and Jesus went up to Jerusalem. (2) Now there is at Jerusalem by the sheep market a pool, which is called in the Hebrew tongue Bethesda, having five porches. (3) In these lay a great multitude of impotent folk, of blind, halt, withered, waiting for the moving of the water. (4) For an angel went down at a certain season into the pool, and troubled the water: whosoever then first after the troubling of the water stepped in was made whole of whatsoever disease he had. (5) And a certain man was there, which had an infirmity thirty and eight years. (6) When Jesus saw him lie, and knew that he had been now a long time in that case, he saith unto him, Wilt thou be made whole? (7) The impotent man answered him, Sir, I have no man, when the water is troubled, to put me into the pool: but while I am coming, another steppeth down before me. (8) Jesus saith unto him, Rise, take up thy bed, and walk. (9) And immediately the man was made whole, and took up his bed, and walked: and on the same day was the sabbath. (10) The Jews therefore said unto him that was cured, It is the sabbath day: it is not lawful for thee to carry thy bed. (11) He answered them, He that made me whole, the same said unto me, Take up thy bed, and walk. (12) Then asked they him, What man is that which said unto thee, Take up thy bed, and walk? (13) And he that was healed wist not who it was: for Jesus had conveyed himself away, a multitude being in that place. (14) Afterward Jesus findeth him in the temple, and said unto him, Behold, thou art made whole: sin no more, lest a worse thing come unto thee. (15) The man departed, and told the Jews that it was Jesus, which had made him whole. (16) And therefore did the Jews persecute Jesus, and sought to slay him, because he had done these things on the sabbath day.*
>
> *(17) But Jesus answered them, My Father worketh hitherto, and I work. (18) Therefore the Jews sought the more to kill him, because he not only had broken the sabbath, but said also that God was his Father, making himself equal with God. (John 5:1-18)*

John 5:1-16 records the sign as the occasion of the sermon; 5:17-18 gives the theme of the sermon, the Oneness of Jesus with God; 5:19-47 gives the sermon itself.

The Sign—the Healing of the Impotent Man, 5:1-18

This feast was most likely the feast of the Passover. See 2:12. "After these things" does not state how long. The feast was the occasion of Jesus' going up since the crowds would be there in the capital city. We do not yet know with certainty the location of this pool, but it is generally believed that we are to find it just north of the temple area. This has been the tradition since the fourth century. We know that in some way it was associated with sheep interests. Was it the gate through which the sheep were brought to Jerusalem? Was it the place of marketing the sheep? Or was it the place at which the priests washed the sheep for the sacrifices? (Adams 1938).

"Five porches"—There was a structure having five porches or wings, "whether in the form of clo sters or colonnades is not known" (Adams 1938).[9]

HUMAN NEED AND THE MISERY OF SIN—A PICTURE OF SIN, 5:1-5

The picture here fittingly illustrates the suffering, selfishness, and sin of the world in contrast to the healing and salvation of Jesus. His is a ministry of redemption (Erdman 1916). Jesus' statement in 5:14 shows that the healing may be applied to sin. Jesus likely chose this man as a case well-known in Jerusalem as hopeless.

Observe: He was utterly helpless in his condition. He could neither heal himself nor put himself into the water. So is the sinner "without strength" (Romans 5:6). He was wholly friendless in the attitude of others toward him. The prodigal lost his friends-in-sin when his money gave out. We must care for men just because they have priceless souls, not just because of what they have in earthly possessions or their standing among men. He was deeply hopeless in his own attitude toward himself. When men come to the end of their own strength in the sense of realizing their helplessness, then they are ready to trust Jesus. So long as men think that they can do something to save themselves, they will never turn to Jesus for salvation. There is a negative side to faith. It grows out of the

---

9. Editor's Note: Some modern translations omit part of John 5:4-5 on the assumption that the earliest and best manuscripts do not contain these verses. The assumption by these scholars is that the copyists of the Scriptures through the centuries made mistakes by adding words to the text. These words had not been a part of the original autographs and therefore are not Scripture. This scholarly assumption is debatable and in this case, especially so. In this particular instance, one of the church fathers sheds light on whether these verses belong in the passage. Tertullian referenced these verses with the disputed words in place. Since Tertullian died in the middle of the third century (his date of death is sometimes given as 240 AD), this gives a very early attestation of the verses. The editor's opinion is that these disputed verses *are* Scripture and should be included in the text of John 5.

fact that man wants to offer his religion to God as having saving power or anything he esteems as worthy to save This must be abandoned.

Divine Love and Compassion—A Picture of Salvation, 5:6-9

Jesus saw with His eyes the man's sad case and knew by divine knowledge that he had for a long time continued thus. Note these lessons:

1. Jesus first got the man's attention by asking a question. This is a good lesson for soul winners. You cannot do much for the man who is not interested in what you are saying.

2. Jesus next appealed to the will or desire of the man. Jesus is "far more ready to save than man is to be saved" (Ryle 1860). The stubborn will of man must be broken. The desire for salvation and life must be awakened. If Jesus bestowed salvation on us without His stirring us to a sense of need, we would not appreciate His gift of love. Conviction for sin is essential in the bestowing of salvation on men.

3. Jesus gave the man a simple test. Along with the command to arise and carry his bed went the power to heal. Note that the healing was instantaneous. Salvation is not a process; deliverance from the guilt of sin occurs the moment one trusts the Savior. Salvation is the instantaneous act of God in rescuing the soul from the brink of hell. Salvation implies three things: a danger; one exposed to the danger; and rescue from that danger.

Human Duty and Gratitude—A Picture of Service, 5:10-15

When he was mercifully healed, this man told others that Jesus did it. Do we? Let us imitate this man in telling even our enemies what Jesus has done for us. Nothing is more needed today among Christians than the habit of daily telling lost people about Christ Jesus Who saves all who trust in Him.

Blind Persecutors and Faultfinder—A Picture of Persecution, 5:16-18

The shame of it is that too many are faultfinders instead of truth-seekers.

Note the reasoning of the man. The man who had power to heal him had the right also to command him. The fact that He is the giver of life argues that He is the regulator of life. The kindness of Jesus to him prompts and elicits the gratitude of the man to Jesus. That is service growing out of a sense of benefit bestowed. Service that looks toward the goal of receiving a benefit is of a lower motive. The love motive is the highest motive known, and the deepest spring to produce such is a sense of benefit received through amazing grace.

The persecutors' first objection: The first thing that attracted their attention was not the marvelous deed of mercy but their false attitude toward the Sabbath (5:16-17). Their minds were already made up against Jesus. Too many are unwilling to investigate the truth and pass it up with a wave of the hand as though it were beneath their dignity. The search and discovery of truth, however, is the most important seeking in the world.

Their charge was twofold: They said He Himself worked on a Sabbath and caused another to work They thus claimed that He broke the fourth commandment. He answered, "I am merely imitating My Father Who, though He rested from creation, is very actively at work even now in redemption and providence, and I am working." "I am working" forms a good motto for every Christian. The motive of it is that *My Father is working*; hence I too must be working.

The persecutors' second objection (5:18): They charged that He made Himself equal to God and that therein He violated the first commandment. They persecuted Him for the first and attempted to kill Him for the second.

The Sermon—The Deity of Jesus; or, Jesus' Oneness or Equality with God, 5:19-47

(19) Then answered Jesus and said unto them, Verily, verily, I say unto you, The Son can do nothing of himself, but what he seeth the Father do: for what things soever he doeth, these also doeth the Son likewise. (20) For the Father loveth the Son, and sheweth him all things that himself doeth: and he will shew him greater works than these, that ye may marvel. (21) For as the Father raiseth up the dead, and quickeneth them; even so the Son quickeneth whom he will. (22) For the Father judgeth no man, but hath committed all judgment unto the Son: (23) That all men should honour the Son, even as they honour the Father. He that honoureth not the Son honoureth not the Father which hath sent him. (24) Verily, verily, I say unto you, He that heareth my word, and believeth on him that sent me, hath everlasting life, and shall not come into condemnation; but is passed from death unto life. (25) Verily, verily, I say unto you, The hour is coming, and now is, when the dead shall hear the voice of the Son of God: and they that hear shall live. (26) For as the Father hath life in himself; so hath he given to the Son to have life in himself; (27) And hath given him authority to execute judgment also, because he is the Son of man. (28) Marvel not at this: for the hour is coming, in the which

all that are in the graves shall hear his voice, (29) And shall come forth; they that have done good, unto the resurrection of life; and they that have done evil, unto the resurrection of damnation. (30) I can of mine own self do nothing: as I hear, I judge: and my judgment is just; because I seek not mine own will, but the will of the Father which hath sent me.

(31) If I bear witness of myself, my witness is not true. (32) There is another that beareth witness of me; and I know that the witness which he witnesseth of me is true. (33) Ye sent unto John, and he bare witness unto the truth. (34) But I receive not testimony from man: but these things I say, that ye might be saved. (35) He was a burning and a shining light: and ye were willing for a season to rejoice in his light. (36) But I have greater witness than that of John: for the works which the Father hath given me to finish, the same works that I do, bear witness of me, that the Father hath sent me. (37) And the Father himself, which hath sent me, hath borne witness of me. Ye have neither heard his voice at any time, nor seen his shape. (38) And ye have not his word abiding in you: for whom he hath sent, him ye believe not. (39) Search the scriptures; for in them ye think ye have eternal life: and they are they which testify of me. (40) And ye will not come to me, that ye might have life. (41) I receive not honour from men. (42) But I know you, that ye have not the love of God in you. (43) I am come in my Father's name, and ye receive me not: if another shall come in his own name, him ye will receive. (44) How can ye believe, which receive honour one of another, and seek not the honour that cometh from God only? (45) Do not think that I will accuse you to the Father: there is one that accuseth you, even Moses, in whom ye trust. (46) For had ye believed Moses, ye would have believed me: for he wrote of me. (47) But if ye believe not his writings, how shall ye believe my words? (John 5:19-47)

John 5:19-47 constitute His full answer. He admits that their charge was true and sets out to prove it. That is indeed hard on any who hold that Jesus claimed to be only a man. He claimed He was God manifest in flesh. "Either Jesus was a blasphemer and a deceiver, or else he was the Son of God" (Erdman 1916).

The sermon falls into three parts:

1. He explains wherein this equality exists (5:19-30).

2. He enumerates the witnesses to this equality (5:31-39).

3. He shows the reasons for their rejection of Him (5:38-47).

He makes His claim or states His case, then proves it by various witnesses, and then applies the matter to His hearers. That is a logical way of development. The three may here be called exposition, argument, and application; and Jesus was artist in each of them.

He explains wherein this equality exists (5:19-30). When Jesus called God His Father, the Jews took it that He thereby made Himself equal with God. If Jesus had not meant to claim deity, here was the time to say it. He could easily have said, as liberals have tried to represent that

He meant, that His hearers misunderstood Him. He did no such thing. Instead of denying such a charge, He claimed it and set out to prove it. If we take the word of Jesus for it, then He is God. If we do not take His word for it, we either charge Him with insincerity or ignorance, and in neither case would He be worthy of our respect.

JESUS IS THE MEDIATOR BETWEEN GOD AND MAN, 5:19-20

Jesus was dependent on the Father, that is, in His mediatorial office. Jesus declares a harmony of doing, feeling, and knowing. And that is not all—greater works remain to be done. "The divine activity which Jesus claimed to share with the Father was twofold, and neither function could be performed by man" (Erdman 1916).

JESUS HAS POWER TO MAKE DEAD MEN ALIVE, 5:21

The word *quicken* means "to make alive." From the original meaning, we get a weakened force of "quicken." The point of Jesus is just this—the Son and the Father do the same miraculous work; they, therefore, are equal. "The Son quickeneth whom He will." His will is sovereign as well as miraculous. This power to make dead men alive is illustrated in 5:1-16. He will return to this point in 5:24-30.

JESUS HAS AUTHORITY TO JUDGE, 5:22-23, 27

His Father committed all judgment to the Son. The purpose was the honor of Jesus. Honoring the Father and the Son cannot be separated (5:23). Jews, Mohammedans, and Unitarians cannot honor the Father so long as they dishonor the Son. The Father loves His Son too well to accept love or honor proffered to Him that spells dishonor to His Son.

As the Son of God, Jesus had inherently, spontaneously, and underivedly this honor, but "because he is a son of man" (5:24, ASV), the Father committed this work into His hands. Only here does this expression "the Son of man," as used by Jesus (all 81 times), stand without the article. It is not here, "the Son of Man," but merely, "a Son of man." The variance is very significant. This shows that the title "the Son of Man" refers to the Messiah and implies His deity, but "a Son of man" emphasizes Jesus as a man. The Jews would not accept the mere man Jesus as the Judge; Jesus claimed that the very fact of His humanity led the Father to make such a committal. The phrase here emphasizes that He will be sympathetic and understanding even in His judgment or sentence of judgment.

The Judge will be both just and sovereign in act and sympathetic and understanding in attitude. The judgment and the incarnation are thus tied together, making the mediatorial work of Jesus universal in this aspect. Not often do we see men making or pointing out this significant relationship. What a relationship! But in reality, all the great doctrines are vitally related; they are a unit, they form complementary threads in the fabric of truth.

Jesus Is the Source of Life, or Resurrection Life, 5:24-30

I have often illustrated John 5:24, this blessed text, thus: The encouraging inscription over the door—in two parts: "verily, verily," an assurance of His sincerity and truthfulness and trustworthiness; "I say to you," the authority of Jesus. The only key to unlock the door is "He that hears My word and believes on Him that sent Me." Do not add other things; they will neither fit nor bring the blessing.

There is a threefold blessing within the room. First, "has everlasting life" in the present. Second, "and shall not come into condemnation" or judgment in the future. The believer will be judged as to his works and the reward he will receive, but not as to his sins nor as to his salvation. His sins are so put away by Christ that they will never be brought up again against him in judgment; they are removed forever. Third, "but is passed from death unto life" for the past. The American Standard Version (1901) more vividly follows the Greek, "but has passed out of death into life." These three blessings take care of all time—past, present, and future. Jesus is the Savior for all ages, in all ages, covering all their sins, for all time. Your case is safe in His hands. He will do to trust.

Two kinds of death are mentioned: spiritual and physical. Physical death is the separation of the soul from the body. Spiritual death is the separation of the soul from God. Eternal death is the eternal separation of the soul from God. Eternal death is the prolongation of spiritual death into eternity. If the sinner lets Jesus save him, his spiritual death ends in eternal life in Christ. The one who rejects Him continues in this state of spiritual death forever. Separation is the chief idea in death, not annihilation.

Two resurrections are pictured: a spiritual resurrection now and a physical resurrection later. The first of these is metaphorical or figurative, just as the first type of death is a metaphor. Physical death and physical resurrection are real.

It is important to note that His voice breaks the reign of death in each case. His voice in thus breaking the reign of death is the strongest voice in the world. Now, He calls the dead in sin into life eternal in Himself (5:24-26). Later, He calls all the physically dead into resurrection—life (5:28-29). In 5:25 He says, "The hour is coming and now is," because He refers to the spiritual resurrection that takes place here and now at faith in Jesus Christ (see also 4:23). In 5:28 it is simply "the hour is coming," because it refers to the future, bodily resurrection.

"They that hear shall live" (5:25). Literally, "the ones hearing," or "the ones who hear." Dods (1908) says, "The insertion of the article indicates that not all, but only a certain class of the *nekroi* (dead) are meant: all the dead hear but not all give ear (Weiss)." All in general hear with the outward ear, but these hear with faith. The construction characterizes those who live as those who hear His voice, who hear in the deepest recesses of the soul and with the enlistment of the faculties of the personality. *Hear* is here a picture of faith. The soul is not dead in the sense of being in non-existence; it is rather that separation of the soul from God, that estrangement of the spirit from its maker, that degradation and defilement and decay brought on by man's sin.

It does not read, "They that live shall hear," or "They that have already been made alive shall hear." That is Hardshellism; it is not Bible and Baptist doctrine. Whether we are able to explain it or not, still the statement of Jesus stands and should not be twisted to suit our ideas or make them more convenient. The simple truth remains that until you have heard the voice of the Son of God in trustful faith, you cannot claim any life from Him. He sets the matter of hearing as prerequisite or conditional to the living. The hearing in faith characterizes those who are so to become alive.

This may be psychologically impossible or un-understandable, but the mighty power of Jesus makes it soluble and possible in actual practice (Dods 1908). The best parallel to it is found in Jesus' miracles. Jesus told the man to stretch forth his withered hand; He called Lazarus to come forth; He ordered the impotent man to arise and walk. With the command went the power to perform and to live. We can believe it whether we can understand it or not. At least, we have not the slightest warrant for changing the order of Jesus.

Both the saved and the lost will be raised from the dead (5:29). Daniel anticipates Jesus, and Paul and John follow Jesus in this declaration. Daniel 12:2 says, "Some to everlasting life and some to shame and everlasting contempt." Jesus spoke of both soul and body as cast into hell

(Matthew 10:28). Paul affirmed a "resurrection of the dead, both of the just and unjust" (Acts 24:15). Revelation 20:5 shows that there will be a space of one thousand years between the resurrection of the just and of the unjust. They will have life in its fullness or damnation according to their character. "Those that have done good" do not inherit life by virtue of their good conduct; they get life from Christ, as is shown clearly in 5:24-25, and their doing good fruits results from the life implanted and imparted at faith. The life of Jesus within us will bear fruit in our doing good (Matthew 7:17-20); but fruit does not make the tree good, it bears fruit of a good character since the tree is good.

He Enumerates the Witnesses to His Equality with the Father, 5:31-39

If Jesus were the only witness concerning Himself, His witness would not be true (5:31). But He had other witnesses.

- John the Baptist (5:32-35): See 1:6-8. Whether "another" in 5:32 refers to the Father or to John the Baptist, it is a tacit way of Jesus' saying that He Himself and this other witness are of the same kind. There is another word for "other" that means another of a different kind. Jesus' estimate of John was that John was a burning and shining lamp.

- "That ye might be saved" (5:34): Jesus' heart was ever on fire for souls. He preached looking toward the salvation of men. Do we? Do our Sunday school teachers, special workers, and preachers teach and preach that men may be saved? The evangelistic purpose in preaching is most important. Jesus was not primarily interested in confuting His enemies; He wanted to give a light that would pierce the armor of prejudice, misunderstanding, and hatred.

- Jesus' works or miracles (5:36): His interpretation of His own miracles is that in them the Father proved that He sent the Son to be the Savior. Every miracle proved His Messiahship. This was their highest purpose. Helping man was a guiding thought, but it was not supreme. Many another was afflicted but was not healed. Those He did heal He intended as "accreditive" (given permission to) witnesses of His Messiahship.

- The Father Himself (5:37): "God is spirit"—God does not have bodily form.

- The Scriptures (5:38): The indicative mood of the American Standard Version (1901) is preferable to the imperative mood of the King James Version. The form in the Greek may be either, only the context can be decisive, and that seems to require some such meaning as the following. They were searching the Scriptures but falsely thought that in the Scriptures themselves they would have life. They thought of the Scriptures as an end in themselves; they are rather a glorious means to a glorious end.

"The grand purpose of all Scripture is to witness concerning Me." Yes, Jesus fills the Old Testament; if you fail to see Him there, you fail to see the grand purpose of the Scriptures. They were devoted to the Scriptures but with the wrong intent. Their motivation was off center. When we read and search the Bible, do we see Jesus in it? We may well emulate their assiduity in searching but not their reason or intent.

He Shows the Reasons for Their Rejection of Him, 5:38-47

Jesus analyzed His hearers and showed them to themselves; that is if they only had power to understand His analysis.

- His Word does not abide in you (5:38-39): "And the word of Him you do not have abiding in you." That is a serious charge; how does Jesus prove or sustain this charge? "For whom that one sent, this one you do not believe." The two demonstratives strongly tie the Father and the Son together. The emphatic "you" puts teeth into the charge. His Word in you would lead you to believe on Him, for the Scriptures bear witness concerning Him, Jesus Christ. He is the heart of the testimony of the Bible. Does His Word abide in you? Faith in Him makes the Word about Him precious to the soul. Faith is that realization of the value and pertinence of Jesus to the needs of everyday life and the life after this.

- Your will is depraved (5:40): Why did they not come to Jesus? "You will not to come." Their will and desire were corrupted. Men today give many excuses as to why they put off salvation. The real cause is found in a will that is set against Jesus. Men go wrong in their sinful lives, but their misconduct is traceable to a depraved will. Jesus does not emphasize here the weakness of the will but the willfulness of it. Conviction is needed to break that stubborn will. Men are not saved until the will is reached. The reason is that the will is the active principle or phase of the personality. Knowing and feeling, the complementary traits of personality, cannot come to focus or become active except through the outlet of the will. They too must be touched and can influence the will, but until the will is reached, no salvation comes. Men are not saved against their wills. They are saved against what their will once was. In repentance, however, the sinful will is so broken that it turns and takes God's side against sin.

Coming to Christ is the only way men get life. They are dead without Jesus Christ (1 John 5:12). No one else has the gift of eternal life except the Savior. John 6:68 says, "Thou hast the words of eternal life." Coming to Christ is just another way of stating faith in Jesus or just another of those varied and rich metaphors of faith. It implies that men are away from Him, being estranged by and in sin; it implies that He has power to save; it implies that contact with Him is necessary for life in Him. Faith is, therefore, that approach of the heart to Him Who alone can make dead men alive. There is no other source of spiritual or eternal life. This coming does not refer to a physical act of coming; the physical act is merely the metaphor or picture portraying simply the spiritual act of the soul.

- The love of God is not in you (5:42): You cannot love God without loving Jesus. Do you really love Him? The curse of God rests on all who do not love Him (1 Corinthians 16:22). Men do not naturally love the Lord; this love must be poured out into their hearts by the Holy Spirit (Romans 5:5).

- Your desire for human honor overmasters you and causes your unbelief (5:43-44): Self-seeking and faith do not grow in the same heart. The soil for faith is humility and penitence. Seek Him and Him alone.

- You do not believe your own Scriptures; therefore you are self-condemned (5:45-47): There was no need for Jesus to condemn them; the law of Moses did that. Sinner, the same law accuses and condemns you. You cannot escape so long as you reject the Lord Jesus. They trusted in Moses in the wrong way. They failed to see that Moses wrote about Jesus Christ (5:46; see

John 1:45). The Old Testament is full of Christ and the gospel. The man who denies Moses' writings cannot believe Jesus' words. The principle is that that one act of unbelief precludes an act of faith. That is hard on evolutionists, higher critics, etcetera. Believing what God says in Genesis to Deuteronomy prepares the heart to receive Jesus as Savior and Lord.

Believing Jesus' words is all-important, for on faith in Him and His Word hangs one's eternal destiny. Of no other person can it be truly said that on one's attitude toward him turns one's eternal destiny. That proves that Jesus is God and the only Savior. Why not believe on Him without delay?

3.2.2 JESUS' FEEDING THE FIVE THOUSAND AND HIS SERMON ON THE TRUE BREAD OF LIFE, CHAPTER 6

The two miracles of this chapter demonstrate the power of Jesus over nature. He is the Master in every realm. The sermon that follows centers around one of His great "I am" declarations.

Jesus Feeds the Hungry Multitude, 6:1-15

(1) After these things Jesus went over the sea of Galilee, which is the sea of Tiberias. (2) And a great multitude followed him, because they saw his miracles which he did on them that were diseased. (3) And Jesus went up into a mountain, and there he sat with his disciples. (4) And the passover, a feast of the Jews, was nigh. (5) When Jesus then lifted up his eyes, and saw a great company come unto him, he saith unto Philip, Whence shall we buy bread, that these may eat? (6) And this he said to prove him: for he himself knew what he would do. (7) Philip answered him, Two hundred pennyworth of bread is not sufficient for them, that every one of them may take a little. (8) One of his disciples, Andrew, Simon Peter's brother, saith unto him, (9) There is a lad here, which hath five barley loaves, and two small fishes: but what are they among so many? (10) And Jesus said, Make the men sit down. Now there was much grass in the place. So the men sat down, in number about five thousand. (11) And Jesus took the loaves; and when he had given thanks, he distributed to the disciples, and the disciples to them that were set down; and likewise of the fishes as much as they would. (12) When they were filled, he said unto his disciples, Gather up the fragments that remain, that nothing be lost. (13) Therefore they gathered them together, and filled twelve baskets with the fragments of the five barley loaves, which remained over and above unto them that had eaten. (14) Then those men, when they had seen the miracle that Jesus did, said, This is of a truth that prophet that should come into the world.

(15) When Jesus therefore perceived that they would come and take him by force, to make him a king, he departed again into a mountain himself alone. (John 6:1-15)

Note four pictures in the headings that follow.

The Gathering of Curious Crowds, 6:1-4

With the statement "after these things," John passes over much material given by the other writers. John 5:1 most probably mentions the second Passover in Jesus' ministry; John 6:4 says that the Passover, the third in His ministry, was near. Hence between chapter 5, when He was in Jerusalem, and chapter 6, when we find Him in Galilee, several months transpired. The record of events of these months are found in Matthew 11:1-14:12, Mark 3:2-6:29, and Luke 6:1-9:9. For the full story of this feeding of the multitude, compare Matthew 14:13-21, Mark 6:30-44, and Luke 9:10-17. Thus this story appears in all four Gospels. John's other signs are peculiar to him.

Following the crisis in Jerusalem, this chapter (John 6) shows that a crisis came within the multitude of His professed followers as well as among the Jewish opposers.

"After these things Jesus went"—our Lord was ever busy, and so should we too be busy for Him.

This sea is given two names, Galilee and Tiberias, and it was further called Genessaret and Chinnereth.

The popularity of Jesus had reached its peak, but they were not interested in Him because of His spiritual message, but from sensation. "Because they saw His miracles." His signs proved that He was what He claimed for Himself; but seeing the signs without trusting the Savior whom they proclaimed, did not save. Do we go to church or otherwise engage in religious activities for the show of it?

Jesus sought rest in the mountain, but they would not permit Him to rest. This is the first and shortest of the four great seasons of retirement for rest and instruction of the twelve in preparation for His death and ascension to the Father.

The Lack of Faith on the Part of His Disciples, 6:5-9

"When Jesus lifted up His eyes"—He sees the world's need and longs to fill it. Let us get the vision of a world hungering and dying without the Bread of Life (John 4:35). The urge in the heart of Jesus was, *These must be fed, not because they deserve it but because they need it.*

"Whence shall we buy bread?" (6:5). Jesus would have us realize that supplying the need of the world is our task. It is not His alone; it is ours too because He has committed it to us. Does a lost world dying in the hunger of sin look up to us unfed when we hold the Bread of Life?

Jesus wanted to test or prove the faith of Philip. He never needs to ask questions for the sake of information; John emphasizes Jesus' full knowledge of what He would do. Philip could figure out that about thirty dollars' worth of bread could not feed them but lacked faith to see that Jesus could handle the situation.

Andrew scouted around and brought this information: "There is a little lad here." Every time we meet Andrew in this Gospel, he is bringing someone to Jesus (1:42; 12:22). Let us ever be busy finding and bringing others to Jesus.

"There is a little lad here!" What a touching statement! Do we have eyes to see the lads and lassies in our midst? Let us get our eyes open to see them and our responsbilities to them. No Sunday school teacher should teach dryly so long as there is a lad in his presence. No preacher should preach half-heartedly so long as there is a lad before him. One should not speak unclean words or indulge in unclean habits so long as he may influence a lad. Oh, the thrill and value of helping the lads in one's presence!

Andrew was practical enough to find the little lad but despaired of doing any good with the little lad's little lunch. If we look to ourselves, we too must exclaim in doubt, "But what are they among so many?" Where is your faith?

JESUS THE MASTER OF THE SITUATION, 6:10-13

Learn several important lessons from Jesus:

1. His orderliness (6:10): He had them sit down in order instead of milling around in confusion. The apostle admonished, "Let everything be done decently and in order."

   The count was about five thousand men. Only those who have no figures worth counting object to counting for His glory. The number is mentioned only to honor Jesus by emphasizing the bigness of what He did.

2. His thankfulness (6:11): Learn from Jesus to give God thanks before you eat your meal. Do not be like the ungrateful hog.

3. His "all-mighty" power (6:10-11): Before the barley was ground into flour or the fish were dressed, agriculture and breeding could have increased them to feed many through long years. Behold the power of Jesus: after the crushing of the barley and the death of the fish, Jesus increased them from a scant meal for a little boy to a surplus for five thousand— immediately. No case is too hard for Him to handle. This is a true action of creative power.

But it was more than an act of power. He felt no resentment at the surging, hungering multitude but only love and compassion.

4. His economy (6:12-13): Jesus would not waste the fragments that were left over. Many people remain in poverty because they do not know how to save what little they do have. The disciples could use these fragments and eat them as reminders of the Teacher's divine act.

5. His use of means and agents: In 6:9 He used the loaves and fishes; in 6:11 He used the apostles to distribute the food. He could have created without the loaves and fishes and could have distributed without their help; but He chooses to use means and agents in His work. He does not miracle foolishly. Why not yield now to His call?

THE EFFECT ON THE PEOPLE, 6:14-15

The people were convinced of His Messiahship, (6:14). That was the great purpose of His signs.

They wanted to make Him king of Galilee (6:15). He did not want this honor; if king in an outward sense, He must be King of all. He wanted to be King of their hearts and lives first of all. Let Him reign within you.

Again He saw that faith was not genuine. He wants to be known and accepted as more than a worker of miracles. They saw Him as a worker of prodigies that would relieve their political and social situation. On the following day, proof came that their faith was thus shallow. He already knew it and did not commit Himself to their enthusiasm, misdirected as it was.

Jesus Walks on the Sea, 6:16-21

(16) And when even was now come, his disciples went down unto the sea, (17) And entered into a ship, and went over the sea toward Capernaum. And it was now dark, and Jesus was not come to them. (18) And the sea arose by reason of a great wind that blew. (19) So when they had rowed about five and twenty or thirty furlongs, they see Jesus walking on the sea, and drawing nigh unto the ship: and they were afraid. (20) But he saith unto them, It is I; be not afraid. (21) Then they willingly received him into the ship: and immediately the ship was at the land whither they went. (John 6:16-21)

Note five pictures:

1. Their imminent danger (6:16-18): The darkness added to the great wind. Sinners are in similar spiritual danger.

Also, dangers and darkness often hover about the saints of God.

2. The mighty Savior (6:19): "The walking on the water is a miracle which offers a striking contrast to the conception of Jesus which the multitudes had shown. It reveals, not a political leader, with power in a restricted, earthly sphere, but a divine Creator Who has supreme authority in the universe. . . . He does not suspend the law of gravitation, but shows Himself superior to natural forces and independent of space" (Erdman 1916).

3. Their groundless fear (6:19b): The One Who came to aid them—it was He that they feared. Do not be afraid to hear the gospel; do not try to drown the voice of conviction in your heart. Do not brush aside the hand that reaches out to you in the dark, nor close your ears to His footfalls as He treads underneath His feet the danger and makes it the very pavement that brings Him to your rescue.

4. His words of comfort (6:20): What comfort for us! Literally, "I am," a reminder of Exodus 3:14. He can cheer, and He can save in the midnight and in the storm.

5. The effect on them (6:21): He can still the troubled seas of your life. Why not trust Him now? He shows His ability to cope with any threatening situation. The troubles of life become the pavement of His feet as He comes to our rescue. He cannot, He will not fail you; "Be not afraid." Faith drives out fears. Try it.

The Sermon on the Bread of Life, 6:22-65

(22) The day following, when the people which stood on the other side of the sea saw that there was none other boat there, save that one whereinto his disciples were entered, and that Jesus went not with his disciples into the boat, but that his disciples were gone away alone; (23) (Howbeit there came other boats from Tiberias nigh unto the place where they did eat bread, after that the Lord had given thanks:) (24) When the people therefore saw that Jesus was not there, neither his disciples, they also took shipping, and came to Capernaum, seeking for Jesus. (25) And when they had found him on the other side of the sea, they said unto him, Rabbi, when camest thou hither? (26) Jesus answered them and said, Verily, verily, I say unto you, Ye seek me, not because ye saw the miracles, but because ye did eat of the loaves, and were filled. (27) Labour not for the meat which perisheth, but for that meat which endureth unto everlasting life, which the Son of man shall give unto you: for

him hath God the Father sealed. (28) Then said they unto him, What shall we do, that we might work the works of God? (29) Jesus answered and said unto them, This is the work of God, that ye believe on him whom he hath sent. (30) They said therefore unto him, What sign shewest thou then, that we may see, and believe thee? what dost thou work? (31) Our fathers did eat manna in the desert; as it is written, He gave them bread from heaven to eat. (32) Then Jesus said unto them, Verily, verily, I say unto you, Moses gave you not that bread from heaven; but my Father giveth you the true bread from heaven. (33) For the bread of God is he which cometh down from heaven, and giveth life unto the world. (34) Then said they unto him, Lord, evermore give us this bread. (35) And Jesus said unto them, I am the bread of life: he that cometh to me shall never hunger; and he that believeth on me shall never thirst. (36) But I said unto you, That ye also have seen me, and believe not. (37) All that the Father giveth me shall come to me; and him that cometh to me I will in no wise cast out. (38) For I came down from heaven, not to do mine own will, but the will of him that sent me. (39) And this is the Father's will which hath sent me, that of all which he hath given me I should lose nothing, but should raise it up again at the last day. (40) And this is the will of him that sent me, that every one which seeth the Son, and believeth on him, may have everlasting life: and I will raise him up at the last day. (41) The Jews then murmured at him, because he said, I am the bread which came down from heaven. (42) And they said, Is not this Jesus, the son of Joseph, whose father and mother we know? how is it then that he saith, I came down from heaven? (43) Jesus therefore answered and said unto them, Murmur not among yourselves. (44) No man can come to me, except the Father which hath sent me draw him: and I will raise him up at the last day. (45) It is written in the prophets, And they shall be all taught of God. Every man therefore that hath heard, and hath learned of the Father, cometh unto me. (46) Not that any man hath seen the Father, save he which is of God, he hath seen the Father. (47) Verily, verily, I say unto you, He that believeth on me hath everlasting life. (48) I am that bread of life. (49) Your fathers did eat manna in the wilderness, and are dead. (50) This is the bread which cometh down from heaven, that a man may eat thereof, and not die. (51) I am the living bread which came down from heaven: if any man eat of this bread, he shall live for ever: and the bread that I will give is my flesh, which I will give for the life of the world. (52) The Jews therefore strove among themselves, saying, How can this man give us his flesh to eat? (53) Then Jesus said unto them, Verily, verily, I say unto you, Except ye eat the flesh of the Son of man, and drink his blood, ye have no life in you. (54) Whoso eateth my flesh, and drinketh my blood, hath eternal life; and I will raise him up at the last day. (55) For my flesh is meat indeed, and my blood is drink indeed. (56) He that eateth my flesh, and drinketh my blood, dwelleth in me, and I in him. (57) As the living Father hath sent me, and I live by the Father: so he that eateth me, even he shall live by me. (58) This is that bread which came down from heaven: not as your fathers did eat manna, and are dead: he that eateth of this bread shall live for ever. (59) These things said he in the synagogue, as he taught in Capernaum.

(60) Many therefore of his disciples, when they had heard this, said, This is an hard saying; who can hear it? (61) When Jesus knew in himself that his disciples murmured at it, he said unto them, Doth this offend you? (62) What and if ye shall see the Son of man ascend up where he was before? (63) It is the spirit that quickeneth; the flesh profiteth nothing: the words that I speak

unto you, they are spirit, and they are life. (64) But there are some of you that believe not. For Jesus knew from the beginning who they were that believed not, and who should betray him. (65) And he said, Therefore said I unto you, that no man can come unto me, except it were given unto him of my Father. (John 6:22-65)

This is another of the marvelous sermons of Jesus, the Master Preacher. The place was at a Capernaum synagogue (6:59). Jesus preached wherever the opportunity presented itself. The method of the sermon is that of a series of dialogues; they ask questions, and He gives the answers. Jesus was not limited to one method of preaching; He suited His message to the hearers. The occasion of the sermon is twofold: remote—the feeding of the multitude (6:1-15); immediate—the multitude that He fed the day before coming into Capernaum by boat (6:22-24).

Despite the four separate dialogues of the sermon, there is an obvious unity of theme (Erdman 1916). Note the direct occasion of each dialogue: a question by the Jews (6:25-40); a murmur of the Jews (6:41-51); a dispute among the Jews (6:52-59); a decision to turn away from Christ (6:60-65).

CONTEXTUAL SETTING OF THE BREAD OF LIFE SERMON, 6:22-25

The multitudes whom He fed beyond the sea came into Capernaum by boat to see Him. The full occasion of the sermon extends through these verses.

JESUS' DIALOGUE WITH THE CARNAL AND CURIOUS MULTITUDE, 6:25-40

Their question (6:25); His Answer (6:26-40). He disregarded their carnal questions as to how He got there and used the occasion to preach spiritual truth. He saw and met their deepest need. He presented Himself as the Bread of Life since they were thinking about natural bread (see John 4). Preacher, learn from Jesus, the Master Preacher, how to preach. This discourse gives the true interpretation of the sign of the feeding of the multitude (see 6:35).

He reveals their carnal purpose (6:26) and exhorts them to labor for the bread that endures (6:27). Their stomachs led them, not their hearts. The sign had no purpose for them. Yet Jesus patiently sought to lift their thought to spiritual levels. Note two kinds of bread: the natural bread that perishes and the spiritual that endures. Jesus drew the same lesson from water in 4:13-14. He hints that He wants to give them this spiritual bread.

From Jesus' use of the word *labor*, they asked what works were essential to salvation (6:28). They believed in salvation by works. By "works of God" they meant the works that God requires from men or what works will please God.

Jesus replied, "Only one; namely, faith in the One sent" (6:29). They thought of *works*, plural, more than one; Jesus used *work*, singular, only one. The only thing that it takes to save a guilty sinner is for him to believe on Jesus. That is Jesus' Word on it and settles it for all who have faith in Him. "The work of God" means "the work that God requires." Faith is not a work of merit; faith saves only instrumentally since the Savior is the source, agent, and cause of salvation. Jesus used the word *work* because they had used it. It is equivalent here to our word *act*, the act of faith. Have you believed on Jesus as the sent One?

Because they saw that He claimed to be the object of saving faith, they required a sign, arguing that their historical bread was miraculous (6:30-31). Read here the story of the manna in Exodus 16.

They had the wrong order: they said that they would believe if they could see (6:30). The order of Christ is believing, then seeing (11:40).

Jesus answered that the Father gives the true Bread, the antitype of the manna, with which Jesus identifies Himself (6:32-33). Do not be afraid of types but only of their abuse. Moses was not the source but merely the agent of the giving of the manna. They needed to get their eyes on God, and then they could see the purpose of God in the true, genuine, antitypical bread, even Jesus.

They, being impressed by this statement, asked for "the genuine bread from heaven," yet they seemingly were unconscious that it referred to Jesus Himself (6:34). Compare the slowness with which the woman in 4:15 grasped the statement of Jesus that He referred to spiritual water. Oh, the blindness of the human heart!

In His answer, He pointed out three facts (6:35-40):

1. He affirmed again, "I am the Bread of Life which satisfies spiritual hunger and thirst" (6:35). "Coming to Christ" and "believing on Him" are the same act of satisfaction in Jesus— to "not hunger" and "never thirst." He returns to the figure of water, as in John 4.

2. He pointed out their willful unbelief (6:36). Their unbelief was all that stood between them and salvation. They had the evidence but would not believe.

3. He taught that the sovereign will of God will accomplish the coming of all those given to Him (6:37-40). Election and

the freeness of the gospel are twins: they stand in the same verse, 6:37. "Coming" is again the metaphor for faith.

Be encouraged, He will "in no wise" cast out anyone that comes. This alone disproves the claim that one can be saved and then lost.

Christ had no will of His own but to do the will of the Father (6:38).

John 6:39-40—Both verses declare the will of the Father. The work of Jesus not only includes giving everlasting life to the believer here and now at faith but the giving of resurrection life to all these later. The gospel deals with the need of the soul and the need of the body. He undoes the work of sin and more. In chapter 5 He had claimed resurrection power, and in chapter 11 it will be largely emphasized.

There are several analogies or parallels between the manna and Jesus:

- Its source—heavenly (6:32-33): Jesus is "the Bread of God." He is also "He Who cometh down from heaven" and "The Bread from heaven." Thus He teaches the doctrines of His deity and His incarnation.

- Its nature—twofold: Life-giving and soul satisfying (6:33, 35, 40). This is the doctrine of salvation, the result of His deity and incarnation. Note "giveth life," "Bread of Life," and "have everlasting life."

- Its effect—enduring forever (6:27, 35): The doctrine of the eternal security of the saint is strongly emphasized. The Bread itself (6:27) causes the appropriator to endure without hungering (6:35).

- Its appropriation—eating: It is more than tasting or admiring; it is such a taking that appropriates and identifies. Eating is assimilating Him in the heart. That is how simple faith is, simple as eating what is set before you. Eat and thy soul shall live. He promises; only believe (6:40).

JESUS' DIALOGUE WITH THE UNBELIEVING AND SELF-RIGHTEOUS MURMURERS, 6:41-51

Their complaint (6:41-42): Murmuring at His claim of supernatural and divine origin, they try to explain His origin as merely human. All other men can be accounted for as human beings only, but Jesus so differs from all others that we are without explanation if we accept Him as only a man. In many churches and pulpits today, these murmurers would be told that it does not matter whether we believe the deity of Jesus or not.

His answer (6:43-51): Note two things: Jesus says, "You need not murmur, for God's sovereign [1] drawing and [2] effectual teaching will bring eternal life now to all who believe on Me" (6:43-47). Jesus mentions the first and last steps in what God does for the human soul. The drawing by the Father is the beginning in conviction; their being raised up by the Son is the climax of it all in glorification. It is grace from the start to the finish.

"Taught of God" means "taught by God." The teaching and drawing are just two pictures of the same gracious work. Note both the human and the divine sides of the matter of salvation: God draws and teaches; man comes and learns. To emphasize only God's side is Hardshellism and fatalism; to mention only man's side is Arminianism and salvation by works. To relate both properly in one's testimony is to trace the Bible and the teaching of our Lord.

The word is *draw*, not *drag*. The distinction is finely maintained in the Greek (see Trench 1854, on *Synonyms*). The sweet compulsion of the Holy Spirit so moves on the soul that one wants to come and does come gladly. One is not saved against his will. The will that once chose sin is sweetly won over by the power of God, gladly to choose Jesus Christ.

Only Jesus has seen God in reality and fullness (6:46). In 6:47 He emphasizes the importance and blessing of believing on Him.

He contrasts the life-giving and life-sustaining effects of the true Bread with the typical manna (6:48-51). Note that Jesus uses both statements, "cometh down from heaven" and "came down from heaven." He came when He was born; that is the historical fact. He is still coming in His vital union with the Father and His outreach toward needy humanity.

The chief point here is that eating manna did not furnish life but that eating of Christ or believing on Him does bring eternal life. Jesus asserts that He gave His life "for the life of the world." Jesus dies for all, but only those who believe will be saved. There is sufficiency in the death of Christ to make alive all who are dead in trespasses and sins. There is life for you if you will only accept His gift. Why not do it now?

JESUS' DIALOGUE WITH THE SCOFFING AND NON-FIGURATIVE LITERALISTS, 6:52-59

They blindly imagined that His reference to His death was a literal eating of His flesh (6:52). Strangely enough, Catholics continue this error in their view of the Lord's Supper. They say that the bread and wine are changed into the actual body and blood of Jesus, even though it appears still to be bread and wine. At this point Jesus had no reference to the Lord's Supper. Eating and drinking are pictures or metaphors of faith in Jesus Christ by which we appropriate or make our own the saving benefits of His death. These illustrations center around the Cross of our Lord Jesus Christ.

Appropriation by faith is the keynote here. *Sharing* tends to put too much emphasis upon us. His Bread and His Blood alone possess merit. He states the absolute necessity of their appropriating the benefits of His sacrifice for the possession of life (6:53-58).

Note certain things about this saving faith:

- Its necessity—"except" (6:53)

- Its object—"His flesh and His blood" signify the saving benefits of His cross.

- Its nature—two illustrations

- Its blessings—fourfold: (1) Life. Note how richly this thought is presented: "Has eternal life," "life in yourself," "shall live because of Me," "shall live forever." This is the same as the New Birth. (2) Full satisfaction, 6:55. "Meat indeed" and "drink indeed"—that is, fulfilling in the truest and fullest sense their office or function of satisfying hunger and quenching thirst. (3) Union with Christ, 6:56 "Dwelleth in Me and I in Him." What blessed union of our souls with Him. Here is a faint illustration of this: I am in the atmosphere, and it is in me. We are so united with Christ as to have the most intimate fellowship and unbreakable security. (4) Resurrection of the body, 6:54. See 6:40. Having eternal life now by faith in Him assures us of our future resurrection. None can be assured except the believer. The source of such a blessing is in His power. The assurance of such is in His work of honor in his promise; the means of our entering into the blessing is by faith.

Jesus' Dialogue with His Untrue and Murmuring Disciples, 6:60-65

They objected that His teaching was too hard (6:60). They were disciples in outward profession but not in the inner possession of the blessing accruing to genuine faith in Him.

"This saying is hard." That puts the emphasis on the difficulty as they felt it, and there was a real difficulty to those who lived and thought only on the material level. Faith in Him lifts one above such a level and enlarges or deepens or transforms one's sense of values. The word *therefore* shows the real ground of their difficulty was in the requirement of faith in Him by eating and drinking His flesh and blood.

Not all of that tribe is dead. The character of one's words reveals what he is. Once a young man was called to view a marvelous piece of art. The young man thought to criticize it. The one who was showing it to him replied, "Young man, this is not on trial. The verdict of the ages favors this work of art. You are on trial." So is every sinner when Jesus is presented, and rejection only proves that the judgment of the sinner is bad.

Jesus answers (6:61-65), "I will tell you something harder yet" (6:61-62). He knew their murmuring. They could not hide the facts from His searching eye. Friend, He knows yours too. He refers to the surprise and bewilderment and unbelief that would follow His ascension to the Father. He leaves the sentence unfinished because the whole story of man's misuse of God's mercy is not yet told, nor can it be told in human words.

"The spiritual is what counts" (6:63). Jesus declared all efforts of depraved flesh or sinful humanity worthless. And there has been no improvement since He uttered these words. All that men try to do to get to heaven is just as futile as ever. His words count; they are spirit, and they are life. The weak effort of Campbellites to make this statement deny the personality of the Holy Spirit is nothing short of dense blindness to what Jesus is saying and to the ample teaching in many Scriptures concerning the Person of the Spirit. They deny the Person of the Holy Spirit in the Bible. Jesus uses the word but is not to be identified with it.

"I knew you were false, hence My hard doctrine to reveal you" (6:64-65). He said what He said with full knowledge of their nature and spirit. They could put nothing over on Jesus. He saw through their spuriousness. It was better for them to own it and get right with Him, but such they did not do.

A Crisis: The Results of His Sermon on the Bread of Life, 6:66-71

(66) From that time many of his disciples went back, and walked no more with him. (67) Then said Jesus unto the twelve, Will ye also go away? (68) Then Simon Peter answered him, Lord, to whom shall we go? thou hast the words of eternal life. (69) And we believe and are sure that thou art that Christ, the Son of the living God. (70) Jesus answered them, Have not I chosen you twelve, and one of you is a devil? (71) He spake of Judas Iscariot the son of Simon: for he it was that should betray him, being one of the twelve. (John 6:66-71)

This wholesale desertion of Jesus by the multitude of His professed disciples constituted a major event in His life and ministry. It can truly be rated as one of the crises of His earthly life. Its importance is not usually emphasized as it should be. Jesus was a man as truly as He was God, and the going away of the great crowds touched Him vitally. He resisted every appeal of a false popularity and preached the truth.

Thereupon He turned longingly to His true disciples and found their attachment to Him heartily and representatively expressed by Peter. He sincerely appreciated their unwavering confidence but revealed that the presence of Judas, a devil, in their number should make them cautious. This crisis in the life of our Lord marks quite clearly the line between growing popularity and increasing hatred. The story illustrates that truth is the greatest divider among men. He drew the line; they showed their colors.

MANY FALSE PROFESSORS WHO WERE THUS REVEALED FORSOOK JESUS, 6:66

"Upon this" is both temporal and causal. They were disciples in name only. They went back; forsaking Christ is never going forward. Literally translated, the phrase used is "into the things behind." This step robbed them of the fellowship of walking with Jesus. What a contrast between what they left when they forsook Him and what they found on their return!

JESUS' SEARCHING QUESTION, 6:67

"Therefore" looks back over the forsaking multitude that could not stand the truth and yet finds inspiration in those who stood around Him. He addressed Himself to their desire. He assured them that He did not feel that they desired to go away (a little particle in the Greek so indicates). "Ye" is emphatic in contrast to the many.

Peter represented the others in this confidence. "Lord, to whom shall we go?" That is saying there is no other one to whom one can go and find truth and satisfaction.

Sinner friend, if you go to another or anything else, you will be disappointed. Jesus alone "has the words of eternal life." Do not go to baptism nor to the priest nor to the church, but to Jesus only. He alone is the One. Brush everything else aside and go to Him. I think I see you clinging to other things. Away with them. I think I see you fearfully bringing along other things to save you. Drop them this minute and come to Jesus. He is the one need of your soul. He is the one and only Savior. He has never turned down one who came to Him. Come to Him now without delay.

His revealing Assertion, 6:70

He perceives the traitor. This was a year before John 13 when Judas betrayed Him. Judas was never converted.

3.2.3 Jesus at the Feast of Tabernacles and His Great Invitation, chapter 7

(1) After these things Jesus walked in Galilee: for he would not walk in Jewry, because the Jews sought to kill him. (2) Now the Jews' feast of tabernacles was at hand. (3) His brethren therefore said unto him, Depart hence, and go into Judaea, that thy disciples also may see the works that thou doest. (4) For there is no man that doeth any thing in secret, and he himself seeketh to be known openly. If thou do these things, shew thyself to the world. (5) For neither did his brethren believe in him. (6) Then Jesus said unto them, My time is not yet come: but your time is alway ready. (7) The world cannot hate you; but me it hateth, because I testify of it, that the works thereof are evil. (8) Go ye up unto this feast: I go not up yet unto this feast; for my time is not yet full come. (9) When he had said these words unto them, he abode still in Galilee. (10) But when his brethren were gone up, then went he also up unto the feast, not openly, but as it were in secret. (11) Then the Jews sought him at the feast, and said, Where is he? (12) And there was much murmuring among the people concerning him: for some said, He is a good man: others said, Nay; but he deceiveth the people. (13) Howbeit no man spake openly of him for fear of the Jews. (John 7:1-13)

John 6 was in the spring near the time of the Passover feast; John 7 was in the fall at the Feast of Tabernacles. This is one of the three great annual feasts of the Jews. "It began on the fifteenth day of the seventh month, or Tishri, answering to our October, and was celebrated a full week. It was followed, on the eighth day, by a holy convocation" (Hovey 1885). Consult Leviticus 23:34-36, 39-43 and Deuteronomy 16:13-15.

The feast had two names: the Feast of Tabernacles and the Feast of Ingathering (Exodus 23:16). It was a season of great joy and signified two things: first, commemoration of their deliverance from bondage by their journey through the wilderness and their dwelling in booths or tents while there; second, the bringing of the fruits at the end of the year. In the late spring or early summer, they brought their firstfruits at the Feast of Weeks, Pentecost, or Feast of Firstfruits. The Feast of Ingathering came at the close of harvest as the first had come at the beginning. "Special sacrifices were offered, and parts of the law were publicly read" (Hovey 1885).

The Trip to the Feast, 7:1-13

JESUS TARRIES IN GALILEE, 7:1-2

Jesus was not afraid of the Jews but would rather not tempt God by unnecessarily running into danger.

THE BROTHERS OF JESUS OFFER HIM WORLDLY ADVICE, 7:3-5

Mark 6:3 lists the names of Jesus' four half-brothers. Their advice was no doubt sincere but was born of unbelief. They left God out of this advice, as the wisdom of this world always does. Religious work to be seen by men has its reward here and now (Matthew 6:1-8). Learn from Jesus to check on the intent and source of the advice you receive.

John 7:5 says that they were not then saved. Such advice had a natural source in their unbelieving hearts. Faith in Him puts a new sense or criterion of value into the heart. The events about the death and resurrection of Jesus brought them to salvation (Acts 1:14). The winning of His brothers, though we know not the details, is a romantic and convincing story.

HE REFUSED THEIR ADVICE, 7:6-9

Learn from Jesus to check on the advice proffered before you take it. He knew beforehand the exact time and nature of His death. This evidence of His deity turns up again and again in this Gospel.

"Your time is already ready." Their harmony with the spirit of the world would not incur its hatred. We may well ask ourselves as His followers if our conduct, temper, and aims arouse the enmity of the world or grieve the Master.

Jesus Was a Faithful Preacher, 7:7

The world is evil, not good, and Jesus never shunned to tell it so. The world still hates preachers who testify against its evils.

Jesus Went Up Secretly Later, 7:10

There was no insincerity in this. Luke 9:51-53 gives a story of the trip.

The Disappointment of the Jews On the Non-Appearance of Jesus, 7:11-13

Note how much the opinions of today resemble these. Jesus has always been the greatest divider of opinions.

His Teaching At the Feast, 7:14-36

(14) Now about the midst of the feast Jesus went up into the temple, and taught. (15) And the Jews marvelled, saying, How knoweth this man letters, having never learned? (16) Jesus answered them, and said, My doctrine is not mine, but his that sent me. (17) If any man will do his will, he shall know of the doctrine, whether it be of God, or whether I speak of myself. (18) He that speaketh of himself seeketh his own glory: but he that seeketh his glory that sent him, the same is true, and no unrighteousness is in him. (19) Did not Moses give you the law, and yet none of you keepeth the law? Why go ye about to kill me? (20) The people answered and said, Thou hast a devil: who goeth about to kill thee? (21) Jesus answered and said unto them, I have done one work, and ye all marvel. (22) Moses therefore gave unto you circumcision; (not because it is of Moses, but of the fathers;) and ye on the sabbath day circumcise a man. (23) If a man on the sabbath day receive circumcision, that the law of Moses should not be broken; are ye angry at me, because I have made a man every whit whole on the sabbath day? (24) Judge not according to the appearance, but judge righteous judgment. (25) Then said some of them of Jerusalem, Is not this he, whom they seek to kill? (26) But, lo, he speaketh boldly, and they say nothing unto him. Do the rulers know indeed that this is the very Christ? (27) Howbeit we know this man whence he is: but when Christ cometh, no man knoweth whence he is. (28) Then cried Jesus in the temple as he taught, saying, Ye both know me, and ye know whence I am: and I am not come of myself, but he that sent me is true, whom ye know not. (29) But I know him: for I am from him, and he hath sent me. (30) Then they sought to take him: but no man laid hands on him, because his hour was not yet come. (31) And many of the people believed on him, and said, When Christ cometh, will he do more miracles than these which this man hath done? (32) The Pharisees heard that the people murmured such things concerning him; and the Pharisees and the chief priests sent officers to take him. (33) Then said Jesus unto them, Yet a little while am I with you, and then I go unto him that sent me. (34) Ye shall seek me, and shall not find me: and where I am, thither ye cannot come. (35) Then said the Jews among themselves, Whither will he go, that we shall not find him? will he go unto the dispersed among the Gentiles, and teach the Gentiles? (36) What manner of saying is this that he said, Ye shall seek me, and shall not find me: and where I am, thither ye cannot come? (John 7:14-36)

JESUS JUSTIFIES HIS AUTHORITY AS A TEACHER; THE JEWS OPPOSE, 7:14-24

John 7:15 means that Jesus was not a school-bred man, "having never learned"—better, "not having been discipled or taught." Jesus' teaching was heavenly (7:16). In 7:17 Jesus offers a challenge to every sincere doubter. I prefer the American Standard Version (1901): "If any man willeth to do His will." Jesus waits to prove Himself to any soul who comes with an open mind and will let Him prove Himself. Willing or desiring to *do* His will is not the same as willing to *know* His will. "Faith has more to do with the moral than the intellectual faculties; it is more a question of spiritual sympathy than of external evidence" (Erdman 1916). Too many want the demonstration without the proper attitude of heart, without the right attitude or desire.

The preacher is not to originate his message but to preach God's message (7:18). "No unrighteousness is in Him." Jesus thus claims sinlessness. Jesus told them that they had not kept their own law (7:19). He did not compromise or dodge the issue; His courage forbad that.

The Jews charged that He was demon possessed because He told what was in their wicked hearts (7:20). Abuse is the weapon of the defeated man. He who will not or cannot answer the facts that expose his sin turns with personal abuse on the man who dares to point out his sin. They objected to His showing mercy and healing a man on the Sabbath day, yet they would circumcise on a Sabbath (7:21-24). How inconsistent!

John 7:24 gives the false and the true ways of judging. Righteous judgment goes beneath the surface. Do we judge according to appearances?

JESUS ASSERTS HIS DIVINE ORIGIN, 7 25-31

The inhabitants of Jerusalem object—literally, "Jerusalemites." Note how they cross themselves. He was immortal until His work was finished (7:30).

JESUS SPEAKS OF HIS APPROACHING DEATH, 7:32-36

The Pharisees feared that the plain teaching of Jesus about His coming from the Father would convince the people. They were not willing for the truth to have its way. They would neither enter into salvation nor permit those to do so that desired to do it. They wanted to mislead the people. Not all their tribe is today out of the pulpits. They were not willing to listen to the One Who knew God and could make Him known to their hearts.

"Yet a little while" refers to the time between then and His death on the cross. It was their day of opportunity but was fast closing. He told them what the climax of His death would be. It would mean His going to the Father; it would not mean His destruction as they desired it. "You will seek Me and will not find Me." What a sad statement! Oh, the toll of neglected opportunity! They were sinning away their day of opportunity. Are we? Regrets and remorse will not bring back the opportunity.

"Where I am, thither you cannot come." That will be one of the keenest pains of hell. He did not bar them out from God's mercy; their sins alone did that. Their unbelief slammed the door in their face. There is no getting to heaven without personal knowledge of Jesus. How sad that they so woefully misunderstood His gracious words (7:35-36). They could repeat His words but could not read their meaning. Do you believe on Him that you may someday be where He is? We have here a kind of negative way of saying what heaven will mean—being where He is. Note the dispersion (7:35).

The Discussion On the Last Day of the Feast, 7:37-52

(37) In the last day, that great day of the feast, Jesus stood and cried, saying, If any man thirst, let him come unto me, and drink. (38) He that believeth on me, as the scripture hath said, out of his belly shall flow rivers of living water. (39) (But this spake he of the Spirit, which they that believe on him should receive: for the Holy Ghost was not yet given; because that Jesus was not yet glorified.) (40) Many of the people therefore, when they heard this saying, said, Of a truth this is the Prophet. (41) Others said, This is the Christ. But some said, Shall Christ come out of Galilee? (42) Hath not the scripture said, That Christ cometh of the seed of David, and out of the town of Bethlehem, where David was? (43) So there was a division among the people because of him. (44) And some of them would have taken him; but no man laid hands on him.

(45) Then came the officers to the chief priests and Pharisees; and they said unto them, Why have ye not brought him? (46) The officers answered, Never man spake like this man. (47) Then answered them the Pharisees, Are ye also deceived? (48) Have any of the rulers or of the Pharisees believed on him? (49) But this people who knoweth not the law are cursed. (50) Nicodemus saith unto them, (he that came to Jesus by night, being one of them,) (51) Doth our law judge any man, before it hear him, and know what he doeth? (52) They answered and said unto him, Art thou also of Galilee? Search, and look: for out of Galilee ariseth no prophet. (John 7:37-52)

The last day of the feast was the eighth day. For seven days, water was brought in a golden pitcher from the pool of Siloam and poured out as an offering before God. This commemorated the water that miraculously gushed from the rock in the wilderness. On the last day the priests returned from the pool without water to signify that the promise of God was yet unfulfilled. How strikingly did Jesus use the occasion to tell them that He Himself filled that lack!

The Great Promise of Jesus; The Great Invitation, 7:37-39

"Cried" speaks of the earnestness and clearness with which Jesus spoke.

There is only one condition of your coming to Christ. You must thirst or feel a sense of sin and a sense of need of Him. You do not have to be good to come; you have only to thirst. Sinners often say they do not feel like coming. "All the fitness He requireth is to feel your need of Him."[10] If you are waiting for a special feeling before you trust the Savior, you already have that feeling He requires. You feel and know that you are lost; that is enough. Just tell out your needs to Him.

What does it mean to trust Christ? There are three pictures here. First, it is coming to Him, yet that does not mean a physical act. The physical act of coming to another illustrates the coming of the heart to Jesus. Second, it is drinking the water of life. The physical act of drinking, by which we appropriate the benefits of water, is a picture of the soul in taking Christ Jesus as Savior. Third, it is believing on Him. Faith is the simple means that puts one into Jesus Christ. Neither is this a physical transfer. Until we believe into Him, we are outside of Him in danger and ruin. The moment we believe into Him, we are then and there sheltered from all danger of hell and judgment; we are then and there united indissolubly with Him Who is our life. Come, drink, believe.

"As the Scripture hath said." Jesus made much of the Scriptures. We are unlike Him insofar as we discredit by any means the authority and sufficiency of the Word of God. Liberalism tries to correct Jesus on this point. It will not follow Him in His attitude toward and use of the Old Testament.

For "belly" read "from within" or "from his innermost being." The water of life first quenches the thirst of the sinner, then flows out from the believer to bless others. The word *flow* speaks of the freeness with which the blessings of God flow through a Christian. It is not forced service that He desires. The word *rivers* speaks of plenty; there can be no necessary lack in the believer's life. Lack comes in blessing others only when we become clogged channels. The word *living* means that our lives will not be parched, dry, and formal.

---

10. Hymn by Joseph Heart: "Come Ye Sinners, Poor and Needy." http://etymologyofhymns.blogspot.com/2013/08/come-ye-sinners.html.

In 7:39 we have the inspired interpretation of this outflowing. "This spake He of the Spirit." Though the Holy Spirit did His work here in the world from the morning of Creation, He was not fully and publicly given until Pentecost. Jesus must first be glorified, which refers to His resurrection, ascension, and seating at the Father's right hand of honor. The gift of the Spirit flows from the crucified and risen Christ. This is the age of the Holy Spirit, as the time of His sojourn here was the age of the Son, and as the Old Testament period was the age of the Father.

Have you received the blessed indwelling power of the Spirit? There should be the continual inflowing of His power and outflowing of His blessing.

Divided Opinion Concerning Jesus, 7:40-44

Jesus is still the ground of the greatest differences. Three opinions prevailed among them. "The Prophet" refers to Deuteronomy 18:15 as in John 1:21. Jesus was born at Bethlehem in Judah but grew up at Nazareth in Galilee.

The Sanhedrin Discusses Jesus, 7:45-52

It has been a frequent thing for courts and councils to discuss Jesus rather than to believe on Him. The officers or policemen were reprimanded for not arresting Jesus.

The report of the officers (7:45-46): It was not from lack of authority nor from lack of mere physical force to do it. Why then did they not do it? The marvelous words and acts of Jesus impressed them powerfully. "Never man spake like this man." What a report! How truly they spoke of Him! But they did not go far enough; they did not believe on Him.

The false argument of the Pharisees (7:47-49): How like the Catholics! They do not believe that the common people can understand the Scriptures. Contrast the attitude of Jesus toward the multitudes. He preached to them and expected them to understand His message.

Nicodemus defends Jesus (7:50-52): John recalls the story of John 3. John 7:51 calls attention to a fair law. A man surely has a right to speak for himself. This is democratic. They failed to answer Nicodemus and dodged the issue (7:52). A prophet did grow up in Galilee though He was born in Bethlehem in Judea. He is the Prophet from Nazareth! Both questions are introduced with a particle in Greek, showing that the questioner expected a negative answer. They expected Nicodemus to say that he was not from Galilee. He indicated that he felt that their answer should be negative.

3.2.4 THE WOMAN TAKEN IN ADULTERY, 7:53-8:11

(7:53) And every man went unto his own house. (8:1) Jesus went unto the mount of Olives. (2) And early in the morning he came again into the temple, and all the people came unto him; and he sat down, and taught them. (3) And the scribes and Pharisees brought unto him a woman taken in adultery; and when they had set her in the midst, (4) They say unto him, Master, this woman was taken in adultery, in the very act. (5) Now Moses in the law commanded us, that such should be stoned: but what sayest thou? (6) This they said, tempting him, that they might have to accuse him. But Jesus stooped down, and with his finger wrote on the ground, as though he heard them not. (7) So when they continued asking him, he lifted up himself, and said unto them, He that is without sin among you, let him first cast a stone at her. (8) And again he stooped down, and wrote on the ground. (9) And they which heard it, being convicted by their own conscience, went out one by one, beginning at the eldest, even unto the last: and Jesus was left alone, and the woman standing in the midst. (10) When Jesus had lifted up himself, and saw none but the woman, he said unto her, Woman, where are those thine accusers? hath no man condemned thee? (11) She said, No man, Lord. And Jesus said unto her, Neither do I condemn thee: go, and sin no more. (John 7:53–8:11)

Jesus On the Mount of Olives, 7:53-8:1

Two things here obscure the message: the chapter division is not good; 8:1 should begin with the word *but*, which the translators left untranslated. The contrast is vividly drawn between the action of Jesus in going to the Mount of Olives and the actions of the people in going to their own homes. Jesus was the uninvited Savior. They thanklessly rejected in their hearts His message. Our homes and our hearts are the two places in which Jesus is needed most of all. Have you shut Him out or invited Him into these two places? Too many leave Him uninvited, as He then was. Alone with His Father, He spent the night in calm repose or in fervent prayer.

Jesus Teaching Again, 8:2

Hard hearts did not make His heart cold: rejection whetted His zeal to do even more. The source of His zeal was deeper than the attitude of the people toward Him. His concern stemmed from His unselfish love for men, from His sense of commission from His Father, and from His understanding of their deep need. How do we react when our message is slighted?

Note two details that enliven the story: He began early in the morning. Jesus was an untiring worker for souls. His zeal ought to put us to shame. The second detail is that He sat while He was teaching. The tense of the verb demands "was teaching"; that is, He continued teaching. The tense means for us to see a painted picture of Jesus in the act of teaching.

Jesus' Refusal to Judge the Woman, 8:3-11

Their Insincere Purpose, 8:3-5

Neither love for God nor zeal for righteousness nor a passion for purity nor indignation against sin moved them. They desired to entrap or entangle Jesus into repudiating the law of Moses or into usurping the office of a civil magistrate. It was the same temptation as is recorded in Matthew 22:17. Their testing Him was not to know the truth but to have a club with which to drive Him away. "They were ready to stoop to any measure in order to accomplish their desired end. We find that the character of men is often revealed by the instruments which they employ to secure their purposes" (Erdman 1916). These things tell on us more quickly than we are aware. Ryle (1860) comments, "What they really desired was not to vindicate the purity of God's law and punish the sinner, but to wreak their malice on Himself."

His Singular Action, 8:6

This is the only time Jesus is said to have written. Conjectures as to what He wrote lead us to no certain truth. I think, however, that His silence is highly significant. His silence indicated that He did not desire to take the office of judge, nor would He be caught in their sly trap.

His Uncomfortable Challenge, 8:7

Some think that when He wrote on the ground, "He lifted the question out of the sphere of mere legal technicalities into the realm of moral realities" (Erdman 1916). The law of Moses required that the witnesses do the stoning. They had not expected Him to bring that up. He put them, so to speak, on the spot. He pressed on them a moral qualification for what they were doing. "He that is without sin" cannot mean just any sin, for the Bible teaches that all without exception have sinned. It must mean the same or similar sin as that for which they were condemning her. No general statement would have produced such results as were here produced.

Jesus does not question the right of human governments to inflict penalties on offenders; He upheld the Mosaic law but convicted these proud accusers of being themselves not only unfit for the task but worthy themselves of condemnation. Nor can this logically be used against church discipline; recall that the temptation was to take the power of the civil magistrate into His hands. The dilemma was this: "Should he acquit the woman, he would then oppose the law of Moses (Leviticus 20:10; Deuteronomy 22:22-24). Should He condemn the woman to death, He could encroach upon the power and authority of the Roman state (John 18:28-31), for the Romans had taken from the Jews the power of inflicting capital punishment" (Erdman 1916). Yet the principle is here that the witness should be pure in life (Matthew 7:1ff). Study this view of the story before rejecting it.

THE POWER OF CONSCIENCE, 8:9

That silent little monitor did its work all unseen except to the penetrating eyes of the Son of God. They pretended high regard for the law; Jesus saw through such veneer. Conscience did its sure work. The oldest went out first, perhaps, because he had more sins and because his conscience made him more miserable. I do not find the cause in the possibility that as the leaders they had led in the evil design. Conscience worked on a deeper principle, that of sin. You may hide your evil work from men, but that little monitor of God, your conscience, will not let you by.

Jesus was left alone as far as the accusers and trappers were concerned. Not one accuser was left to do his evil work, though the multitude remained. How blessed to be alone in the presence of Jesus!

HIS WORDS TO THE WOMAN, 8:11

We must exercise great caution here. Jesus did not in any wise condone the breach of the seventh commandment against unchastity. If He did that, He was caught in one of their traps. Impossible! Jesus meant merely that He would not be caught in their trap. He was no civil judge (see also John 3:17). He would not condemn as they chose. If Jesus forgave her, He taught that forgiveness should bear fruit in an amendment of life. She escaped only because of lack of evidence. If He had meant to condone her sin, He would have said, "Live as you please." He said the very opposite. Jesus could never condone sin in anyone because He is everlastingly the Righteous One.

Lessons to emphasize:

- Jesus' untiring teaching

- The hypocrisy of His enemies

- The revelation of our character by our deeds

- The power of conscience to convict of sin

- Jesus' triumph over His enemies

- Jesus' condemnation of sin

- "He did not speak the word of pardon, for she had not come to Him in penitence and in faith, as had the woman whose story is given in Luke 7:37-50. He merely warned the woman and gave her time to repent and believe. His word, however, was full of encouragement, and we cannot but conclude that she must have gone away to a new and better life" (Erdman 1916).[11]

3.2.5 Jesus as the Light of the World Proclaimed and Illustrated, 8:12-9:41

(12) Then spake Jesus again unto them, saying, I am the light of the world: he that followeth me shall not walk in darkness, but shall have the light of life. (13) The Pharisees therefore said unto him, Thou bearest record of thyself; thy record is not true. (14) Jesus answered and said unto them, Though I bear record of myself, yet my record is true: for I know whence I came, and whither I go; but ye cannot tell whence I came, and whither I go. (15) Ye judge after the flesh; I judge no man. (16) And yet if I judge, my judgment is true: for I am not alone, but I and the Father that sent me. (17) It is also written in your law, that the testimony of two men is true. (18) I am one that bear witness of myself, and the Father that sent me beareth witness of me. (19) Then said they unto him, Where is thy Father? Jesus answered, Ye neither know me, nor my Father: if ye had known me, ye should have known my Father also. (20) These words spake Jesus in the treasury, as he taught in the temple: and no man laid hands on him; for his hour was not yet come. (21) Then said Jesus again unto them, I go my way, and ye shall seek me, and shall die in your sins: whither I go, ye cannot come. (22) Then said the Jews, Will he kill himself? because he saith, Whither I go, ye cannot come. (23) And he said unto them, Ye are from beneath; I am from above: ye are of this world; I am not of this

---

11. Editor's Note: The text of John 7:53 to 8:11 is another disputed passage in John's Gospel. Some scholars believe that the text either is misplaced or should not be in John's Gospel at all. I was a student of Dr. Beaman's in his Advanced Greek Grammar class in the spring of 1987. I believe it was here that he discussed this issue with us. Beaman related how he had travelled to Europe to see important ancient New Testament texts for himself. After viewing the manuscripts, he believed that this passage of Scripture was authentic and, further, that it was correctly located in its current place in the Gospel of John.

world. (24) I said therefore unto you, that ye shall die in your sins: for if ye believe not that I am he, ye shall die in your sins. (25) Then said they unto him, Who art thou? And Jesus saith unto them, Even the same that I said unto you from the beginning. (26) I have many things to say and to judge of you: but he that sent me is true; and I speak to the world those things which I have heard of him. (27) They understood not that he spake to them of the Father. (28) Then said Jesus unto them, When ye have lifted up the Son of man, then shall ye know that I am he, and that I do nothing of myself; but as my Father hath taught me, I speak these things. (29) And he that sent me is with me: the Father hath not left me alone; for I do always those things that please him. (30) As he spake these words, many believed on him. (31) Then said Jesus to those Jews which believed on him, If ye continue in my word, then are ye my disciples indeed; (32) And ye shall know the truth, and the truth shall make you free. (33) They answered him, We be Abraham's seed, and were never in bondage to any man: how sayest thou, Ye shall be made free? (34) Jesus answered them, Verily, verily, I say unto you, Whosoever committeth sin is the servant of sin. (35) And the servant abideth not in the house for ever: but the Son abideth ever. (36) If the Son therefore shall make you free, ye shall be free indeed. (37) I know that ye are Abraham's seed; but ye seek to kill me, because my word hath no place in you. (38) I speak that which I have seen with my Father: and ye do that which ye have seen with your father. (39) They answered and said unto him, Abraham is our father. Jesus saith unto them, If ye were Abraham's children, ye would do the works of Abraham. (40) But now ye seek to kill me, a man that hath told you the truth, which I have heard of God: this did not Abraham. (41) Ye do the deeds of your father. Then said they to him, We be not born of fornication; we have one Father, even God. (42) Jesus said unto them, If God were your Father, ye would love me: for I proceeded forth and came from God; neither came I of myself, but he sent me. (43) Why do ye not understand my speech? even because ye cannot hear my word. (44) Ye are of your father the devil, and the lusts of your father ye will do. He was a murderer from the beginning, and abode not in the truth, because there is no truth in him. When he speaketh a lie, he speaketh of his own: for he is a liar, and the father of it. (45) And because I tell you the truth, ye believe me not. (46) Which of you convinceth me of sin? And if I say the truth, why do ye not believe me? (47) He that is of God heareth God's words: ye therefore hear them not, because ye are not of God. (48) Then answered the Jews, and said unto him, Say we not well that thou art a Samaritan, and hast a devil? (49) Jesus answered, I have not a devil; but I honour my Father, and ye do dishonour me. (50) And I seek not mine own glory: there is one that seeketh and judgeth. (51) Verily, verily, I say unto you, If a man keep my saying, he shall never see death. (52) Then said the Jews unto him, Now we know that thou hast a devil. Abraham is dead, and the prophets; and thou sayest, If a man keep my saying, he shall never taste of death. (53) Art thou greater than our father Abraham, which is dead? and the prophets are dead: whom makest thou thyself? (54) Jesus answered, If I honour myself, my honour is nothing: it is my Father that honoureth me; of whom ye say, that he is your God: (55) Yet ye have not known him; but I know him: and if I should say, I know him not, I shall be a liar like unto you: but I know him, and keep his saying. (56) Your father Abraham rejoiced to see my day: and he saw it, and was glad. (57) Then said the Jews unto him, Thou art not yet fifty years old, and hast thou seen Abraham? (58) Jesus said unto them, Verily, verily, I *say unto you, Before Abraham was, I am. (59) Then took they up stones to cast at him: but Jesus hid himself, and went out of the temple, going through the midst of them, and so passed by. (9:1) And as Jesus passed by, he saw a man which was blind from his birth. (2) And his disciples asked him, saying, Master, who did sin, this man, or his parents, that he was born blind? (3) Jesus answered, Neither hath this man sinned, nor his parents: but that the works of God should be made manifest in him. (4) I must work the works of him that sent me, while it is day: the night cometh, when no man can work. (5) As long as I am in the world, I am the light of the world. (6) When he had thus spoken, he spat on the ground, and made clay of the spittle, and he anointed the eyes of the blind man with the clay, (7) And said unto him, Go, wash in the pool of Siloam, (which is by interpretation, Sent.) He went his way therefore, and washed, and came seeing. (8) The neighbours therefore, and they which before had seen him that he was blind, said, Is not this he that sat and begged? (9) Some said, This is he: others said, He is like him: but he said, I am he. (10) Therefore said they unto him, How were thine eyes opened? (11) He answered and said, A man that is called Jesus made clay, and anointed mine eyes, and said unto me, Go to the pool of Siloam, and wash: and I went and washed, and I received sight. (12) Then said they unto him, Where is he? He said, I know not. (13) They brought to the Pharisees him that aforetime was blind. (14) And it was the sabbath day when Jesus made the clay, and opened his eyes. (15) Then again the Pharisees also asked him how he had received his sight. He said unto them, He put clay upon mine eyes, and I washed, and do see. (16) Therefore said some of the Pharisees, This man is not of God, because he keepeth not the sabbath day. Others said, How can a man that is a sinner do such miracles? And there was a division among them. (17) They say unto the blind man again, What sayest thou of him, that he hath opened thine eyes? He said, He is a prophet. (18) But the Jews did not believe concerning him, that he had been blind, and received his sight, until they called the parents of him that had received his sight. (19) And they asked them, saying, Is this your son, who ye say was born blind? how then doth he now see? (20) His parents answered them and said, We know that this is our son, and that he was born blind: (21) But by what means he now seeth, we know not; or who hath opened his eyes, we know not: he is of age; ask him: he shall speak for himself. (22) These words spake his parents, because they feared the Jews: for the Jews had agreed already, that if any man did confess that he was Christ, he should be put out of the synagogue. (23) Therefore said his parents, He is of age; ask him. (24) Then again called they the man that was blind, and said unto him, Give God the praise: we know that this man is a sinner. (25) He answered and said, Whether he be a sinner or no, I know not: one thing I know, that, whereas I was blind, now I see. (26) Then said they to him again, What did he to thee? how opened he thine eyes? (27) He answered them, I have told you already, and ye did not hear: wherefore would ye hear it again? will ye also be his disciples? (28) Then they reviled him, and said, Thou art his disciple; but we are Moses' disciples. (29) We know that God spake unto Moses: as for this fellow, we know not from whence he is. (30) The man answered and said unto them, Why herein is a marvellous thing, that ye know not from whence he is, and yet he hath opened mine eyes. (31) Now we know that God heareth not sinners: but if any man be a worshipper of God, and doeth his will, him he heareth. (32) Since the world began was it not heard that any man opened the eyes of one that was born blind. (33) If this man were not of God, he could do nothing. (34) They answered and said unto him, Thou wast altogether born in sins, and dost thou teach us? And they cast him out. (35) Jesus heard that they had cast him out; and when he had found him, he said unto him, Dost thou believe on the Son of God? (36) He answered and said, Who is he, Lord, that I might believe on him? (37) And Jesus said unto him, Thou hast both seen him, and it is he that talketh with thee. (38) And he said, Lord, I believe. And he worshipped him. (39) And Jesus said, For judgment I am come into this world, that they which see not might see; and that they which see might be made blind. (40) And some of the Pharisees which were with him heard these words, and said unto him, Are we blind also? (41) Jesus said unto them, If ye were blind, ye should have no sin: but now ye say, We see; therefore your sin remaineth. (John 8:12-9:41)*

The Light of the World is the theme in chapters 8 and 9. In chapter 8 Jesus is proclaimed as the Light of the World; in chapter 9 He is illustrated as the Light of the World. "Jesus spoke again" (8:12). What an untiring preacher He ever was.

Jesus Preaches Himself as the Light of the World, 8:12-59

THE LIGHT OF THE WORLD, 8:12-20

The declaration of Jesus (3:12) is one of the truly great texts of Jesus (see also 7:37). Compare "I am the Bread of Life," "I am the Resurrection and the Life," etc.

The declaration: "I am the Light of the World." This implies that man is in moral and spiritual darkness. Sin blinds men (2 Corinthians 4:4; Ephesians 4:18). Jesus is the only remedy. John 8:12 refers to the rising of the sun. What the sun was to the earth, He came to be to mankind. The court of the women in the temple building was brilliantly lighted during this feast. This was a memorial of the pillar of fire in the wilderness. How fitting as a type of Jesus! Either of these gives a good setting for this famous saying. Prefer the latter view, however.

Not for a few but for all mankind. The sun shines on all whether men use its light or not. Let us make sure it blesses us.

The promise:

- The condition of the promise: It is not enough to gaze on or to admire the Light. "Following," suggesting their following the pillar of fire, is another picture of "believing." The "following" is not physical. One must follow in faith, not unbelief. Let us make sure that we follow Jesus instead of our own opinions or the mere opinions of men.

- The substance of the promise: It is twofold: deliverance from darkness and the possession of living, unquenchable light. How blessed and full is what Jesus gives us! It not only removes the curse but brings positive blessing. Notice how closely light and life are related; it is light that brings life, and it is life that brings light. Both are spiritual (see also John 1:4).

The discussion with the Pharisees (8:13-19):

- Their charge (8:13): They counted His testimony as unreliable. They held that a man could not tell the truth on Himself. They must have been measuring Him by their own crookedness!

- The answer of Jesus (8:14-19): My testimony is trustworthy (8:14). The reason is that He had full consciousness of His origin, mission, and destiny. Jesus contrasted their ignorance and His knowledge. There is a gulf between Jesus and every man that no man can span.

    Your judgment is fleshly: mine is the same as My Father's (8:15-16). It was not Jesus' business to judge at His first coming (John 3:17). Again He draws a contrast: this time it was between their fleshly judgment and His divine judgment. What a testimony Jesus had. "I am not alone" (8:16). Would we come nearer, saying it all the time?

    Your law requires the testimony of only two (8:17-18; see also John 5:31-39). This was a knockout blow. He quoted their own scriptures against them. His witness and that of His Father made the two required witnesses.

Their question (8:19): "Where is Thy Father?" They were not serious but sarcastic. They probably looked around as if to say that He had meant an earthly father.

The answer of Jesus (8:19): Knowing the Father and the Son come inseparably.

The deliverance of Jesus from His enemies (8:20): In John 7:30 "His hour" means the hour of the Cross. As they wickedly attempted to lay hands on Him to His hurt, an Invisible Hand overruled their wickedness of plan to the good of Jesus. "Man is immortal till his work is done." This did not breed carelessness in the heart of Jesus but rather fuller trust. Divine care and human duty happily harmonize for the man who has faith.

DYING IN SIN (WITHOUT THE LIGHT OF THE WORLD), 8:21-30

Their unbelief (8:21-24): His warning (8:21). Jesus never tired in teaching; He spoke "again" to them. He warns them of the terrible remorse of seeking too late (Proverbs 1:28-29). His going refers to His cross and His ascension. To "die in your sins" is to die as a result of sin, to die without God and without hope in the world, to die without being saved out of the wreck of sin, to go down to hell without Christ as Savior.

Their objection (8:22): They suggested that He would commit suicide, a thing so horrible to the Jews. And suicide ought to be a horrible thing to all. Be patient until He calls.

His explanation (8:23-24): Jesus gives a striking contrast between Himself and unbelievers (8:23). They differ in both nature and origin. The repetition is for emphasis. John 8:24 explains more fully the sin of unbelief mentioned in 8:21. "I am" probably refers to Exodus 3:14. One must believe the deity of Christ to be saved. "If ye believe not," there is no other way. Never does the Bible say that if you are not baptized, you will die in your sins. We have no right to put things between the soul and the sinner that the Lord did not put there.

Their misunderstanding (8:25-30):

- Their insincere question (8:25)

- His answer (8:25b-26): He has no new truth to say to them. He is the unvarying Jesus. He did not have to change what He taught. This "beginning" refers to the beginning of His ministry. Jesus knew them perfectly; that is why He said that He had many things to say and to judge concerning them. But He would leave that to the One Who sent Him; He could trust the Father to take care of His own personal interests. Let us learn the lesson from Jesus not to take things into our own hands but to trust our case to the Father. Let us speak to the world what He tells us.

- Their misunderstanding (8:27): What ignorance exceeds that of unbelief? If they misunderstood the message of Jesus, why should we marvel if they misunderstand ours?

- His answer (8:28-29) Jesus foretells the new light and understanding that would come to them after His death on the cross (8:28). On two other occasions, He speaks of His death under the metaphor of a lifting up (John 3:14; 12:32). He told them that they would be guilty of His death. He did nothing of His own independent authority (John 5:19, 30). Their knowing may be twofold: in conversion, as at Pentecost, and in judgment, as on Jerusalem in 70 AD when the armies of Titus destroyed the city. Note "I am."

- Jesus calls attention to His sinless life (8:29): He was always conscious of the Father's presence; His presence was so dear to Him that He expressed it twice in one verse. Jesus never allowed one thought that was not pleasing to the Father. Though we can never please Him perfectly here, yet our great desire should be to strive to please Him.

- The result (8:30): Let us be sure that we believe on Jesus from the heart. Only heart faith saves. Faith that saves is more than believing the truth about Jesus; it actually trusts the soul into His hands for salvation and life. Trust Him without delay.

True Freedom and Spiritual Sonship, 8:31-47

True freedom or liberty (8:31-36); what is it? How and where is it found?

- Perseverance proves discipleship (8:31-32): The word *then* has the force of *therefore* (ASV) and refers to those in 8:30 who professed to believe on Jesus. There is just one way for others to know whether our believing on Christ is head faith or heart faith. The one who has believed with the heart as well as with the head will abide in Jesus' Word. That means that he will enjoy feasting on the Word of God. He will seek to be at church to hear it preached. He will shape his life by it and be obedient to what the Word of God demands of him. Obedience is not faith but results from and proves faith. According to this test of Jesus, many of His so-called disciples are such only in name.

- Spiritual slavery (8:33-35): They boasted political freedom. They did not care for the truth, for at that moment they were suffering under the galling yoke of Rome. At different times, they had been crushed under the power of Egypt, Assyria, Babylon, Persia, Greece, and others. Jesus pointed out a worse slavery than political slavery; that is, spiritual slavery. The proof was not hard to give; their committing sin as a habitual thing proved that they were slaves to sin (8:34). Jesus emphasized this by His emphatic "verily, verily, I say to you," which occurs twenty-five times in this Gospel.

- John 8:35 contrasts them as bond-servants of sin and Jesus as the Son. Ruin for them; safety for Him. Such can be said of every saint of God; He will not cast out those that are His (6:37).

- True freedom (8:36): Note six things about it: (1) the Agent of it—the Son; (2) the Means of it—the truth (8:32); (3) the degree of it—"free indeed," really and eternally; (4) the Nature of it—freedom from being cast out; (5) the Condition of it—knowing the truth (8:32); and (6) the Proof of it—doing the truth (8:32).

Spiritual Sonship (8:37-47):

- Jesus' contrast (8:37-38): Jesus acknowledged that they were natural children of Abraham but denied that they were spiritual children. Each one, Jesus and the Jews, did what he learned from his father. Their said plight was that Jesus' Word had no place or room in them; their hearts were full of sin.

- Their claim (8:39): They surely meant more than physical children of Abraham. That was true, but they were not his spiritual children.

- Jesus' reply—you do not do His works (8:39-41): You must act like Abraham to prove that you are his spiritual children. You do not convince people that you are his spiritual children. You do not convince people that you are a Christian by mere profession; daily practice is the acid test. Their seeking to kill Jesus proved they were lost.

- "If you were spiritual seed of Abraham, you would love Me" (8:42-43): Love for Jesus—that is the test (1 Corinthians 16:22).

- The devil is your spiritual father (8:44): All are naturally children of the devil (Genesis 5:3; Job 14:4; Psalm 51:5; Ephesians 2:3). Not to love Jesus is to prove that one is a child of the devil. To love Him is to prove that God is our Father. Can you stand this strong test?

- Jesus' unmet challenge (8:45-47): They did not want the truth—they rejected Him just because He told them the truth

(8:45). That is a strange reason for unbelief. His sinlessness stands unstained (8:46). Many may have attempted to show that Jesus was a sinner but have utterly failed. John 8:47 gives another strong test. Do you hear God's Word? Do not dodge this test. Do you hear it gladly, believingly, unquestioningly, wholeheartedly?

The One Greater than Abraham, 8:48-59

You may prefer one of these titles: *The One Greater than Death*, or *Honoring Jesus Christ.*

- The false charge of the Jews (8:48): By their calling Him a Samaritan, they meant that He was not a true Jew and that He was a half-breed and despised by them (see also John 4:9). By saying that He had a devil, they meant that He was acting under demonic influence. To lose one's temper and to turn to personal abuse proves a defeated cause. Only defeated men abuse their opponent.

- The calm answer of Jesus (8:49-51): Note three things in 8:49: (1) A calm denial—"I have not a devil." In vindicating ourselves, we must not become personal but seek always to honor God. (2) A solemn claim—"I honor My Father." He never did otherwise. (3) A pointed charge—"ye do dishonor Me." Jesus' meaning in 8:50 is, "My Father, not I by self-seeking, will care for My honor and bring you Jews to judgment."

- A glorious promise (8:51)—the One Who is greater than death. An emphatic introduction—"verily, verily": The Greek for this is "amen, amen," meaning "of a truth, of a truth." A definite condition: *My saying* is another term for *My gospel. Keep* means to receive into the heart and prove by a life of obedience. Heaven and hell turn on the attitude and treatment men give Jesus and His message. A striking blessing: Death, since the sin of Adam, has been the peculiar enemy of man. But Jesus holds out a glorious prospect to the saint. "He shall never see death"—that is, never experience it. This means at least three things to the saint of God: (1) Deliverance from the condemnation of spiritual death. John 6:47 gives the positive side of this as eternal life. (2) Removal of the fear and sting of death (Hebrews 2:15). The worst of death is taken out; resurrection will destroy the grave forevermore. (3) Deliverance from the second death of eternal ruin in hell (Revelation 21:3). The second death does not mean annihilation; it does not put the sinner out of existence and out of his pains. It rather prolongs the separation, degradation, and pains of death forevermore. O sinner, turn to Jesus. O saint, rejoice in what you have in Jesus.

- Their ignorant reply (8:52-53): They thought or pretended that they thought that He referred to physical death. Compare the woman's question in John 4:12 with John 8:53. If they had only known that there stood in their presence One greater than either Jacob or Abraham.

- Jesus' answer (8:54-56): In 8:54 He disclaimed all self-sought honor and claimed only what His Father bestowed. His Father honored Him by giving signs and by giving Him His words. In 8:55 He contrasts their ignorance of God and His conscious knowledge of God. The Greek is interesting here: "I shall be like to you, a liar." Pause at the comma and feel the stunning effect of these words.

    In 8:56 He tells what clear knowledge of Himself Abraham had. He saw by faith. He looked forward to Christ for salvation just as we look back. There is only one way of salvation then, now, and evermore—that is, in seeing by faith Jesus Christ as one's personal Savior.

- Their perversion of His words (8:57): They pretended that He meant that Abraham saw Him in person. Evidently, this they did to entrap Him in His words. All He claimed was that Abraham saw His day. Since He was discussing the spiritual topic of salvation, He left them to gather the evident spiritual meaning of His words. Their action only shows their blindness in spiritual things.

- In His answer, Jesus declares His preexistence (8:58): They asked, "Are you greater than Abraham?" He answered twofoldly: I am the eternal One; Abraham was born as a mere creature of time. Literally, "Before Abraham came into being, I am." That means that He claims to be Jehovah of Exodus 3:14. "I am" is stronger than "I was" would have been. It signifies full eternity, which is more than mere priority, and belongs only to Godhood. This is hard on those who claim that Jesus never claimed to be more than a mere man.

- The sequel (8:59): They understood His claim of being Jehovah God and proceeded to stone Him for blasphemy. He did not court death—"He hid." He did not hide in a corner—"through their midst." He did not retaliate to get even—"He passed by." Infinite discretion and patience were His.

Emphasize the two "verilys" in 8:51 and 8:58; the deity of Jesus (8:58); joy in seeing Jesus' day (8:56); our being saved as Abraham was (Romans 4:23-24); our looking back to Christ's day as Abraham looked forward to His day. Have you looked to Him by faith?

3.2.6 JESUS OPENS THE EYES OF THE MAN BORN BLIND, CHAPTER 9

Jesus opens the eyes of the man born blind. The Jews examine and excommunicate him, but Jesus saves him. Jesus was always busy (e.g., 8:59; 9:1). Jesus "saw" this man (9:1). Thank God, He sees or looks on the ills of human life and cares.

Jesus healed this man, unasked. This is grace indeed. Compare this with John 5. This is a special illustration of Jesus' claim: "I am the Light of the world." The reformer Martin Bucer (1491-1551) said, "This chapter is a sermon in act and deed, on the words, 'I am the light of the world.'"[12]

Dean of Chichester Cathedral, John Burgon (1813-1888), observed, "More of our Savior's miracles are recorded as having been wrought on blindness than on any other form of human infirmity. One deaf and dumb man is related to have had speech and hearing restored to him; one case of palsy, and one of dropsy, find special record; twice was leprosy, and twice was fever expelled by the Savior's word; three times were dead persons raised to life; but the records of His cures wrought on blindness are four in number, at least, if not five."[13]

A Case of Need: The Disciples' Question and Jesus' Answer, 9:1-5

SIN AS BLINDNESS, 9:1-3

Jesus denied that this man's blindness was the direct result of his personal sins. But blindness is a fitting picture of men in the darkness of

---

12. This quote from Bucer is cited in the following title (although the original source is unnamed): Rev. J.C. Ryle, *Expository Thoughts on the Gospels*, vol. 2, *St. John* (New York: Robert Carter & Brothers, 1860) 156.

13. Ryle, "J.C. Ryle's Notes on the Gospel of John: 9:1-12" in *Expository Thoughts on the Gospels*, 2 (http://rediscoveringthebible.com/Ryle9vv1-12.pdf).

sins, bereft of joy, made helpless, and dependent on others. Every sinner needs Jesus as this man did.

The purpose of God in afflictions (9:3): The blindness of this man was permitted that it might be the platform for the manifestation of a work of divine mercy and power. Be quiet; do not complain; He may be working out His purpose through you.

There are several reasons for sickness:

1. As chastisement for specific sin (1 Corinthians 11:30)

2. For God's glory, as here

3. To test our faith, as Job's troubles and Paul's thorn

4. To get the dross out of us, as Job

USE OF OPPORTUNITIES, 9:4-5

Our one great lesson from human suffering is the need of diligence on our part. What a rebuke to the curious disciples. The word *day* refers to the span of life; the term *night* means death has closed earthly opportunity. Be busy, now! Do not put it off!

The Cure Itself, 9:6-7

His almighty power to do the impossible: Why should we ever despair in the presence of such a One? A blind multimillionaire of New York City offered a million dollars cash to any scientist, savant, or surgeon in the world who would restore his sight. What man cannot do, that very thing Jesus did.

His pity toward the man's miserable condition: Our true condition in sin would repel Him, but His inward kindness compels Him toward us.

His sovereign use of means: He did as He pleased; He spoke the word or touched the afflicted or used means as here. He was never tied to the use of one particular instrument. That is the limitation of a charlatan or one mildly efficient. There could be no healing virtue in what the man did in going to the pool. How strange was Jesus' action in adding clay, an artificial blindness, to the natural blindness! When He was working miracles on those deprived of the natural sense, Jesus used some object that would let them know that the cure emanated from His blessed Person (Godet 1886).

The Man and His Neighbors, 9:8-12

How prone curiosity is to pry in where angels dare not tread! Three questions were aroused by the man's return home. First, is this the beggar (9:8)? (Note three answers, 9:9). Second, how were your eyes opened (9:10-11)? Third, where is Jesus (9:12)?

Christian, be busy during your day of opportunity. May we feel the urge that Jesus felt when He said, "I must work" the Father's works. Sinner, let Jesus open your spiritual eyes. Do not boast of what you know mentally. You are blind spiritually. Jesus is the only one Who can make you see things divine. Look now and live. Do not strive to save yourself; let Jesus do it. Do not try; just trust.

The Man and the Pharisees, 9:13-17

Those of 9:9 that said, "He is like him," pushed for an investigation until they got it.

The Man On Trial Before the Pharisees, 9:13-15

They scrupulously and wrongfully observed the Sabbath; we, taking the other extreme, make it a day of pleasure, indulgence, and business.

Divided Opinion: Three Opinions Concerning Jesus, 9:16-17

Some opposed the work of mercy because it was a Sabbath. Others said Jesus was good because they saw the miracle (John 3:2). This is the first glimpse of faith in the healed man; he exclaimed, "He is a prophet."

His Parents and the Pharisees, 9:18-23

Their Testimony as to His Identity and Original Blindness, 9:18-20

"Called" in 9:18 means the same as summons to appear in court.

Their Fear of the Jews, 9:21-23

There are too many cowards today! Prejudice closed the minds of the Jews to the truth and led to persecution. They should have contented themselves with knowing the miraculous fact, for reason always shatters itself in trying to know the *how* of miracles. I cite this instance from the words of Voltaire, the leading French infidel: "If in the market of Paris, before the eyes of a thousand men and before my own eyes, a miracle should be performed, I would much rather disbelieve the two thousand eyes and my own two, than believe it."[14] What a fallacious reasoning! Yet liberals want us to think that they are great thinkers and open-minded!

The Man and the Pharisees, Again, 9:24-34

They acknowledge the fact of the miracle and set out to discredit Jesus as the doer of it (9:24). It is to be noted that these men testified to the reality of the miracle, but they did not want Jesus to have the glory or credit for it.

The testimony of experience (9:25): He did not know the *how* but could not be driven from the two facts his sense taught him. So it is with Christians. They know that they are saved, though they cannot explain all about it.

His opposers turned from arguments to abuse and violence (9:28). Godet (1886) gives this paraphrase of 9:30: "There is here a miracle greater than even my cure itself; it is your unbelief."

John 9:31 has often been misinterpreted. The Old Testament teaches that God does not hear a wicked man when he prays for a miracle. Let this illustration suffice: Elijah and the Baalites. In using this verse against penitent sinners' asking for mercy through Jesus Christ, "Campbellites" and "Hardshells" unquestionably err. Always study the context. Furthermore, this was praying about an outward miracle, not salvation. Finally, these are not the words of Jesus and should not be quoted as such.

Then the critics tried to discredit the man (8:34). How inconsistent! They first denied the man's blindness; then they blamed him as a great sinner. "Thus unbelief ends by giving the lie to itself" (Godet 1886). They used any tool that seemed to carry their point—that was their policy. They reasoned that God could not favor a Sabbath violator; therefore, the miracle does not exist. Liberals reason that miracles are impossible; therefore, Jesus wrought none. Both start wrong, and both end wrong.

Jesus and the Man, 9:35-38

This is the most touching scene in this fast-changing drama of the conflict of honesty and dishonesty, almighty mercy, and blind unbelief. How different the Jews and Jesus! How cruel they! How merciful He! Note how

---

14. Editor's Note: This quote probably came from J. C. Ryle's commentary, *Expository Thoughts*, 1860, on page 156. Ryle relates the Voltaire quote via Besser.

clearly Jesus revealed Himself to the man (cf. John 4). "O happy man! Having lost the synagogue, he finds heaven" (Burkitt 1844). "The Jews cast him out of the temple, and the Lord of the temple found him" (Chrysostom).[15] This was the first confessor who suffered for the sake of Jesus Christ.

He was saved just at this point. Jesus' acceptance of his worship shows that He is either God or that He is not a good man—for Peter and John were mere men who refused worship. The pope is not as good as Peter and John or he would refuse to be worshipped. Worship stems from faith. Worship does not thrive in the soil of unbelief. May we all say with this man, "Lord, I believe!" He is worthy of the faith of everyone in the world.

Jesus and the Pharisees, 9:39-41

Jesus' reflection on the incident gives it interpretation and general application. The twofold result of Christ's message was this: Light revealed to babes, light withheld from the proud. Much depends on the attitude of the heart toward the Savior (2 Corinthians 2:15-16). "The same fire that melts wax hardens clay" (Ryle 1860).

The ones who "see not" are the ones who feel that they do not see and therefore turn to Jesus for spiritual sight; the ones "who see" are the proud who will not acknowledge their deep spiritual blindness. This class will not let Jesus make them see. Oh, that we may ever be willing to own our blindness and go to Jesus for spiritual sight!

3.2.7 Jesus: The True Door and the Good Shepherd, 10:1-21

(1) Verily, verily, I say unto you, He that entereth not by the door into the sheepfold, but climbeth up some other way, the same is a thief and a robber. (2) But he that entereth in by the door is the shepherd of the sheep. (3) To him the porter openeth; and the sheep hear his voice: and he calleth his own sheep by name, and leadeth them out. (4) And when he putteth forth his own sheep, he goeth before them, and the sheep follow him: for they know his voice. (5) And a stranger will they not follow, but will flee from him: for they know not the voice of strangers. (6) This parable spake Jesus unto them: but they understood not what things they were which he spake unto them. (7) Then said Jesus unto them again, Verily, verily, I say unto you, I am the door of the sheep. (8) All that ever came before me are thieves and robbers: but the sheep did not hear them. (9) I am the door: by me if any man enter in, he shall be saved, and shall go in and out, and find pasture. (10) The thief cometh not, but for to steal, and to kill, and to destroy: I am come that they might have life, and that they might have it more abundantly. (11) I am the good shepherd: the good shepherd giveth his life for the sheep. (12) But he that is an hireling, and not the

---

15. Editor's Note: This Chrysostom may have come from Philip Schaff's, *A Select Library of the Nicene and Post-Nicene Fathers of the Christian Church*, 1889.

shepherd, whose own the sheep are not, seeth the wolf coming, and leaveth the sheep, and fleeth: and the wolf catcheth them, and scattereth the sheep. (13) The hireling fleeth, because he is an hireling, and careth not for the sheep. (14) I am the good shepherd, and know my sheep, and am known of mine. (15) As the Father knoweth me, even so know I the Father: and I lay down my life for the sheep. (16) And other sheep I have, which are not of this fold: them also I must bring, and they shall hear my voice; and there shall be one fold, and one shepherd. (17) Therefore doth my Father love me, because I lay down my life, that I might take it again. (18) No man taketh it from me, but I lay it down of myself. I have power to lay it down, and I have power to take it again. This commandment have I received of my Father. (19) There was a division therefore again among the Jews for these sayings. (20) And many of them said, He hath a devil, and is mad; why hear ye him? (21) Others said, These are not the words of him that hath a devil. Can a devil open the eyes of the blind? (John 10:1-21)

Note the connection with chapter nine. Jesus tells the excommunicated man of John 9 who has power to give entrance into the true fold or to exclude from it (Dods 1908). This message consoled the man born blind and instructed the Pharisees. The violence of climbing over the wall reminds us of the deceptive Pharisees, and the sheep that followed the shepherd pictures the man born blind following the true Shepherd. The sacrifice of the Good Shepherd is in line with the tenderness of Jesus to the man born blind. The allegories or metaphors set forth a series of contrasts.

The Shepherd, 10:1-6

The fold, in that land, was a walled, unroofed enclosure to which various shepherds led their sheep and left them for the night and then led them out the next morning. It pictures Judaism, out of which Jesus led men to Himself. The door, therefore, is the office of the Messiah. The porter is probably the forerunner of Jesus, John the Baptist; of course, it may be meant merely to fill out the story. A thief suggests secret deception; a robber suggests open violence.

There are two things by which we know the True Shepherd:

1. His using the legitimate entrance: One climbs over the wall; the other appeals to the regular keeper of the fold. Jesus did not just of Himself assume the office of the Messiah; the Father sent Him.

2. His treatment of the sheep: The robber, true to his evil nature, uses violence; Jesus, true to His loving nature, calls tenderly.

This is a morning scene. He leads them out, not drives them out. Sheep in the East often answer to their names as dogs and horses do with us. A Scottish traveler changed clothes with a Jerusalem shepherd and tried to lead the sheep, but the sheep followed the shepherd's voice, not his clothes (Plummer 1902).[16]

Knowledge of His sheep and tenderness toward them are the two points to emphasize. "The history of each sheep, its state, qualities, worth, age, are known to the shepherd, and its special name suggests his knowledge, interest, and affection towards itself" (Reith 1889, 39). The sheep hears the voice of the actual shepherd and flees from strangers. The man born blind listened to Jesus and fled from strangers, the devouring Pharisees.

By their failure to catch the drift of His words, the Pharisees proved that they were not His sheep (10:6).

The Door, 10:7-10

"Then" or "therefore" in 10:7 indicates that, in consequence of their darkness of understanding, Jesus made another gracious effort to reach them ("again"). He changed the picture, and soundness of interpretation depends on observing this.

The scene shifts to midday and to the pasture to show us the way in which Jesus feeds His flock. The fold here is in the pasture and is individual to each shepherd and not general as in 10:1-6. The Pharisees, with their teaching of salvation by works, were thieves and robbers. Such are any who teach salvation by works today (Matthew 7:15; 23:13-14; Luke 11:39). Jesus declared that all who claim to be saviors are thieves and robbers. That includes Confucius, Buddha, and all others before Christ's day. That includes Mohammed, the Pope of Rome, Mrs. Mary Baker Eddy, Mrs. Ellen G. White who founded Adventism, Joseph Smith, Father Divine, "Pastor" Charles Taze Russell, "Judge" Joseph Franklin Rutherford, the Fox Sisters (Leah, Margaret, and Kate) who started Spiritualism, and all others who pose as bringing to light new truth about salvation. All these deny the Bible's way of salvation by grace through faith in Jesus Christ. All who claim to stand between Christ and men are thieves and robbers.

"The term, the door of the sheep, naturally means: the door which the sheep uses for going in and out" (Godet 1886). Jesus declares, "I am the Door." The pronoun is emphatic. He alone is; He is the only Door. He is more than a Door, there being no other. You cannot come any other way. Neither the church nor baptism nor good life nor keeping commands nor anything else is the door. If baptism were the door, Jesus

16. Editor's Note: This may have come from Plummer's *A Critical and Exegetical Commentary on the Gospel According to St. Luke* (1902). See the selected bibliography for more information.

would not be the Door. He is not discussing the door into the church but into salvation. Reith (1889) mistakes this, as do others.

Note three definite blessings in 10:9:

1. Deliverance or salvation through Christ Jesus: "By Me" or "through Me." Do not try anything else. Anything else tried for salvation leads to hell and ruin. Not "he may be saved" but he "shall be saved." The next phrase must not be so interpreted as to contradict this statement.

2. Freedom or liberty in Christ: The going in and out reminds us of the free, unhampered use of a house. One goes in for shelter and rest and out for sustenance or food. "The expression, go in and out, does not mean that the sheep will go out of salvation to enter into it again" (Godet 1886). To claim that this teaches that one can be saved and then lost twists the words terribly. You cannot be saved and then lost. If you can save yourself, you can lose your salvation; but since the Lord alone saves, He does the keeping too. The statement is the language of assurance, confidence, and fellowship.

3. Sustenance or pasturage: Read Psalm 23. How graciously, tenderly, and satisfyingly He feeds our souls. Do you stay in His pasture, or do you stray to the sinful pleasures of the world?

Contrast Jesus with false religious teachers in 10:10. His purpose is never bad; theirs is. He gives life, abiding life; that saves from sin. He does more than merely readjust our lives; He gives us a life we did not have. We are naturally dead in sins; He makes us alive in Himself. O sinner, receive life from Him as His gracious gift. He comes to give; the thief comes to get.

But His words go further. Life can be increased in three ways: by the creation of a new life, by lengthening life, and by deepening life. He creates us anew in Christ Jesus, and that is an eternal life. He gives more abundant life, abounding life, life with fuller meaning; that is the life of overflowing service in the lives of the saved. Do you have abiding life? Then is that abiding life the abounding life? These two sum up the all-inclusive picture of Jesus respecting life—its origination and its deepening, broadening, and expanding of force and meaning.

The Good Shepherd, 10:11-18

These verses complete what Jesus says about Himself as the Shepherd. Other occupational names are given Him to indicate the fullness of His glories—Sower, Vinedresser, Judge, Mediator, Prophet, Priest, Lawgiver, Physician—but none excels in charm and beauty the title of Shepherd. Study here Psalm 23 and Luke 15:1ff.

The Good Shepherd is known by two things:

1. Sacrifice (10:11-13): The New Testament uses three adjectives to describe our Savior's work for us as a Shepherd—good, great, chief. The Good Shepherd is the life-giving Shepherd. This points to His death. He gave His life for us. Who is He? The Good Shepherd, having every perfection. The word *good* sometimes means "courageous" in Greek, and that meaning is suggestive here. What does He do? He gives, not selfishly withholds. What does He give? "His life," not just a little but all. For whom does He give His life? "For the sheep." All false teachers are hirelings; they are in it because of what they get out of it. On the other hand, Christ Jesus sees how much He can do for the sheep because of love and because they are His own. Christ cares for His own property. "The wolf" represents all enemies: in particular, false religious leaders.

   Jesus tells us in 10:13 why false religious leaders will not make any sacrifice for the sheep. The two reasons are that (1) they work only for pay and (2) are without love for the sheep. Let the ministers of Christ test themselves by these two standards.

   Also, Jesus is the Great Shepherd, Who was raised from the dead for us (Hebrews 13:20). If the wolf slays the human shepherd, he lies dead and helpless. The Divine Shepherd, the Great Shepherd, could not be kept dead; His greatness lies in the fact that He lives—lives forevermore in spite of death and all foes. In human affairs, a wolf might kill the shepherd and then get his sheep; Jesus is the Shepherd that cannot, since His resurrection, be killed and cannot be overpowered by all combined foes.

Also, He is the Chief Shepherd, Who will come for us (1 Peter 5:4). He died for us, He lives for us, and He is coming again for us.

2. Mutual knowledge (10:14-15): An Eastern shepherd said that he could tell each one of his sheep by the feeling of its face. The world may not know, friends may not misunderstand, but Jesus understands.

Who are the "other' sheep in 10:16? He refers to the Gentiles: in fact, to all that were yet to be saved. Jesus said that He already had or possessed them, yet they were not yet brought to Him as a personal Savior. They were unsaved and most of them yet unborn but were already His own sheep by the purpose, choice, and gift of the Father.

Note the expressions, "other sheep" and "them also." His great missionary heart was always thinking of someone else. Let us learn the missionary spirit from Him. "I must bring"—Jesus Christ must save all His sheep. The mark of a shepherd of the East was his faithfulness; Jesus says that He Himself will not let up until every one of the sheep the Father gave Him is led or brought to Himself in salvation. He is not a failing shepherd but the victorious One. The word *bring* is properly "lead." Study the story in Luke 15. Note the response of Jesus' followers, His sheep: "They shall hear My voice." Whose voice do we hear?

The grand result will be "one fold, one shepherd" (10:16). All His sheep, the saved ones and the lost ones and the yet unborn ones, will all be brought one day into one fold with Christ Jesus as their Shepherd. That fold is ever growing and will be completed when He comes again.

His motive in all this was love (10:15-18). He gave up His life freely. There was no coercion. This assertion alone proves His deity; no one else but God could lay down or take up His life at will. We can do neither. Suicide is not voluntarily laying down life; it is violent taking of what we cannot give or bring back. No dead man can say, "I will arise" and actually arise. But Jesus could and did. In His hands He held the power to let go of life and to return to life. Jesus laid down His life at the Cross and took it up again in resurrection. This voluntariness of Jesus is very important. If He had been forced to die on the cross contrary to His will, His death could not atone for us.

The Result: Another Division, 10:19-21

Note the two opinions concerning Jesus. Nothing so sifts hearers as plain truth about Jesus. "What do you think of Christ?" (Matthew 22:42). Too many worry about the many opinions about Christ when they ought to be concerned to search and to believe for themselves what the Bible says.

3.2.8 JESUS AT THE FEAST OF DEDICATION, 10:22-42

(22) And it was at Jerusalem the feast of the dedication, and it was winter. (23) And Jesus walked in the temple in Solomon's porch. (24) Then came the Jews round about him, and said unto him How long dost thou make us to doubt? If thou be the Christ, tell us plainly. (25) Jesus answered them, I told you, and ye believed not: the works that I do in my Father's name, they bear witness of me. (26) But ye believe not, because ye are not of my sheep, as I said unto you. (27) My sheep hear my voice, and I know them, and they follow me: (28) And I give unto them eternal life; and they shall never perish, neither shall any man pluck them out of my hand. (29) My Father, which gave them me, is greater than all; and no man is able to pluck them out of my Father's hand. (30) I and my Father are one. (31) Then the Jews took up stones again to stone him. (32) Jesus answered them, Many good works have I shewed you from my Father; for which of those works do ye stone me? (33) The Jews answered him, saying, For a good work we stone thee not; but for blasphemy; and because that thou, being a man, makest thyself God. (34) Jesus answered them, Is it not written in your law, I said, Ye are gods? (35) If he called them gods, unto whom the word of God came, and the scripture cannot be broken; (36) Say ye of him, whom the Father hath sanctified, and sent into the world, Thou blasphemest; because I said, I am the Son of God? (37) If I do not the works of my Father, believe me not (38) But if I do, though ye believe not me, believe the works: that ye may know, and believe, that the Father is in me, and I in him. (39) Therefore they sought again to take him: but he escaped out of their hand, (40) And went away again beyond Jordan into the place where John at first baptized; and there he abode. (41) And many resorted unto him, and said, John did no miracle: but all things that John spake of this man were true. (42) And many believed on him there. (John 10:22-42)

The Historical Setting, 10:22-23

The Feast of Dedication was instituted in 167 BC by Judas Maccabaeus to commemorate the purification of the temple from the defilement of Antiochus Ephiphanes in the period between the Old and New Testaments. It came in December, about the middle, and was a time of great joy. The corruptions of the temple by Antiochus were unspeakably terrible.

It had been two months since the Feast of Tabernacles (John 7:2), during which time comes much of the material of Luke. The feast was celebrated for eight days, beginning with the twenty-fifth day of Kislev, corresponding roughly to our December. (Read 1 Maccabees 4; 2 Maccabees 1, 10.) Josephus says that the feast was also called the "Feast of Lights," supposing that the name was given from the joy of the nation at their unexpected liberty.

John mentioned that it was winter to explain why Jesus walked under a porch or veranda. This detail does not at all look like an invention but like the word of an eyewitness.

Jesus' First Address, 10:24-31

THEIR QUESTION, 10:24

They charged that He held them in suspense.

JESUS' ANSWER, 10:25-30

They were insincere; "I told you and ye believed not" (10:25). He charged them pointedly with unbelief. His works proved His claims.

"My sheep." How precious the thought of being His sheep! Christ's sheep have two special marks: (1) An ear mark—they hear His voice. Do you hear him? (2) A foot mark—they follow Him (10:27). Two things are said of His attitude toward the sheep: He knows them tenderly and fully, and He gives to them. His gift to them is nothing short of "eternal life" (10:28). It is life, life for souls dead in sins. It is eternal life. Eternal means something that has no beginning and no end. Our eternal life has no beginning because Jesus Christ, Who is eternal, is our life. It can have no end because it will last as long as He lives. "Because I live, ye also shall live" (John 14:19).

How could eternal security be made stronger? Dwell on these gracious promises. The Father is greater than the Son in position in the scheme of redemption; not in nature, essence, and being. Illustrate this by the Double Divine Grip. Let a coin represent Christ's sheep. Have a child take the coin in its grip; that represents Christ. Have a strong man grip the hand of the child; that pictures God the Father. To get that coin you must break both grips. For a person to go to hell after he has been saved would mean that the grip of Christ and of the Father has to be broken. Jesus says that that cannot be done.

Apostatizers say that no one can pluck us out but that we may fall out. How come? Is not the grip of Jesus and the Father strong enough to keep us? Does His Word not pledge that He will not let us go? Who can incline Him to break His word of oath and promise? We are kept by the power of God through faith (1 Peter 1:5).

The expression *any man* or *any one* is broad enough to include the sheep himself, the devil, or any conceivable foe. It may sound too good to be true, but believe it because God said it. The old story illustrates this truth: put a five-gallon keg in a thirty-gallon keg or half barrel; then put the half barrel in the full barrel, with both of them headed up. That pictures the Christian hid with Christ in God (Colossians 3:3). You would have to break both barrels in order to get the keg; you would have to break through God the Father and the Son to get one believer to be lost again.

In John 10:26, prefer the "fore" of evidence rather than "because." Ryle (1860) comments, "Not being Christ's sheep was not the cause of the unbelief of the Jews; but their unbelief was the evidence that they were not Christ's sheep."

The Result, 10:31

Cruelly, they attempted persecution.

Jesus' Second Address, 10:32-39

He answers the accusation of blasphemy (10:32-36). His question (10:32)—their reply (10:33). They testified that they could find no evil work in Jesus. He answered (10:34-36). Note how strongly Jesus believed that the very words of Scripture are inspired (10:36).

He shows that His works prove His deity (10:37-38). The result— their attempt at arrest and His escape (10:39).

Historical Conclusion, 10:40-42

He retires away from their unbelief and persecution. Jesus gave the proof of the truth of what John preached. Many believed.

3.3 The Climax of His Signs: The Raising of Lazarus, chapter 11

(1) Now a certain man was sick, named Lazarus, of Bethany, the town of Mary and her sister Martha. (2) (It was that Mary which anointed the Lord with ointment, and wiped his feet with her hair, whose brother Lazarus was sick. (3) Therefore his sisters sent unto him, saying, Lord, behold, he whom

thou lovest is sick. (4) When Jesus heard that, he said, This sickness is not unto death, but for the glory of God, that the Son of God might be glorified thereby. (5) Now Jesus loved Martha, and her sister, and Lazarus. (6) When he had heard therefore that he was sick, he abode two days still in the same place where he was. (7) Then after that saith he to his disciples, Let us go into Judaea again. (8)nHis disciples say unto him, Master, the Jews of late sought to stone thee; and goest thou thither again? (9) Jesus answered, Are there not twelve hours in the day? If any man walk in the day, he stumbleth not, because he seeth the light of this world. (10) But if a man walk in the night, he stumbleth, because there is no light in him. (11) These things said he: and after that he saith unto them, Our friend Lazarus sleepeth; but I go, that I may awake him out of sleep. (12) Then said his disciples, Lord, if he sleep, he shall do well. (13) Howbeit Jesus spake of his death: but they thought that he had spoken of taking of rest in sleep. (14) Then said Jesus unto them plainly, Lazarus is dead. (15) And I am glad for your sakes that I was not there, to the intent ye may believe; nevertheless let us go unto him. (16) Then said Thomas, which is called Didymus, unto his fellowdisciples, Let us also go, that we may die with him. (17) Then when Jesus came, he found that he had lain in the grave four days already. (18) Now Bethany was nigh unto Jerusalem, about fifteen furlongs off: (19) And many of the Jews came to Martha and Mary, to comfort them concerning their brother. (20) Then Martha, as soon as she heard that Jesus was coming, went and met him: but Mary sat still in the house. (21) Then said Martha unto Jesus, Lord, if thou hadst been here, my brother had not died. (22) But I know, that even now, whatsoever thou wilt ask of God, God will give it thee. (23) Jesus saith unto her, Thy brother shall rise again. (24) Martha saith unto him, I know that he shall rise again in the resurrection at the last day. (25) Jesus said unto her, I am the resurrection, and the life: he that believeth in me though he were dead, yet shall he live: (26) And whosoever liveth and believeth in me shall never die. Believest thou this? (27) She saith unto him, Yea, Lord: I believe that thou art the Christ, the Son of God, which should come into the world. (28) And when she had so said, she went her way, and called Mary her sister secretly, saying, The Master is come, and calleth for thee (29) As soon as she heard that, she arose quickly, and came unto him. (30) Now Jesus was not yet come into the town, but was in that place where Martha met him. (31) The Jews then which were with her in the house, and comforted her, when they saw Mary, that she rose up hastily and went out, followed her, saying, She goeth unto the grave to weep there. (32) Then when Mary was come where Jesus was, and saw him, she fell down at his feet, saying unto him, Lord, if thou hadst been here, my brother had not died. (33) When Jesus therefore saw her weeping, and the Jews also weeping which came with her, he groaned in the spirit, and was troubled. (34) And said, Where have ye laid him? They said unto him, Lord, come and see. (35) Jesus wept. (36) Then said the Jews, Behold how he loved him! (37) And some of them said, Could not this man, which opened the eyes of the blind, have caused that even this man should not have died? (38)nJesus therefore again groaning in himself cometh to the grave. It was a cave, and a stone lay upon it. (39) Jesus said, Take ye away the stone. Martha, the sister of him that was dead, saith unto him, Lord, by this time he stinketh: for he hath been dead four days. (40) Jesus saith unto her, Said I not unto thee, that, if thou wouldest believe, thou shouldest see the glory of God? (41) Then they took away the stone from the place where the dead was laid. And Jesus lifted *up his eyes, and said, Father, I thank thee that thou hast heard me. (42) And I knew that thou hearest me always: but because of the people which stand by I said it, that they may believe that thou hast sent me. (43) And when he thus had spoken, he cried with a loud voice, Lazarus, come forth. (44) And he that was dead came forth, bound hand and foot with graveclothes: and his face was bound about with a napkin. Jesus saith unto them, Loose him, and let him go. (45) Then many of the Jews which came to Mary, and had seen the things which Jesus did, believed on him. (46) But some of them went their ways to the Pharisees, and told them what things Jesus had done. (47) Then gathered the chief priests and the Pharisees a council, and said, What do we? for this man doeth many miracles. (48) If we let him thus alone, all men will believe on him: and the Romans shall come and take away both our place and nation. (49) And one of them, named Caiaphas, being the high priest that same year, said unto them, Ye know nothing at all, (50) Nor consider that it is expedient for us, that one man should die for the people, and that the whole nation perish not. (51) And this spake he not of himself: but being high priest that year, he prophesied that Jesus should die for that nation; (52) And not for that nation only, but that also he should gather together in one the children of God that were scattered abroad. (53) Then from that day forth they took counsel together for to put him to death. (54) Jesus therefore walked no more openly among the Jews; but went thence unto a country near to the wilderness, into a city called Ephraim, and there continued with his disciples. (55) And the Jews' passover was nigh at hand: and many went out of the country up to Jerusalem before the passover, to purify themselves. (56) Then sought they for Jesus, and spake among themselves, as they stood in the temple, What think ye, that he will not come to the feast? (57) Now both the chief priests and the Pharisees had given a commandment, that, if any man knew where he were, he should shew it, that they might take him. (John 11)*

3.3.1 The Preparation for His Raising Lazarus, 11:1-16

D. L. Moody said, "Jesus broke up every funeral He attended."[17] He raised many from the dead, but only three of the stories are detailed for us (Luke 7:11-17; Luke 8:49-56; John 11). This is the last of the seven miracles or signs in John (2:1-11; 4:46-54; 5:9; 6:1-13; 6:16-21; 9; 11). This sign and the first in John (2:1-11) concerned intimate family life, manifested divine glory, and strengthened the faith of the disciples.

A Case of Need, 11:1-3

Bethany is on the southeastern slope of the Mount of Olives, nearly two miles from Jerusalem. "Two good women can give a character to a community so that the Savior loves to come to it" (Speer 1915; see Luke 10:38-42). John 11:2 refers to John 12:3. Sickness is real, and

---

17. Editor's Note: It is unknown where this quote was sourced. It can be found in the *Encyclopedia of 15,000 Quotations.*

Christians may be sick. Here is an example of true prayer. They simply told the need without suggesting what for Him to do. They trusted that He would do what was best. They would not suggest His coming to Judea because they knew the Jewish hatred. In trouble, the best friend is Jesus; the first thing to do is to send a message to Him by prayer. Nothing else is needed but to tell a father that his child is in the fire or in a ditch. So did they feel toward Jesus, that He would act.

Jesus' Wise Delay, 11:4-6

He knows best *when* to do. That is why patience becomes us. He awaited the prompting of His Father. Note Christ's love for Christians; He loved all three in this home. It took most of one day for the messengers to get to Jesus; Lazarus died that day. Two days Jesus tarried, then returned on the fourth day. The purpose in this sickness was the glory of God (11:4). "A great sorrow was to Jesus a great opportunity" (Speer 1915). Death was not to be the final issue of this sickness. Both the messengers and the disciples heard this statement. The raising of Lazarus glorified Jesus in that some believed, and it led to His death.

A Talk with His Disciples, 11:7-16

Jesus' talk with His disciples falls into three dialogues:
1. The first dialogue (11:7-10):
   a. His statement (11:7): He mentioned Judea, not Bethany, and the word *again* so as to bring out their fears of persecution that He might overcome them. He knew how they would take His statement.
   b. Their objection (11:8): They are thinking only of the danger.
   c. His answer (11:9-10) The illustration—It is morning; a good day's journey is ahead of them and twelve hours of daylight. During this they can go without danger and reach Bethany before the dangers of night. The lesson—If Jesus cowardly stayed away from Judea to add another hour to His life, He would have stumbled (sinned) and lost the Father's care.
2. The second dialogue (11:11-13): Jesus pictures the death of a saint as *sleep*; the Bible never describes the death of a sinner as *sleep*. The disciples sought a pretext against going to Judea. They argued that the sleep would heal Lazarus without any special help from Jesus.

3. The third dialogue (11:14-16): Seeing that they did not yet grasp His meaning, Jesus explained that He referred to death as sleep and gave the order to depart. When He spoke without any figure, they understood (11:14). Their faith needed to grow. Jesus knew supernaturally that Lazarus was dead. This increase or training in faith in Jesus should have prepared them to have stood at the tomb of Jesus with joy and faith.

The brave words of Thomas (11:16): We see a side of Thomas here that is not mentioned again. His words indicate bravery, attachment to Jesus, and determination. He was afraid of the outcome but would share the worst with Jesus. Yet I can see in this no morbid pessimism. His fears were justified, for this return to Judea occasioned the death of Jesus.

3.3.2 His Talk with Martha and Mary, 11:17-32

The Conditions when Jesus Arrived, 11:17-19

The nearness of Bethany to Jerusalem explains the presence of so many Jews (11:19). The distance of fifteen furlongs would be about two miles or about a forty-minutes' journey. A furlong was one-eighth of a mile or 600 feet.

His Conversation with Martha, 11:20-27

The temperament of the two sisters (11:20): Martha—active, stirring, busy, demonstrative. Mary—quiet, gentle, retiring, contemplative. (See Luke 10:38-42.) You can be too crushed by affliction for your own good and the good of your friends.

Her words indicated mingled faith and sorrow (11:21-22). She hardly meant to reproach Him but rather to express a regret, love, and devotion to Him, faith that He might have helped if He had been there, but unbelief that He could do anything while absent. Yet she had confidence in His prayers and hoped that He would yet do something. Still it seems that she regarded Jesus as no more than a prophet; she did not grasp the truth that Jesus held in Himself the key to the situation.

Jesus makes His promise general to develop her faith (11:23), "Thy brother shall rise again" (Daniel 12:2).

She derives no present comfort from His promise (11:24); whatever of hope she seems to show in 11:22 is gone now. She thinks of the event of the resurrection and not of Jesus as the agent of resurrection.

She fails to take in that all resurrection power is lodged in Jesus alone (John 5:25-29).

He declares that He is not merely a teacher of resurrection, but the very Author of resurrection (11 25-26). He carried within Himself the power to raise dead men. This bold utterance comes from a sense of His deity. "The resurrection" refers to the outward fact, the result; "the life" tells of the inward source, the cause. Jesus is both the resurrection and the life. Notice the importance of faith in these two verses. "Though he were dead" as Lazarus and other departed saints. Death claims them physically, but they shall live in resurrection. "Whosoever liveth and believeth" refers to Martha and other believers, alive physically. They never die the eternal death, the sting of death is removed, and resurrection is ahead for them. (See John 6:50 and 8:51.) Let Jesus' question of application, "Believest thou this?" sink down into your heart.

John 11:27 gives her confession. She claimed that He was all to her and that she was ready to believe all He might say. Her understanding may have been vague, but she evidently meant to be trustful. Note the three titles she gives Jesus: Christ, Son of God, Coming One.

His Conversation with Mary, 11:28-32

The call (11:28): Jesus called her to prepare her for the experience ahead. Martha called Mary secretly so that Mary might have an unhindered interview with Jesus. Note two things: the presence of Jesus and His call. He is calling for you; why not listen? He calls in and through sorrow. His call was no less His because He sent it through Martha. The voice of the preacher or another that calls you to Jesus is His call.

Her response (11:29-32): Grief did not so blind and deafen her that she could not hear His call. Have a listening ear in sorrow. Note "as soon as" and "quickly." This is the kind of response Jesus deserves from our hearts. Her weeping comforters misinterpreted her actions; she was not going to the grave, but to Jesus. Where you go in sorrow is the thing that counts. Go to Jesus.

Mary uttered exactly the same words to Jesus as Martha did (11:21, 32). Note this difference: Mary fell at His feet. Was this an act of worship or was it a breakdown under grief and emotion? Most probably worship (Luke 10:39; John 12:3). If Mary wished to say more, comers disturbed her. Jesus dealt with the two differently: He taught Martha; He expressed full sympathy with Mary. He wept with Mary. Such sympathy and tenderness (Hebrews 2:18; 4:15)! It is not sinful to

150

sorrow, but it is sinful to question God's goodness and wisdom because of sorrow.

The word for "weep" in 11:31 and 11:33 means loud sighs, wailing; but the one in 11:35 speaks of a calm and gentle grief expressed in many tears. "He shed tears" well translates the idea.

A. T. Robertson suggested that "burst into tears" fits the aorist tense.[18] The weeping of Jesus proves His humanity. He "teaches us by His own example the due measure of joy and grief. The absence altogether of sympathy and sorrow is brutal; the excess of them is womanly (Theophylact)."[19]

Emphasize that Jesus is the resurrection and the life. Jesus is just as able to save, though not bodily present, as if He were present in body. Believe on Him now and live forever!

3.3.3 His Raising of Lazarus, 11:33-44

Jesus Wept with Those He Loved, 11:33-38

"Therefore" in 11:33 shows that their weeping led to His weeping. Note three expressions of Jesus' feeling and attitude:

1. "He groaned in the spirit" (11:33): The word signifies a shudder of indignation. Pain and anger are mingled. Anger with Jesus could never be other than righteous indignation. Some think that He was indignant towards death that brought this sorrow. Others think that He was seized by horror as He foresaw how His enemies would use this act of sympathy to crucify Him. Probably both are true.

2. "He was troubled" (11:33): There was a visible shudder. But He threw off these agitations of His spirit and asked resolutely, "Where have ye laid him?"

3. "Jesus wept" (11:35): See comments above. This is a sign of His full humanity. He wept because of pure love and sympathy. The ravages of sin and death and the unbelief of those around Him may be remote causes. The onlookers took it as the weeping of love (11:36). Was their question about Jesus' power to miracle (11:37) asked sincerely or in unbelief? The word *therefore* in

---

18. Editor's Note: There are two sources for Robertson used in this commentary, and Beaman did not provide which source was used for each Robertson reference.

19. Editor's Note: Probably Theophylact of Ohrid who lived about 1100 AD and wrote several commentaries on books of the Bible.

11:38 shows that this suspicious question again disturbed the spirit of Jesus. But the command to take away the stone shows that He soon threw off this new soul disturbance (11:39).

The Removal of the Stone, 11:39-41a

Jesus miracled only when it was necessary. He gave man something to do—not the man to be raised but others. They were thus made strong witnesses to the miracle and could say, "I know Jesus raised Lazarus, for I helped roll away the stone and smelled the fumes of decay." "Christ approached the sepulcher as a champion preparing for a contest" (John Calvin).[20]

Martha objects to rolling away the stone (11:39). Did her statement indicate unbelief or a sense of embarrassment and confusion at seeing her brother in such a condition of decay? Both, but chiefly a breakdown in faith as the answer of Jesus shows (11:40). Jesus exhorts her to raise her faith to take hold of His promise. Compare 11:4 and 11:25. The world says, "Seeing is believing." Jesus and faith say, "Believing is seeing." (See Psalm 27:13.) Which do we follow? The world's attitude is to look to the material first. Faith, however, takes the Word of God for it and goes ahead even when the eye cannot see and when the mind cannot understand. Faith is not presumption because it is based on the promise of God.

The Prayer of Jesus, 11:41b-42

Jesus' prayer proves His humanity and shows His assurance in prayer. His communion with the Father was constant. He did it for their good; He thought of the bystander who needed to be brought to faith. It was a challenge to His enemies: "If God does not respond, it will prove Me an impostor; but if God grants the miracle, it proves He sent Me and that I am the Messiah."

His Calling Lazarus from the Tomb, 11:43

This came only after He prepared His disciples, the sisters, and the crowd to behold God's glory. This was a moment of thrilling and breathless interest. What wonder filled the heart of the whole company! What astonishment for them! "A living man in costume of the dead."[21] What perfect composure on the part of Jesus! The loud voice was a tone of victory; it was not the mutterings of a sorcerer. It illustrates John 5:25-29.

---

20. Editor's Note: This John Calvin quote probably comes from J. C. Ryle's (1860) work on John. See the Selected Bibliography for more details.

21. Editor's Note: No citation is given for this quote.

Here was public proof that Jesus had absolute power over the material world and the world of spirits.

Colonel Robert G. Ingersoll (1833-1899), a well-known skeptic, used to tell this story: "I was nonplussed but once. I was lecturing one night and took occasion to show that the resurrection of Lazarus was probably a planned affair to bolster the waning fortunes of Jesus. . . . Lazarus was to feign death 'til Jesus should come and say, 'Lazarus, come forth.' I said, 'Can anyone here tell me why Jesus said, "Lazarus, come forth"?' A man said, 'If my Lord had not said, "Lazarus, come forth," the whole graveyard would have come forth.'"[22]

His Final Command, 11:44

Godet (1886) paraphrased Jesus' command, "Each to his office; I have raised to life; it is for you to loose him." No doubt the modest Lazarus desired to go away form the curiosity of the crowd.

Jesus uttered three definite commands at the tomb of Lazarus, which have a striking message for us: (1) "Take ye away the stone" (11:39). The Lord calls His people into fellowship with Him and His work (Mark 16:20; 2 Corinthians 6:1); (2) "Lazarus, come forth" (11:43); (3) "Loose him and let him go" (11:44). Christians, encourage young converts!

The skeptic Spinoza declared that he would accept Christianity if he could be convinced of this miracle. I quote this to show the importance of our believing this story. Impress on your pupils the power of Jesus, for this miracle displays Jesus as the God-Man; God in power, man in sympathy and prayer.[23]

3.3.4 The Results of His Raising Lazarus, 11:45-57

The Immediate Effect, 11:45-46

A division—some believed; some reported to the Pharisees (11:45-46). Observe two contrasts: many believed versus some opposed. "Believed" versus "went away." What is your attitude toward Jesus and His power?

The More Remote Effect, 11:47-53

The Sadducees and the Pharisees join against Jesus (11:47-53). Jesus' raising Lazarus occasioned their decree of condemnation.

---

22. Editor's Note: No citation is given for this quote, but it can be located in *Australasian Record and Advent World Survey*, vol. 65:45, (Warburton: Victoria, 1961). 15.

23. Editor's Note: No citation is given for this quote, but it can be located in Charles Pettit M'Ilvaine's *The Evidences of Christianity: In Their External, or Historical, Division, Exhibited in a Course of Lectures* (Philadelphia: Smith & English, 1852).

The Council Meets, 11:47-48

Jesus said that they would not believe if one rose from the dead (Luke 16:31). Their unbelief fulfilled His statement. The word *council* means that the Sanhedrin court of the Jews had a meeting. They admitted His miracles. Study the unwitting testimony of His enemies to what He truly was. Even the testimony of the bitterest enemies whom Jesus had favors His miracles. This admission only made their rejection of Him so much more wicked (11:47). They acknowledged His signs as facts but sought to erase Jesus. They did not want people to believe on Jesus. Because of what they did to Him, Rome did destroy them in 70 AD.

The Speech of Caiaphas and Its Meaning, 11:49-52

We need to study it from two angles:

1. As Caiaphas meant it: It was a contemptuous remark of a Sadducee against the wild policy of the Pharisees. Note, "Ye know nothing at all" (11:49). He wanted to preserve the nation and argued that the death of Jesus would be a public benefit. He was moved by personal and diabolical motives but, strangely enough, uttered divine truth. He would get rid of Jesus and obtain favor with Rome.

2. As John applies it: "This spoke He not of Himself . . . He prophesied" (11:51). Like Balaam, Caiaphas uttered divine truth unconsciously. Note "that same year" (11:49) and "that year" (11:51). John means that unique, memorable, decisive, and fateful year in which Jesus was put to death and Judaism died. Caiaphas spoke the truth of the substitutionary death of Jesus. He argued that it was best to kill one man for the good of the nation. How expedient or profitable the death of Jesus really is! On His death for our sins hangs our souls for time and eternity. There is nothing so profitable as that He did die that we might live.

"Not for that nation only" (11:52). John sees the worldwide scope of the death of Jesus. The word *also* breaks national bounds and reaches out to all classes. "The children of God" refer to the Gentiles or unsaved, elect children by the intent and purpose of God but as yet unconverted and many yet unborn (John 10:16).

Caiaphas wanted to preserve the nation as a unit, but Jesus would bring into one the children of God, making a truer solidarity than any nation. Instead of securing what the priest Caiaphas wanted, the death of Jesus brought to an end the priesthood of Caiaphas and all other priesthood, sounded the death of Judaism that would not accept the Messiah, and established Jesus as the Great High Priest on His throne. In seeking to maintain his office, Caiaphas abolished forever a merely human priesthood.

The Decree to Put Jesus to Death, 11:53

Note the emphatic statement, "From that day forth." This marked a turn in the events in opposition to Jesus. They formed a set and permanent plan to put Jesus to death. From then on, they merely watched for an opportune time and means to carry out their horrible deed. This meeting was very important, and indirectly so was the raising of Lazarus, in the events that led to His death.

The raising of Lazarus was Jesus' greatest miracle. Not that it was more difficult, for divine omnipotence knows no difficulty. Not that it was any more miraculous. But it had greater influence than any of His miracles. It crystallized Jewish hatred into the Sanhedrin decree to kill Jesus; all that follows, on their part, was merely the seeking of an opportunity to entrap Jesus. The course of Jesus was altered; He sought more privacy until the Father's time came for Him to face the greatest crisis—His death on the cross.

It is true that Jesus died as a martyr to the truth; but more is true—He died as the substitute for guilty and hopeless sinners.

Jesus Retires to Ephraim, 11:54-57

These were Jesus' last quiet days with His disciples. His unrecorded days were not filled with idleness (11:54). He confined Himself to training the twelve (11:56). Note the restless curiosity of the country people. "Commandment" in 11:57 refers to the decree in 11:53.[24]

------- ❧ ----- ❧ -------

---

24. Editor's Note: The final chapters of this commentary will reveal even more of Dr. Beaman's fascination with languages and how this study can enhance Bible knowledge. He planned an updated reference work on Greek based on A. T. Robertson's *Word Pictures*. He planned on calling his book *Word Windows in the Greek New Testament*. Alas, this book was never completed.

3.4 Questions on John 2–11

3.4.1 John 2

1. Explain what is meant by the double-miracle in the birth of Jesus.
2. What are the two lessons from Jesus' first sign?
3. What are the three great annual feasts of the Jews?
4. What sign did Jesus say was sufficient?
5. When did Jesus refuse to count the professions that were made?

3.4.2 John 3

1. Explain what is conveyed by the metaphor of a birth.
2. What are the other metaphors for the same experience?
3. What is meant by the kingdom of God?
4. List at least four proofs that "water" in John 3:5 does not refer to baptism.
5. What are the three parallels between the wind and the work of the Spirit?
6. To what Old Testament story does 3:14 refer?
7. What is the difference in "eternal" and "everlasting?"
8. Why prefer "for" instead of "because" in 3:18?
9. Explain "Jesus baptized."
10. Discuss "obeyeth not" as a substitute translation for "believeth not" in 3:36.
11. Define the "wrath of God."

3.4.3 John 4

1. From John 4, discuss Jesus' method of personal work.
2. Discuss how Jesus brought to the woman conviction of sin.
3. Discuss briefly the expression "God is spirit" and its implications for our worship of Him.

4. Why call this passage (4:31-34) a great missionary message?

5. What is significant about the title the Samaritans gave our Lord?

6. Discuss briefly the three phases of the courtier's faith.

7. Discuss the two crises indicated in these two miracles.

3.4.4 John 5

1. On what two points did the Jews object to Jesus?

2. Why does Jesus once call Himself "a son of man?"

3. Give the outline of John 5:24.

4. Distinguish three kinds of death.

5. What two resurrections does Jesus mention?

6. Discuss the words, "they that hear shall live."

7. What witnesses does Jesus call?

8. Discuss the evangelistic note in preaching.

9. Discuss the translation of 5:38.

10. What are the three essential traits of personality?

3.4.5 John 6

1. What is meant by the statement, "after these things"?

2. What two instances of shallow faith do we find in this chapter?

3. Discuss Jesus as a preacher, from this chapter.

4. Why will the Augustinian interpretation of "work of God" not hold here?

5. What parallels may be drawn between the manna and Jesus?

6. Explain "taught of God."

7. What is the difference between cometh and came?

8. Refute the Catholic error on eating Jesus' flesh and drinking His blood.

9. Discuss the crisis in 6:66-71.

3.4.6 JOHN 7

1. How much time transpired between John 6 and John 7?
2. Describe the Feast of Tabernacles.
3. Develop the thought of the winning of Jesus' brothers.
4. Indicate the practical use of 7:17.
5. What three dispensations may be justified?

3.4.7 JOHN 8–9

1. What two things obscure the meaning of John 8:1?
2. How did Jesus respond to coldness?
3. Explore the moral, political, ecclesiastical, and evangelistic possibilities of 8:3-11.
4. What is the connection between chapters 8 and 9?
5. What is the allusion in Jesus' metaphor, "the Light of the World"?
6. What is it to die in one's sins?
7. How did Jesus say one proves true freedom and spiritual sonship?
8. What would Jesus say of the popular phrase, "the universal fatherhood of God and the universal brotherhood of men"?
9. Summarize what Jesus taught about His sinlessness.
10. What are the doctrinal implications in His sinlessness?
11. Explain the words *never see death*.
12. How does Jesus teach His preexistence?
13. Discuss the various reasons for life's afflictions.
14. Why did Jesus use clay on the man's eyes?
15. What did Voltaire say about miracles?
16. How strong is the argument from experience?
17. Interpret 9:31.
18. Show some fallacies in the reasoning of Jesus' foes.

3.4.8 John 10

1. What is the connection between chapter 9 and chapter 10?

2. What two applications did Jesus make of both "door" and "fold"?

3. Why did He shift His emphasis or application?

4. Contrast the hired man and the genuine Shepherd.

5. What are the three blessings of 10:9?

6. By what three ways can life be increased?

7. What are the two traits of the "Good" Shepherd?

8. What three adjectives does the New Testament apply to Jesus as a shepherd?

9. Who are the "other" sheep?

10. What was the Feast of Dedication?

11. What two marks have Christ's sheep?

12. Explain the Double Divine Grip.

3.4.9 John 11

1. What are the three narrations of Jesus' raising the dead?

2. Why did Jesus tarry after He knew of Lazarus' death?

3. Contrast and compare Martha and Mary.

4. Explain the word *wept* and what it proves.

5. Discriminate the three commands of Jesus at Lazarus' tomb.

6. Explain "groaned in the spirit."

7. Wherein may Jesus' raising Lazarus be called "Jesus' greatest miracle?"

3.5 SERMON SUGGESTIONS

3.5.1 JOHN 2

Some choose to spiritualize the story. I prefer the explanation of 2:11. Use the divisions for expository sermons.

- "Mine Hour;" carry through to the end.
- Zeal for God's House
- Professions One Cannot Count
- The Master Psychologist

On special occasions, you may wish to discuss the social life of Jesus. See the section on the Wedding at Cana.

3.5.2 JOHN 3

- I took John 3 for a series on the New Birth—the need, the necessity, the nature, the fruit, the means and agent.
- The Birth from Above
- The Uplifted Serpent
- On 3:16, preach from various angles. The Pictures in John 3:16—a picture of God's heart, a picture of a lost world, a picture of the Cross, a picture of the individual heart, a picture of hell, a picture of heaven.
- Sermons on 3:18 and 36
- A sermon for preachers on 3:30
- 3:34, Jesus and the Holy Spirit

3.5.3 JOHN 4

- The Master Soul Winner (4:10): Make much of this idea in soul winning and in preaching.
- Spiritual Worship
- The Best Food

- The Call of White Fields
- Our Benefactors
- The Faith of the Samaritans
- The Faith of the Nobleman

3.5.4 John 5

- Would You Be Made Whole?
- The Deity of Jesus Christ (5:24)
- Two Kinds of Resurrection
- Purpose in Preaching (5:34)
- Christ and the Old Testament

3.5.5 John 6

- Jesus as Administrator
- Jesus, Master over Troubled Seas
- The Break of Life, or the Heavenly Manna
- Attachment to Christ (6:66ff)
- To Whom Shall We Go?

3.5.6 John 7

- The Closed Door (7:36)
- The Secret of Christian Living (7:37-39)
- How to Know (7:17)

3.5.7 John 8–9

- The Uninvited Savior
- The Light of the World
- The Unvarying Jesus
- The Sinlessness of Jesus (8:46)
- One Greater than Abraham

- One Greater than Death; Why the Godly Suffer
- Worshipping Jesus Christ
- True Freedom
- Power of Conscience
- The Witness Within
- Dying in Sin
- The Enlightenment of the Cross (8:28)
- Who Is Truly Free?

3.5.8 JOHN 10

- Only One Door
- The Good Shepherd
- The Double Divine Grip
- Marks of God's Sheep

3.5.9 JOHN 11

- A Full Biography of Thomas (11:16)
- Jesus as Resurrection and Life (11:25-26)
- The Call of Jesus (11:28)
- The Shortest Verse in the Bible (11:35)
- Two Shibboleths
- Three Commands of Jesus at Lazarus' Tomb
- Jesus and the Bystander (11:42)—Never forgotten by Jesus, often forgotten by us. How sobering is this fact! How much we may turn the bystander rightly or wrongly!)

4: The Results in both Faith and Unbelief: Conclusion, Chapter 12

(1) Then Jesus six days before the passover came to Bethany, where Lazarus was, which had been dead, whom he raised from the dead. (2) There they made him a supper; and Martha served: but Lazarus was one of them that sat at the table with him. (3) Then took Mary a pound of ointment of spikenard, very costly, and anointed the feet of Jesus, and wiped his feet with her hair: and the house was filled with the odour of the ointment. (4) Then saith one of his disciples, Judas Iscariot, Simon's son, which should betray him, (5) Why was not this ointment sold for three hundred pence, and given to the poor? (6) This he said, not that he cared for the poor; but because he was a thief, and had the bag, and bare what was put therein. (7) Then said Jesus, Let her alone: against the day of my burying hath she kept this. (8) For the poor always ye have with you; but me ye have not always. (9) Much people of the Jews therefore knew that he was there: and they came not for Jesus' sake only, but that they might see Lazarus also, whom he had raised from the dead. (10) But the chief priests consulted that they might put Lazarus also to death; (11) Because that by reason of him many of the Jews went away, and believed on Jesus. (12) On the next day much people that were come to the feast, when they heard that Jesus was coming to Jerusalem, (13) Took branches of palm trees, and went forth to meet him, and cried, Hosanna: Blessed is the King of Israel that cometh in the name of the Lord. (14) And Jesus, when he had found a young ass, sat thereon; as it is written, (15) Fear not, daughter of Sion: behold, thy King cometh, sitting on an ass's colt. (16) These things understood not his disciples at the first: but when Jesus was glorified, then remembered they that these things were written of him, and that they had done these things unto him. (17) The people therefore that was with him when he called Lazarus out of his grave, and raised him from the dead, bare record. (18) For this cause the people also met him, for that they heard that he had done this miracle. (19) The Pharisees therefore said among themselves, Perceive ye how ye prevail nothing? behold, the world is gone after him. (20) And there were certain Greeks among them that came up to worship at the feast: (21) The same came therefore to Philip, which was of Bethsaida of Galilee, and desired him, saying, Sir, we would see Jesus. (22)

Philip cometh and telleth Andrew: and again Andrew and Philip tell Jesus. *(23) And Jesus answered them, saying, The hour is come, that the Son of man should be glorified. (24) Verily, verily, I say unto you, Except a corn of wheat fall into the ground and die, it abideth alone: but if it die, it bringeth forth much fruit. (25) He that loveth his life shall lose it; and he that hateth his life in this world shall keep it unto life eternal. (26) If any man serve me, let him follow me; and where I am, there shall also my servant be: if any man serve me, him will my Father honour. (27) Now is my soul troubled; and what shall I say? Father, save me from this hour: but for this cause came I unto this hour. (28) Father, glorify thy name. Then came there a voice from heaven, saying, I have both glorified it, and will glorify it again. (29) The people therefore, that stood by, and heard it, said that it thundered: others said, An angel spake to him. (30) Jesus answered and said, This voice came not because of me, but for your sakes. (31) Now is the judgment of this world: now shall the prince of this world be cast out. (32) And I, if I be lifted up from the earth, will draw all men unto me. (33) This he said, signifying what death he should die. (34) The people answered him, We have heard out of the law that Christ abideth for ever: and how sayest thou, The Son of man must be lifted up? who is this Son of man? (35) Then Jesus said unto them, Yet a little while is the light with you. Walk while ye have the light, lest darkness come upon you: for he that walketh in darkness knoweth not whither he goeth. (36) While ye have light, believe in the light, that ye may be the children of light. These things spake Jesus, and departed, and did hide himself from them. (37) But though he had done so many miracles before them, yet they believed not on him: (38) That the saying of Esaias the prophet might be fulfilled, which he spake, Lord, who hath believed our report? and to whom hath the arm of the Lord been revealed? (39) Therefore they could not believe, because that Esaias said again, (40) He hath blinded their eyes, and hardened their heart; that they should not see with their eyes, nor understand with their heart, and be converted, and I should heal them. (41) These things said Esaias, when he saw his glory, and spake of him. (42) Nevertheless among the chief rulers also many believed on him; but because of the Pharisees they did not confess him, lest they should be put out of the synagogue: (43) For they loved the praise of men more than the praise of God. (44) Jesus cried and said, He that believeth on me, believeth not on me, but on him that sent me. (45) And he that seeth me seeth him that sent me. (46) I am come a light into the world, that whosoever believeth on me should not abide in darkness. (47) And if any man hear my words, and believe not, I judge him not: for I came not to judge the world, but to save the world. (48) He that rejecteth me, and receiveth not my words, hath one that judgeth him: the word that I have spoken, the same shall judge him in the last day. (49) For I have not spoken of myself; but the Father which sent me, he gave me a commandment, what I should say, and what I should speak. (50) And I know that his commandment is life everlasting: whatsoever I speak therefore, even as the Father said unto me, so I speak. (John 12)*

4.1 Mary's Anointing of Jesus at the Supper in Bethany, 12:1-11

(See also Matthew 26:6-13; Mark 14:3-9.)

4.1.1 The Setting, 12:1-2

Now, Bethany is known by what Jesus did there in raising Lazarus. What a fine reputation for the town! The fact that it was the town of Mary and Martha (John 11:1) gives way to a more glorious reason. Note that emphasis is placed on the miracle of raising Lazarus.

John 12:2 shows Jesus' social life—the difference between clean and unclean in social relations. Jesus and Lazarus were the prominent ones at the table.

4.1.2 Mary's Sacrifice of Love, 12:3, 5

Martha served; Mary anointed. Each one honored Jesus in her characteristic way. (See also Luke 10:38-42.)

In 12:5, three hundred pence amounts to "a year's wage for a working man" (Matthew 20). "Alabaster box" (Matthew 26:7) means a vase, white and semi-transparent, used for perfumes—very costly. A pound of perfume is no small amount. Spikenard means pure nard; that is, it was unmixed or unadulterated. Nard is a juice of delicious odor that the ancients extracted from the head or spike of a fragrant East Indian plant belonging to the genus Valeriana (see Buckland).[25] There was more honor given when used on head than on the feet. Mary anointed both (12:3 and Matthew 26:7). "House filled"—this shows abundance.

4.1.3 The Objection of Judas, 12:4-5

Judas made the suggestion; others caught it up and repeated it thoughtlessly. (See also Clark and Pendleton 1884 on Matthew 26:8.) Judas had no sense of the dignity of the Person of Christ and of the sacredness of obligation and love to Him. He is a lasting proof of human corruption. "Privileges alone convert nobody" (Ryle 1860). This gives the true character of Judas as always dishonest. He was too deceptive to say that this ought not to have been done but suggests what he felt was something better. He made

---

25. Editor's Note: This reference may refer to Francis Buckland, 1826-1880, an English natural historian.

much ado about this when he was on the verge of selling Jesus for about one-third this amount. We can never give too much to Christ.

4.1.4 THE COMMENT OF JOHN, 12:5-6

The heart of a man who says such is bad, says John. Judas's interest in the poor was merely professed. "He wanted Mary's love expressed in cash which he could steal" (Speer 1915). Many today excuse themselves from giving to Christ and missions on the ground of giving to the poor. It is the successors of Mary, instead of the successors of Judas who thus "care for the poor." In John 12:6, the ASV translation is better than the KJV translation in rendering "took away" instead of "bare"; that is, Judas actually "stole" out of the funds he oversaw. Judas's character as a thief was coming out.

4.1.5 JESUS' PRAISE OF MARY 12:7-8

Jesus warmly approved of Mary's gift of love. Though He went away in physical presence, we have His spiritual presence (Matthew 28:20; John 12:8 with Matthew 26:10). Giving is a work, a good work, one of moral beauty and fitness. It was the memorial of Mary (Matthew 26:13). Note "on Me." Jesus was the object of the gift. Mark 14:6-8: She did what she could, "now let her alone." Jesus comes to the aid of those who are criticized for doing things for Him. Poverty will always exist. Helping the poor is an everlasting opportunity.

4.1.6 INTEREST CENTERING AROUND LAZARUS, 12:9-11

Another division. How strong their curiosity! Lazarus drew people to Jesus by what Jesus did for him. He also received (shared in) the bitterness directed at Jesus. "Haters of the truth hate even those who are benefited by the truth" (Clark and Pendleton 1884). Lazarus was inconvenient standing evidence; remove him, they argued. They would close his mouth and remove him as a witness by killing him.

4.2 Christ's Triumphal Entrance Into Jerusalem, 12:12-19

4.2.1 Making Jesus King, 12:12-13

This "great multitude" (ASV) was composed largely of Passover visitors from various parts of the land. The highest point of prejudice against Jesus was in the "holy" city. The branches were probably from the date palm, which abounded on the sides of the Mount of Olives. These palm branches "were symbols of victory and peace" (Hovey 1885). The people of the day understood the significance of the palm branches. "Hosanna" is a particle of entreaty and means "Save, I entreat." Psalm 118:25-26, which they had in mind, "Save, I pray." Thayer (1977) renders it, "Save, I pray. . . . Be propitious." (Compare Matthew 21:4-9; Mark 11:7-10; Luke 19:35-38 for details not in John.)

4.2.2 His Triumphal Ride, 12:14-15

The details of procuring the colt are not given by John. Almost every act of Jesus confirmed an Old Testament Scripture. John 12:15 is a "free quotation of Zechariah 9:9" (Hovey 1885).

4.2.3 A Twofold Testimony, 12:16-18

His Disciples, 12:16

The resurrection threw new light on pre-Calvary events. Their memories and spiritual perception were enlivened. They regarded His death and resurrection as His glorification not as His defeat.

Those Who Saw Him Raise Lazarus, 12:17-18

So vividly and unforgettably did that majestic act impress some who saw it that they repeatedly witnessed (the Greek has the imperfect) and could not be silenced by priestly threats. In 12:18, their fervid testimony inclined many who were lingering in Jerusalem for the time of the Passover to go toward Bethany to meet Jesus.

4.2.4 The Despair of the Pharisees, 12:19

The testimony of Jesus' friends and His success irritated these prejudiced Pharisees. Their tone was bitter; their wicked cause was shattering; and they feverishly exaggerated Jesus' popularity. Did any of these people join in the cry, "Crucify Him"? The demonstration terrified His enemies.

Certain ones of the multitudes were not participating in either the praise or the throwing down of the branches for Him to ride on, and these said, "Master, rebuke thy disciples. They are applying to you the words that belong to the Messiah. Rebuke them." He replied, "If these shall hold their peace, the stones shall cry out." Why? Because this is the day that marks the winding up of the probation of the Jewish people, and if nobody should cry out, "Hosanna to the Son of David," then the rocks their lasting silence should break and cry out, "Hosanna to the Son of David" (Carroll 1948, *The Four Gospels*, II, 241ff).

Lessons to emphasize:

- Are we making Jesus King? Imitate these people. He longs to be King of our hearts and lives. Let Him in, and He will push all else out. Jesus and self cannot both be your king at the same time. They made Him Lord outwardly; let us make Him Lord inwardly. "Bow the knee" to Jesus now.

- Wicked plotters do not like to see Christ and Christians prosper (12:19). It will be one sad disappointment to them when He, Whose right it is, comes back to reign and to put down all rebellion.

- Gratitude bears witness. Those who appreciated Jesus' raising Lazarus "bare record" or witnessed (12:17). Hearts that love Jesus will not keep quiet about Him.

4.3 "We Would See Jesus," 12:20-36

4.3.1 The Request of the Greeks, 12:20-22

In John 12:20 we see that these Greeks were Gentiles, "earnest heathen who, disowning their outworn idolatries, had turned to the Jewish faith in one living and true God" (Smith 1928). When men are losing faith in their native religions, it is an exceptionally good time to give them the blessed gospel.

John 12:21: His teaching in the temple that His house should be called for all nations the house of prayer may have emboldened them to come (Mark 11:17). His teaching and miracling fame had gone abroad and created in their minds the conviction that He had the satisfaction they were craving in their deepest souls.

Every time Andrew is mentioned in John, he is introducing someone to Jesus (12:22). What a fine trait for our earnest emulation! Philip probably felt the need of Andrew because of the seeming unwillingness of Jesus to hear the Syrophoenician woman (Matthew 15:24). They seemed not to see that He was glad to welcome her when she came aright and that His mission was all-inclusive and world-encircling.

4.3.2 The Message of Jesus & the Significance of this Hour, 12:23-36

His Declaration, 12:23

He gave these Gentiles a glad welcome. They were a symbol of the larger work that would follow the Cross. The horizon of His work was broadening. The time for the triumph over Jewish prejudice was at hand. This was just the hour for which He had waited. He was glad to look beyond the Cross to the gathering of the Gentiles. These were "forerunners as they were of the myriads of heathendom whom He would yet win, the other sheep whom he must bring (see also 10:16), the scattered children of God whom by His sacrificial death He would gather home (see also 11:52)" (Smith 1928).

His Illustration, 12:24-26

Here is the law of harvest. This is accurate science. It declares the necessity and the glorious results of the Cross. He saw seeming failure fruiting in victory and fruitfulness. So it is with our lives.

The Darkness of this Hour, 12:27-30

He faces it determinedly: God honored Him. If ever it was appropriate for the Voice divine to come from the Most Excellent Glory and pierce the veil sense, it was now when His Son was laying down Himself on the altar as a willing sacrifice for the sin of the world. They misunderstood the voice. Godet (1886) compares this to the effect of a human voice on a man, a trained animal, and a wild animal. Jesus hastens to explain; He does not wish them to miss the deep meaning and encouragement of this voice.

The Crisis of the Cross, 12:31-34

The cross would be a throne of judgement for the eviction or casting out of Satan. The cross would be a divine magnet for the drawing of the multitudes. The cross was to be the lifting up of Jesus, as in the case of the Brazen Serpent. How little they understood (12:34)! Jesus' repeated "now" indicates the importance of the event. The drawing is explained by 12:33. Its primary reference was to His death. The word for "draw" does not speak of mechanical or arbitrary drawing. It is that sweet and mighty compelling love that melts the heart into wanting to be drawn.

A Final Warning Word, 12:35-36

Such pathos Jesus put into His words. He knew that He was preaching His last to them. David Smith (1923) calls these verses (12:20-50) His "last scene of His public ministry."

Do you have the desire of these Greeks, namely to see Jesus? Do not be one who closes his eyes against seeing the true gospel. Jesus said that He would draw men to Himself. Are you fighting against His drawing? If you feel His wooing in your heart, follow it and do not fight it. Out of Jesus' death comes our life. This is the heart of the gospel.

4.4 THE UNBELIEF OF THE JEWS, 12:37-50

The theme of John's Gospel is Jesus' self-revelation of manifestation of the Father. John 5–12 gives us the public manifestation of Jesus to the world. John 13–17 give us His private manifestation to His disciples. John 12:37-50 comes between as an explanation of the mystery of the unbelief of the Jews. Compare with Romans 9–11, which develops this theme. Be sure you are not an unbeliever.

4.4.1 John's Meditation on the Causes of Unbelief, 12:37-43

Two causes of unbelief are mentioned here: the blindness of the human heart and man's fear of criticism or opposition.

Blind Unbelief, 12:37-41

Unbelief in the Face of Many Signs, 12:37

Seeing wonderful sights does not convert anyone. Jesus said that a resurrection from the dead would not convince critical Pharisees (Luke 16:30-31). (On "many," see John 20:30.) How sad that they were so near and yet so far away! Jesus' signs were convincing except for their unbelieving hearts.

God's Word Explaining the Mystery, 12:38-41

There are two quotations: Isaiah 53:1 and Isaiah 6:9-10. The fact of the Jews' unbelief in Jesus was foretold by God but not desired by Him. He predicted it but did not cause it (Augustine).[26] Probably "that" has the force of "so that." Anyway, whether we understand it or not, we know that it does not destroy human responsibility or make God the author of their sin.

John 12:40 teaches by contrast that salvation is an experience of the heart. John 12:38 applies Isaiah 53 to Jesus. Unbelief in the blessed Savior is always an alarming and terrible thing. You cannot be guilty of a greater sin than unbelief.

Isaiah saw the glory of Christ in the vision in Isaiah 6:1-8 (John 12:41). Glory, not shame only, shines from the Cross of Jesus.

Fearful Unbelief, 12:42-43

Belief was the exception, and they who believed were ashamed of Him. How we fear the world and love its applause! Does your faith fruit in confessing Christ even when it costs?

4.4.2 Jesus' Comments on the Results of Unbelief, 12:44-50

They rejected God's testimony of Jesus in His miracles and Jesus' testimony of Himself in His message.

---

26. Editor's Note: No citation is given for Augustine.

The Privilege and Blessings of Faith, 12:44-46

One's attitude toward either the Father or the Son is one and the same (12:44-45). One cannot believe in the Father truly without believing in the Son. Christ removes the darkness of sin (12:46). Seeing and believing Christ are the same spiritual act of the soul.

The Condemnation Which Falls on Unbelief, 12:47-48

Jesus came on a mission of salvation (12:47). It is a fearful thing to reject the Word of God about Jesus.

The Reason for such Blessing on Faith and such Curse on Unbelief, 12:49-50

Note Godet (1886) on 12:49: "What I should say and how I should say it." God gave Jesus both the matter and method, both the what and the how of His message. Jesus did not speak of His own authority; He was commissioned by the Father. The statement, "His commandment is life everlasting," means that the intent of what God says is that men may have eternal life. "Life everlasting," not life that lasts for a short time but that has no end. It is hard for men to believe that Christ gives eternal life, but this is the only kind of life that He does give. You cannot be saved one day and lost the next. The life that one gets when he is saved can no more end than Christ can end.

4.5   QUESTIONS ON JOHN 12

1. Why may Mary's gift be truly termed a sacrifice?
2. Was Judas alone in his covetous suggestion?
3. How did Jesus apply "the law of harvest"?
4. How did Jesus explain unbelief?

4.6   Sermon Suggestions

- Giving to Jesus (12:8)
- Believing Because of Lazarus (12:10)
- What Jesus Did for Lazarus (chapter 11)
- What the Priest Consulted (12:10)
- Led to Believe (12:11)
- The Post-Resurrection Faith of the Disciples (12:16)
- Jesus as His Enemies Saw Him (12:19)
- "We Would See Jesus"
- Dying to Live
- Jesus and the Bystander (12:29-30)
- "Voices from the Excellent Glory" (12:28; see also the section on His baptism and transfiguration.)
- Jesus' Interpretation of His Death (12:24; 32:33)
- The Uplifted Christ (12:32; 34:36)
- Seeing Christ's Glory (12:41)
- Two Kinds of Love (12:43)
- The Mission of Jesus (12:47)
- Jesus Explains Faith (12:44-50)

PART III:

HIS SELF-REVELATION TO HIS DISCIPLES, CHAPTERS 13-17

5: Two Faith-Developing Acts, Chapter 13

One sees three singular movements in Jesus' revelation to His disciples. He developed faith in the hearts of His disciples by the two acts of chapter 13, by several discourses in 13:31–16:33, and by His prayer in chapter 17. Jesus replied to several questions in these hours—that of Peter (13:36–14:4); that of Thomas (14:5-7); that of Phillip (14:8-21); and that of Judas (14:22-24). Hence one sees the chapters in prospectus thus:

(1) Now before the feast of the passover, when Jesus knew that his hour was come that he should depart out of this world unto the Father, having loved his own which were in the world, he loved them unto the end. (2) And supper being ended, the devil having now put into the heart of Judas Iscariot, Simon's son, to betray him; (3) Jesus knowing that the Father had given all things into his hands, and that he was come from God, and went to God; (4) He riseth from supper, and laid aside his garments; and took a towel, and girded himself. (5) After that he poureth water into a bason, and began to wash the disciples' feet, and to wipe them with the towel wherewith he was girded. (6) Then cometh he to Simon Peter: and Peter saith unto him, Lord, dost thou wash my feet? (7) Jesus answered and said unto him, What I do thou knowest not now; but thou shalt know hereafter. (8) Peter saith unto him, Thou shalt never wash my feet. Jesus answered him, If I wash thee not, thou hast no part with me. (9) Simon Peter saith unto him, Lord, not my feet only, but also my hands and my head. (10) Jesus saith to him, He that is washed needeth not save to wash his feet, but is clean every whit: and ye are clean, but not all. (11) For he knew who should betray him; therefore said he, Ye are not all clean.

(12) So after he had washed their feet, and had taken his garments, and was set down again, he said unto them, Know ye what I have done to you? (13) Ye call me Master and Lord: and ye say well, for so I am. (14) If I then, your Lord and Master, have washed your feet; ye also ought to wash one another's feet. (15) For I have given you an example, that ye should do as I have done to you. (16) Verily, verily, I say unto you, The servant is not greater than his lord; neither he that is sent greater than he that sent him. (17) If ye know these things, happy are ye if ye do them. (18) I speak not of you all: I know whom I have chosen: but that the scripture may be

fulfilled, He that eateth bread with me hath lifted up his heel against me. (19) Now I tell you before it come, that, when it is come to pass, ye may believe that I am he. (20) Verily, verily, I say unto you, He that receiveth whomsoever I send receiveth me; and he that receiveth me receiveth him that sent me.

(21) When Jesus had thus said, he was troubled in spirit, and testified, and said, Verily, verily, I say unto you, that one of you shall betray me. (22) Then the disciples looked one on another, doubting of whom he spake. (23) Now there was leaning on Jesus' bosom one of his disciples, whom Jesus loved. (24) Simon Peter therefore beckoned to him, that he should ask who it should be of whom he spake. (25) He then lying on Jesus' breast saith unto him, Lord, who is it? (26) Jesus answered, He it is, to whom I shall give a sop, when I have dipped it. And when he had dipped the sop, he gave it to Judas Iscariot, the son of Simon. (27) And after the sop Satan entered into him. Then said Jesus unto him, That thou doest, do quickly. (28) Now no man at the table knew for what intent he spake this unto him. (29) For some of them thought, because Judas had the bag, that Jesus had said unto him, Buy those things that we have need of against the feast; or, that he should give something to the poor. (30) He then having received the sop went immediately out: and it was night.

(31) Therefore, when he was gone out, Jesus said, Now is the Son of man glorified, and God is glorified in him. (32) If God be glorified in him, God shall also glorify him in himself, and shall straightway glorify him. (33) Little children, yet a little while I am with you. Ye shall seek me: and as I said unto the Jews, Whither I go, ye cannot come; so now I say to you. (34) A new commandment I give unto you, That ye love one another; as I have loved you, that ye also love one another. (35) By this shall all men know that ye are my disciples, if ye have love one to another.

(36) Simon Peter said unto him, Lord, whither goest thou? Jesus answered him, Whither I go, thou canst not follow me now; but thou shalt follow me afterwards. (37) Peter said unto him, Lord, why cannot I follow thee now? I will lay down my life for thy sake. (38) Jesus answered him, Wilt thou lay down thy life for my sake? Verily, verily, I say unto thee, The cock shall not crow, till thou hast denied me thrice. (John 13:1-38)

5.1 ACT ONE: JESUS' WASHING THE DISCIPLES' FEET, 13:1-20

5.1.1 THE GRACIOUS INTRODUCTION, 13:1-3

John 13:1 introduces chapters 13-17. Note both "moreover" and the time note. Jesus ate the regular Passover. This is better than my former view that He ate the Passover in anticipation.

The Holy Spirit calls attention to Jesus and His place in the approaching days. "Since Jesus knew"—He alone was fully conscious of His hour of departure. The perfect tense really reflects a state of knowing. "He was not stumbling into the dark" (Robertson).

"To the Father"—He knew the outcome of His departure. His was no leap into the dark after death.

"Since He loved"—the causal participle gives the reason for a new proof of love, the abiding love of Jesus (see also Romans 8:31-39). He gives them a fresh expression of His love for them. Since He saw the hour of separation, He redoubled His tender love for them. "His Own"—how precious! That is, how precious are the ones gained by His love and the ones who are objects of His love.

John 13:2-3 refers definitely to the following narrative and stresses three things: first, the time. I prefer the ASV, "And during supper." That means the Passover supper. Second, the condition of Judas under the power of Satan. Hatred from Judas, love from Jesus—what a contrast! Third, Jesus' knowledge—His sovereign position, His divine origin, and His divine destiny. All these things are recorded to impress us with the greatness of the One Who would stoop to do such humble service. Grasp the full picture. Because of the momentous and crisis character of the coming events, John gave us a backward and forward glance.

5.1.2 The Solemn Example of Jesus, 13:4-11

The Occasion, 13:4-5

The occasion was a dispute (Luke 22:24-27). He puts on the garb of a slave (13:4). He does the service of a slave (13:5). Jesus wished to free their hearts of pride. Jesus taught them that the one who would outstrip the other in the divine art of humility and self-effacement would be greatest.

The Interruption, 13:6-11

In 13:6 Peter's seeming respect was actually lack of respect. (See also Matthew 16:22.) He was not seated at the head as the Pope. John 13:7 is Jesus' answer, and 13:8 is Peter's refusal. Peter first questioned; now he boldly refuses. His modesty became self-will and pride in refusing Jesus. Compare our pleas that we are not worthy. An overweening emphasis on our littleness can be a positive sin.

Jesus' answer (13:8): Peter's refusal would prove that he had no part with Jesus. Thank God for such a part as we have with Him. Jesus put the matter concretely to shock Peter to an awareness of his absurdity.

Impetuous Peter (13:9): How quickly he changed. But he went from one extreme to another. The danger of extremes is always, everywhere.

Jesus' answer (13:10). That would deny the work already done in Peter. See Trench (1854) on the two words for "wash." The morning bath pictures full cleansing in salvation; washing the sand from the feet at stopping illustrates the need of cleansing from daily defilement, which hinders communion but does not sever union with Christ.

Jesus rises from the material to the spiritual. Here is salvation and fellowship. Salvation is once for all; cleansing is occasional and constant. "Altogether clean" is full salvation. Judas was not clean; he was not saved (13:11). This was a last effort of Jesus to show Judas his need of salvation. Dwell on this.

5.1.3 THE EXPLANATION OF THE ACTS, 13:12-20

Jesus taught by act and word. He interpreted His act. Jesus feared nothing among the disciples as much as position seeking. The way to mount high is to descend from our position of pride. A check-up question, oft used by the wise teacher, is given in 13:12. He commended His blundering disciples whenever He could (13:13). Note the change of order (13:14). Lord of our lives, Master to teach us. Believing in Jesus can master two impulses in the heart of every person: rebellion and ignorance.

His example of humble service (13:15-17). Note "as," not "what," in 13:15. Jesus means for us to do likewise; there is no hint that foot-washing is a church ordinance.

John 13:17 expresses the Gestalt view of Christian living. One, the intellectual—"know." Two, the emotional—"happy." Three, the volitional or practical—"are doing." Our experience must touch each facet of our personalities. Another warning for Judas (13:18-20). How hard the heart that was never touched by the tender entreaties of Jesus! Jesus was explicit. "Not concerning all of you am I speaking," "I know the ones whom I picked out for Myself."

5.2 Act Two: Jesus' Comment on the Betrayal of Judas, 13:21-38

5.2.1 Detecting the Traitor, 13:21-30

A Betrayer Announced, 13:21

Betrayal troubled His spirit; it was the sin of ingratitude, and that of the deepest dye.

The Disciples Wondering, 13:22

Compare with Matthew 26:20-25. The disciples wondered or were puzzled. The tense is very vivid: "The disciples were looking toward one another."

Peter Suggesting to John a Sign, 13:23-24

John was closer to Him in physical fact (in His bosom) and in fellowship. Secrets belong to the inner circle. "Beckoneth" means "nods the head"—part of the sign language of communication.

Jesus Giving the Decisive Sign, 13:25-27

These are the last words that passed between Jesus and Judas. Behold the adamant hardness of the heart of false profession. Giving the sop or piece of bread in the Orient was a sign of honor. Judas made it a sign of guilt. "The act was another appeal to Judas's conscience and his sense of honor" (McClymont 1901). The meaning of the sign as explained by Jesus was known to John only. This was the last appeal of Jesus to Judas. Jesus appealed that Judas give up the idea of betrayal (13:21).

It was a decisive moment for Judas, and his soul was in the balance. He closed his soul to Jesus Christ and opened it wide for Satan. Satan had been in Judas's heart; Satan now possessed it fully. Until this point Judas had played with Satan; at this he dedicated his soul to serve Satan.

Note John 13:27: "And it was night." Compare with Luke 22:53. How true this was spiritually as well as physically. There is melancholy in this note. If Judas would not take the first lesson in humility, he must depart. It was night for Judas, for Jesus, and for the disciples. Following John in his spiritual emphasis is not the wrong kind of spiritualizing in interpretation. His metaphor draws a striking analogy between the physical darkness and its reminding one of spiritual darkness.

Jesus Dismissing Judas, 13:27b-30

"Then" in 13:27 is "therefore"; that is, because Judas had chosen Satan against Jesus, the betrayer must be removed so that Jesus could be alone to unbosom His heart to the eleven.

5.2.2 COMMENTING ON HIS GOING OUT, 13:31-38

Judas was present at the Passover supper (13:1-20) but went out before the institution of the Lord's Supper, a story which John did not tell. "As long as Judas was present, His heart was under restraint and could not give vent to all the feeling of which He was full" (Godet 1886). Now, He was alone with faithful eleven. How marvelously He taught them in the following chapters. The sweets were for His own.

God Was Glorified in the Betrayal by Judas and in Jesus' Atoning Death, 13:31-32

Jesus was glorified in the separation from a soul that was dedicated to Satan. The Cross had its shadow of darkness but its glorious victory also. Light came out of darkness.

The Supreme Proof in the Absence of Jesus, 13:33-35

This is the acid test of Christianity. Men may not understand our doctrine but always measure our lives. How neglected this profoundly simple test is. This commandment was new in that it had a new emphasis. The expression, "little children," reminds of the tenderness of a parent.

The universal proof (13:35): Sound doctrine is very important, but sound doctrine must fruit in practical living. Jesus puts major emphasis on loving one another. Instead, many professed Christians hate one another or hold grudges against one another. We do not become His by loving one another, but His is the way to make others know it. Does your life prove you are Christ's disciple?

Boastful Peter, 13:36-38

The delay in the going of Peter was only temporary; that of the unbelieving Jew was eternal (John 7:34; 8:21).

5.3 Questions on John 13

1. What three movements characterize John 13-17?

2. How broad is sentence one in John 13?

3. What is the central lesson in Jesus' washing the feet of His apostles?

4. What was Peter's blunder?

5. Discuss the breadth of John 13:17.

6. Why did Jesus give Judas "the sop"?

7. What is the threefold application of, "and it was night?"

5.4 Sermon Suggestions

*   Love to the End

*   "Altogether Clean"

*   Lord and Teacher (13:13-14)

*   Full Christian Living (13:17)

*   "And It Was Night": (1) For Judas; (2) For Jesus' Disciples—Their Blunderings and Short-Sightedness; (3) For Jesus—Luke 22:53

*   Seeking Sympathy in Gethsemane, But They Could Not Watch

*   The Agony of Calvary

*   Loneliness When Forsaken By the Father to Pay Our Sin Debt

6: THE UPPER ROOM DISCOURSES, CHAPTERS 14-16

6.1 DISCOURSE ONE: THE GOING AWAY OF JESUS, 14:1-15

(1) Let not your heart be troubled: ye believe in God, believe also in me. (2) In my Father's house are many mansions: if it were not so, I would have told you. I go to prepare a place for you. (3) And if I go and prepare a place for you, I will come again, and receive you unto myself; that where I am, there ye may be also. (4) And whither I go ye know, and the way ye know. (5) Thomas saith unto him, Lord, we know not whither thou goest; and how can we know the way? (6) Jesus saith unto him, I am the way, the truth, and the life: no man cometh unto the Father, but by me. (7) If ye had known me, ye should have known my Father also: and from henceforth ye know him, and have seen him. (8) Philip saith unto him, Lord, show us the Father, and it sufficeth us. (9) Jesus saith unto him, Have I been so long time with you, and yet hast thou not known me, Philip? he that hath seen me hath seen the Father; and how sayest thou then, Show us the Father? (10) Believest thou not that I am in the Father, and the Father in me? the words that I speak unto you I speak not of myself: but the Father that dwelleth in me, he doeth the works. (11) Believe me that I am in the Father, and the Father in me: or else believe me for the very works' sake. (12) Verily, verily, I say unto you, He that believeth on me, the works that I do shall he do also; and greater works than these shall he do; because I go unto my Father. (13) And whatsoever ye shall ask in my name, that will I do, that the Father may be glorified in the Son. (14) If ye shall ask any thing in my name, I will do it. (15) If ye love me, keep my commandments. (John 14:1-15)

6.1.1 COMFORT FROM HIS GOING, 14:1-3

His departure should have filled their hearts with the sweetest hope. He states the true purpose of His departure.

Faith Is the Cure for Trouble, 14:1

Trouble is an old heart disease; faith is the agelong cure. Jesus exhorts them to confident faith. Faith in God leads to faith in His Son (note, "in Me also").

A Picture of Heaven: The Father's House, 14:2

The Father's house is home. The chief idea is spaciousness; it is wide enough for all—"as many as there are believers." Illustration: Consider an oriental palace with rooms for the king, queen, the heir to the throne, and all the king's sons and daughters. Let's prefer "dwelling places" to "mansions." Jesus was not deceiving them; He would have told them if the separation was to be eternal.

Jesus' Preparation of the Place, 14:2b

Jesus as our forerunner went ahead to prepare for us (Hebrews 6:20). He went to heaven with the merit of His sin-atoning death and publicly demonstrated that merit. Whatever was necessary in preparation, He did it. We could not by our merit make the preparation. Heaven is truly a prepared place for a prepared people.

His Coming for His Own, 14:3

Heaven is a place and a state; both are blessed. It is not a question of either/or; it is both. "Again I am coming" may vividly translate the futuristic present, but it is truly a future tense put into the present for vividness. It is Jesus' way of stooping over His own and whispering assuringly that His coming for them is not at all doubtful.

He assures us of the place and of our reaching it. Jesus takes the believer into the Father's presence at the end of His earthly career, whether it be at the moment of death of the believer or at His Second Coming. "Unto Myself"—"He presses him to His heart, so to speak, while bearing Him away. There is an infinite tenderness in these last words. It is for Himself that He seems to rejoice in and look to His moment which will put an end to all separation' (Godet 1886). Jesus is the center of it all. "Where Jesus is will be heaven for me." "You also" is far better than "be also." The "also" links "I" and "you."

6.1.2 Knowing the Way, 14:4-7

Jesus says that His own know both the end and the way (14:4). Thomas raised a doubt. They knew Jesus, Who was the Way, but they did not know He was the Way. They were likely confused by looking for an earthly kingdom. "The Way" is the way that leads to the Father and His house, not so much the way to be saved. He is the only Way. He is the way to the Father in that He is both the Truth and the Life. A man may point out the way, but Jesus only is the Way. Men come to God only through Jesus, know God only through Jesus, and live only through Jesus.

The article *the* stands with each of the three metaphors. He is more than a way; He is the Way, the only way. This is not narrow in the wrong sense, but it is being as narrow as Jesus in affirmation of the truth. There is no going to the Father apart from Jesus, the Way; there is no knowing the Father aside from Jesus, the Truth; there is no living unto nor living with the Father without Jesus, the Life. These three descriptions of Jesus present His fullness for human need. These tremendous declarations on the lips of any other but Jesus would be the height of blasphemy. On His lips, such utterances are most appropriate; they are final and definitive and trustworthy affirmations.

My friend made 14:6 refer to the "cosmic Christ," by which he separated between the divine in Jesus and the historical Jesus. Such, as he stated to me, utterly disregards the context.

6.1.3 Seeing the Father, 14:8-11

Phillip gets his question from the last part of 14:7.

The Fact, 14:8-9

Knowing and seeing Jesus and the Father are one (see also Exodus 33:18). Jesus was God; no mere man can say, "He who has seen Me has seen the Father."

The Proof, 14:10-11

Note the union between the Father and the Son. There are two signs: His words and His works. "Of His Own wisdom, nothing! By the strength of God, everything!" (Godet 1886).

6.1.4 COMFORT FROM HIS WORKING THROUGH THEM FROM HEAVEN, 14:12-15

John 14:5-11 is a digression from the words of encouragement. "You will do greater works because I go to My Father" (14:12). "Greater" does not mean better or more stupendous works. But greater in number. Greater in quantity rather than greater in quality. His going included His death and ascension; from the throne above—and through us when we pray—He keeps on working.

Prayer is the secret of these greater works (14:13-14). "The believer asks, and the all-powerful Christ works from the midst of His glory" (Godet 1886).

The condition is obedience (14:15). This is a moral condition essential to answered prayer. Westcott and Hort (1881) put 14:15 with the following discourse. The connection is truly close.

6.2 DISCOURSE TWO: THE COMING OF THE HOLY SPIRIT, 14:16-31

(16) And I will pray the Father, and he shall give you another Comforter, that he may abide with you for ever; (17) Even the Spirit of truth; whom the world cannot receive, because it seeth him not, neither knoweth him: but ye know him; for he dwelleth with you, and shall be in you. (18) I will not leave you comfortless: I will come to you. (19) Yet a little while, and the world seeth me no more; but ye see me: because I live, ye shall live also. (20) At that day ye shall know that I am in my Father, and ye in me, and I in you. (21) He that hath my commandments, and keepeth them, he it is that loveth me: and he that loveth me shall be loved of my Father, and I will love him, and will manifest myself to him. (22) Judas saith unto him, not Iscariot, Lord, how is it that thou wilt manifest thyself unto us, and not unto the world? (23) Jesus answered and said unto him, If a man love me, he will keep my words: and my Father will love him, and we will come unto him, and make our abode with him. (24) He that loveth me not keepeth not my sayings: and the word which ye hear is not mine, but the Father's which sent me. (25)

These things have I spoken unto you, being yet present with you. (26) But the Comforter, which is the Holy Ghost, whom the Father will send in my name, he shall teach you all things, and bring all things to your remembrance, whatsoever I have said unto you. (27) Peace I leave with you, my peace I give unto you: not as the world giveth, give I unto you. Let not your heart be troubled, neither let it be afraid. (28) Ye have heard how I said unto you, I go away, and come again unto you. If ye loved me, ye would rejoice, because I said, I go unto the Father: for my Father is greater than I. (29) And now I have told you before it come to pass, that, when it is come to pass, ye might believe. (30) Hereafter I will not talk much with you: for the prince of this world cometh, and hath nothing in me. (31) But that the world may know that I love the Father; and as the Father gave me commandment, even so I do. Arise, let us go hence. (John 14:16-32)

This closeness must be particularized. We poorly perceive the coming of the Holy Spirit because we do not set it in the background of Jesus' official and public going away. We seek to interpret according to our own viewpoint the Spirit's coming.

6.2.1 The Actual Coming of the Holy Spirit, 14:16-17

He came in answer to the intercession of Christ (14:16; compare with 15:26). Jesus asked for Him on our part and sent Him on the Father's part. "Another" means another of the same kind, not another of a different kind. This asserts some common feature between Jesus Christ and the Holy Spirit. Both are comforters; the implication is that they are the same kind in nature.

He is the gift of the Father. Since the Father is the planner of redemption, the Holy Spirit is His gift.

He is the Spirit of Truth. That is, He explains and makes it real to us. He is not the truth but the Author and Teacher of truth. The Bible never confuses truth and the Spirit.

He is the disciple's comforter (14:17). He is the One Who is called in as the sustaining help or support, ever within their reach, ever ready to come to their aid at the first call in their conflict with the world. He is our support in moments of weakness, our counselor in the problems of life, and our consoler in suffering. The world cannot receive the Holy Spirit as comforter because it is not saved, but this does not deny the work of conviction (John 14:8).

He came at Pentecost to stay until Christ's Second Coming. This is the age of the Holy Spirit, the Old Testament was the age of the Father, and the ministry of Jesus was the age of the Son.

Christ came publicly and officially; in the same manner He went away. The coming of the Spirit was to be of the same quality, likewise official and public. He did not need to come really but only to take over the work of Christ. Here is the deepest interpretation of Pentecost.

"You know Him." The "You" is emphatic. "Know" speaks of experiential knowledge. "Because" gives the reasons for their knowing the Holy Spirit. Note each.

"With you He is abiding." "And in you is" or "shall be." The last must be discussed from two angles:

1. Its tense: The manuscripts are divided between the present and the future, perhaps more strongly for the present. In any case, however, the ambiguity disallows one's building a pervasive teaching on such a situation. Some have argued that the future means that Old Testament saints were not indwelt by the Holy Spirit. If other teaching made such clear, one might use this passage. If, however, other passages are almost conclusive that the Old Testament believer was indwelt by the Holy Spirit, it is precarious to set this passage against both clear teachings and clear implications.

2. Its meaning: Grant for a moment that the future is preferred; what is the meaning? It can mean that He will come to be in you but does not say so specifically. It may as truly mean that He will go on being in you.

If Jesus meant to say what some claim, why did He not use a specific verb? The Greek *to be* is far more general or non-specific than several other verbs available to Him.

6.2.2 CHRIST THROUGH THE HOLY SPIRIT GIVES HIS DISCIPLES A NEW AND DEEPER CONSCIOUSNESS OF HIM, 14:18-24

The Declaration of Jesus, 14:18-21

A new consciousness of Jesus in the Person of the Holy Spirit (14:18). "Comfortless" means "orphans." This is the comforting word of a departing Father. How happy is He that could amply provide!

A new union in the spiritual and inward coming of the Son and Father into the heart of the believer (14:19-20). They were losing His bodily presence, but He would make His real presence more abiding and real. The world sees only the bodily; the saint sees the more abiding and real, spiritually (2 Corinthians 3:18).

Translate, "Because I live, ye also shall live." This is the relation of cause and effect. It means eternal security because of Christ. Again, the "also" is often not given its proper position. It is not "live also" in addition to something else. It is rather "you also" in relation to Christ Jesus!

The condition (14:21): There are three stages in this mystical fellowship. All three are made effective by the Holy Spirit:

1. Loving obedience to Christ

2. Increasing sense of the Father's love

3. Growing knowledge of Christ as the revelation of God

The Interrogation of Judas, 14:22

This was Judas the brother of James (Luke 6:16; Acts 1:13); he was called also Thaddaeus or Lebbaeus (Matthew 10:3; Mark 3:18). He was expecting an outward manifestation to Israel. How profitable for us that He asked the question.

The Explanation of Jesus, 14:23-24

This is almost a repetition of 14:21. He was ready to reveal Himself to all, but they rejected Him. Martin Luther stated, "We will be daily His guests, yea house and table companions."[27] Note the Oneness of the Father and the Son. The condition of the Father and the Son in the conscious experience of the believer is love, and that love fruits in obedience.

6.2.3 THE WORK OF THE HOLY SPIRIT, 14:25-31

His work of teaching the disciples all the truth (14:25-26): Here is a promise of the inspiration of the New Testament Scriptures. Here is also a general illumination of their minds to know the truth—all the truth. One may debate as to which is primary in the context, but both inhere in principle in the very wording of Jesus' statement.

His bequest of peace amidst their trouble (14:27-29): What kind of peace? "My peace": the same untroubled and unfearful peace which He enjoyed in the midst of conflict because of communion with the Father.

Victory over the prince of this world, the devil (14:30-31; see also John 12:31; Ephesians 6:10-12): There was no weak point in the nature of Christ to which the tempter could fasten his temptation.

---

27. Editor's Note: No citation was given for this quote.

6.3   DISCOURSE THREE: FRUIT BEARING, 15:1-17

(1) I am the true vine, and my Father is the husbandman. (2) Every branch in me that beareth not fruit he taketh away: and every branch that beareth fruit, he purgeth it, that it may bring forth more fruit. (3) Now ye are clean through the word which I have spoken unto you. (4) Abide in me, and I in you. As the branch cannot bear fruit of itself, except it abide in the vine; no more can ye, except ye abide in me. (5) I am the vine, ye are the branches: He that abideth in me, and I in him, the same bringeth forth much fruit: for without me ye can do nothing. (6) If a man abide not in me, he is cast forth as a branch, and is withered; and men gather them, and cast them into the fire, and they are burned. (7) If ye abide in me, and my words abide in you, ye shall ask what ye will, and it shall be done unto you. (8) Herein is my Father glorified, that ye bear much fruit; so shall ye be my disciples. (9) As the Father hath loved me, so have I loved you: continue ye in my love. (10) If ye keep my commandments, ye shall abide in my love; even as I have kept my Father's commandments, and abide in his love. (11) These things have I spoken unto you, that my joy might remain in you, and that your joy might be full. (12) This is my commandment, That ye love one another, as I have loved you. (13) Greater love hath no man than this, that a man lay down his life for his friends. (14) Ye are my friends, if ye do whatsoever I command you. (15) Henceforth I call you not servants; for the servant knoweth not what his lord doeth: but I have called you friends; for all things that I have heard of my Father I have made known unto you. (16) Ye have not chosen me, but I have chosen you, and ordained you, that ye should go and bring forth fruit, and that your fruit should remain: that whatsoever ye shall ask of the Father in my name, he may give it you. (17) These things I command you, that ye love one another. (John 15:1-17)

6.3.1   THE VINE AND THE BRANCHES: THE UNION OF CHRIST AND HIS DISCIPLES, 15:1-10

The Figure of Relation and Union, 15:1-3

THE FIGURE STATED, 15:1

This is the seventh "I Am" of Jesus in John. Compare with Isaiah 5:1-7. "Husbandman" means "vinedresser."

THE WORK OF THE VINEDRESSER, 15:2

"Every branch in Me" means "united with Me by the profession of faith" (Godet 1886). We must never forget that fruit bearing is His theme and not press this to teach apostasy. All true branches will bear fruit. Non-fruit-bearing proves they are spurious. "They that perish may have looked like believers, but they were not believers in reality" (Ryle 1860).

The casting of the spurious branch into the fire is a part of the drapery of the metaphor. In no wise is this passage discussing the way of salvation either as to how to obtain salvation or as to how to keep saved. The only topic is fruit bearing. Note the Father's care; purging refers to chastisement. If you are being chastised, that proves you are bearing some fruit.

APPLICATION TO HIS DISCIPLES, 15:3

"Clean" means "in a condition to bear fruit" (Dods 1908). Note the cleansing power of the "word." (Compare with Ephesians 5:26; 1 Peter 1:22.) "Trial is the instrument by which our Father in heaven makes Christians more holy" (Ryle 1860).

The Condition of Fruit Bearing, 15:4-6

"The vine needs the branch for its fruitage; the branch must be part of the vine for the production of fruit" (Morgan 1960). "Abide" or "remain" occurs ten times in 15:1-11. What does it mean to "abide in Him?" The answer of Jesus is clear.

The Fruits or Evidence of Abiding, 15:7-8

Answered prayer (15:7): Fellowship with Jesus Christ and obedience to His Word are conditions of answered prayer.

Abounding fruitfulness (15:8): No one should suppose that he is saved if he never bears any fruit. Note the degrees in fruit—"fruit" and "more fruit" in 15:2, and "much fruit" in 15:8.

The Pattern or Example, 15:9-10

We are to abide in His love for us, not our love for Him. The pattern (15:9): The Father loved the Son. The Son loved His disciples. The measure and nature of His love for them is the measure and nature of the love of the Farther for the Son. The one condition is the keeping of Jesus' commandments (15:10). Christ's example of obedience to the Father is the pattern for our obedience.

6.3.2 JESUS AND HIS DISCIPLES, IN THEIR BOND OF UNION AND FRUIT BEARING, 15:11-17

- Its purpose: full joy for the disciples (15:11). "My joy" means the joy Jesus constantly felt in doing His Father's will.

- Its condition: love for one another (15:12-13). The pattern of our love for one another is the way Jesus loved and loves us. What unselfishness and sacrifice this enjoins toward one another!

- Its relation: friends (15:14-15). Jesus' disciples were not a plantation of slaves and He their master; but they were a family of friends, companions, and lovers.

- Their proof of friendship for Him: obedience (15:14).

- His proof of friendship for them: sacrifice (15:13) and sharing with them the secrets His Father gave Him (15:16).

- Its appointment: election to service (15:16). This is divine, not human, choice. This choice may refer to their election to salvation, and the appointment may refer to their appointment as apostles; or both may refer to their choices as apostles. It is hard to say. Two fruits of election: fruit bearing and answered prayer. Compare with Matthew 28:19.

6.4   Discourse Four: The World's Hatred of Jesus and His Disciples, 15:18–16:4

(18) If the world hate you, ye know that it hated me before it hated you. (19) If ye were of the world, the world would love his own: but because ye are not of the world, but I have chosen you out of the world, therefore the world hateth you. (20) Remember the word that I said unto you, The servant is not greater than his lord. If they have persecuted me, they will also persecute you; if they have kept my saying, they will keep yours also. (21) But all these things will they do unto you for my name's sake, because they know not him that sent me. (22) If I had not come and spoken unto them, they had not had sin: but now they have no cloak for their sin. (23) He that hateth me hateth my Father also. (24) If I had not done among them the works which none other man did, they had not had sin: but now have they both seen and hated both me and my Father. (25) But this cometh to pass, that the word might be fulfilled that is written in their law, They hated me without a cause. (26) But when the Comforter is come, whom I will send unto you from the Father, even the Spirit of truth, which proceedeth from the Father, he shall testify of me: (27) And ye also shall bear witness, because ye have been with me from the beginning. (16:1)These things have I spoken unto you, that ye should not be offended. (2) They shall put you out of the synagogues: yea, the time cometh,

that whosoever killeth you will think that he doeth God service. (3) And these things will they do unto you, because they have not known the Father, nor me. (4) But these things have I told you, that when the time shall come, ye may remember that I told you of them. And these things I said not unto you at the beginning, because I was with you. (John 15:18-16:4)

6.4.1 A Picture of the World's Hatred of Believers; The World's Guilt, 15:18-25

In John 15:18 He sets in contrast the love of the disciples for one another and the hatred they would receive from the world. He had already experienced such. They would be identified with Him.

The ground for their hatred (15:19). "Not of the world." That is, saints are heaven born; their origin is higher and nobler than that of the world. "The world has no faith in unselfishness. It knows its own heart so well that it does not believe in the reality of that of which it is itself incapable" (Speer 1915).

They treated Jesus so; we are not better than He (15:20).

It is for the sake of Jesus (15:21). That makes many heavy burdens light, makes many rough roads smooth, makes many dark clouds bright, makes many storms a calm.

The coming refers to the coming of Jesus as Messiah (15:22). He spoke enlightening words; therefore, they knew their sin. They now had conscious sin. It was not mere ignorance but willful hatred. (Study the cloaks or excuses that men make for their sins.)

Jesus and the Father are one—not one person but one in nature, essence, and being (15:23-24). The Greek neuter, not the masculine, decrees this interpretation. To hate one is to hate the other. To hate the Son is to hate the Father.

Compare John 15:25 with Isaiah 53:9. Men have never been able to explain why they rejected and crucified Jesus.

6.4.2 Comfort in the Work of Witnessing, 15:26-28

See the ASV. "He shall bear witness of Me; and ye also shall bear witness." Here is the joint witnessing of believers and the Holy Spirit. (Compare with Acts 2:32; 5:32; 15:25.) Let every personal worker ponder and be encouraged by this gracious truth. The idea of joint witnessing rests upon two facts: the word *also* and the use of the same verb.

The child of God should rejoice that the Holy Spirit confirms His testimony because the Holy Spirit can find access to the minds and hearts of those who hear. Both are witnesses of Jesus Christ. That is the one subject for personal workers, Sunday school teachers, preachers—all.

The word *witness* indicates that the child of God tells what is divinely revealed, eye-witnessed, and heart experienced.

Jesus spoke for a moment concerning the power that would sustain them in their terrible conflict that was ahead. (Compare with 16:5-16 for fuller treatment of this point.)

6.4.3 THE WORLD'S HATRED OF BELIEVERS; THE BELIEVER'S SUFFERINGS, 16:1-4

"Be offended" is rendered in the ASV, "be made to stumble" (16:1). It is about the same as our "tripped up."

For an illustration of John 16:2, see Paul (Acts 26:9).

The reason—moral blindness (16:3). This condition on their part should elicit on our part tenderness and sympathy. They lacked experiential knowledge of both the Father and the Son.

Lessons to emphasize:

- No marvel that saints are persecuted.

- Those who hear the gospel have no cloak for their sins.

- The Holy Spirit goes with those who do personal work.

- Sincerity is not enough. 16:2 says that the persecutors think that they are doing God a service. Sincere, but wrong—that is what Christ says about it.

- It is better to suffer here a little for Christ than there, much and forever without Christ.

6.5 DISCOURSE FIVE: VICTORY OVER THE WORLD THROUGH THE HOLY SPIRIT, 16:1-15

(1) These things have I spoken unto you, that ye should not be offended. (2) They shall put you out of the synagogues: yea, the time cometh, that whosoever killeth you will think that he doeth God service. (3) And these

things will they do unto you, because they have not known the Father, nor me. (4) But these things have I told you, that when the time shall come, ye may remember that I told you of them. And these things I said not unto you at the beginning, because I was with you. (5) But now I go my way to him that sent me; and none of you asketh me, Whither goest thou? (6) But because I have said these things unto you, sorrow hath filled your heart. (7) Nevertheless I tell you the truth; It is expedient for you that I go away: for if I go not away, the Comforter will not come unto you; but if I depart, I will send him unto you. (8) And when he is come, he will reprove the world of sin, and of righteousness, and of judgment: (9) Of sin, because they believe not on me; (10) Of righteousness, because I go to my Father, and ye see me no more; (11) Of judgment, because the prince of this world is judged. (12) I have yet many things to say unto you, but ye cannot bear them now. (13) Howbeit when he, the Spirit of truth, is come, he will guide you into all truth: for he shall not speak of himself; but whatsoever he shall hear, that shall he speak: and he will shew you things to come. (14) He shall glorify me: for he shall receive of mine, and shall shew it unto you. (15) All things that the Father hath are mine: therefore said I, that he shall take of mine, and shall shew it unto you. (John 16:1-15)

6.5.1 SUFFERINGS OF THE DISCIPLES AT THE HANDS OF THE WORLD; THE NEED OF VICTORY, 16:1-4

See the last portion of the previous discourse. In correlation of ideas, the passage of John 16:1-4 belongs with both discourses.

6.5.2 THE COMING OF THE COMFORTER, 16:5-7

His mission was finished, and His work was done—He knew where He was going (16:5). No one asked in the right sense or proper spirit. Some advantages of His going: expedient means profitable, beneficial, advantageous. The glorified Christ working through His disciples is more important than His bodily presence. "The going of the Savior was as blessed as His coming . . . The cross and the open grave gave God in Christ to the world forever . . . They had Him in reality a thousand times more fully and truly after He had gone" (Speer 1915).

His coming on Pentecost awaited Christ's ascension. The Holy Spirit's "dwelling among men was a gift purchased by the Son" (Ryle 1860).

Jesus' body could be in only one place at a time. Through the Holy Spirit, He could be everywhere at one and the same time.

His ascension was necessary to His appearance in heaven to intercede.

Faith is a higher and more blessed principle than sight (John 20:29).

6.5.3 THE CONVICTION OF THE COMFORTER, 16:8-11

Since this is the most pervasive passage on the Holy Spirit conviction, it should be studied much in detail. All other passages on the Holy Spirit conviction dovetail into this classic passage.

This conviction is to be through His disciples as agents (16:7). The "world" is thus limited to wherever the gospel is preached.

Its extent or object: "The world" means so far and only so far as the gospel is preached. The awesome fact in our stewardship is that more would be convicted if we gave them the gospel. The Holy Spirit does not work apart from the gospel. The missing link of Hardshellism is that no person can be found with a knowledge of the gospel who did not hear it through some means. The Century Bible (CB) says, "Whether the world will follow the dictates of conscience and surrender to the claims of Christ is a different question."[28] "The reproof given by the Spirit may lead either to conversion or to hardening. Compare 2 Corinthians 2:15-16" (Godet 1886). Such is not our responsibility. It is our stewardship to get the message out to the world.

Its nature: *Reprove*; better, *convict* (ASV); better still, *convince*. It is no mere rebuke; it "expresses the idea of pressing home a conviction" (Dods 1908). (Compare its use in John 3:20 and 8:46.) It is such a conviction that brings one to see and feel the matter as it is and as the Holy Spirit sees it.

The three subjects or topics of this conviction:

1. Sin (16:9): The Holy Spirit points to unbelief as proof of the general state of sin. (Compare Godet 1886.) "The deepest sin is the sin of unbelief" (Speer 1915). "It is the world's crowning sin and the very essence of guilt" (CB). Conscience and the law awaken men on many sins. The Holy Spirit seeks to put His finger on one's wrong relation to Jesus Christ since only when one's heart gets right with Jesus is one saved.

2. Righteousness (16:10): His going vindicated His righteousness against Jewish slander, shows that it took Him to the Father, and proves to men that they need His righteousness and must have it to go to the Father in heaven. Men have been slow to catch these words of Jesus because they fail to see the principle involved in His concrete language.

3. Judgement (16:11): Not "to come." It is past, took place on the cross, was against Satan and sin, and is the ground of

---

28. *The Century Bible* (London: Caxton Publishing, 1910).

the justification of the believer. To cling to Satan, sin, and the world is to cling to a doomed cause and a sinking ship.

Jesus was the simplest preacher in the world in wishing that all understand. He announced all three items and stopped to explain each one. Each could have been quite general until Jesus specified what He meant. How we need to follow His example!

6.5.4 THE COMPLETION OF THE COMFORTER'S WORK, 16:12-15

The abundance of truth (16:12a): "Much remains unsaid" (Dods 1908). Jesus had not taught them fully all truth, but He was perfect as far as He went.

The inability of the disciples (16:12b): Spiritual life is a life of growth. Truth does not grow, but we grow in our grasp of the truth.

The Holy Spirit as a safe guide to complete what Jesus began (16:13-15). (See John 14:25-26 for this idea.)

The word *spirit* (Greek, *pneuma*) is neuter, but the gender is grammatical, not natural. Therefore, Jesus could jump over the neuter word *spirit* back to *paraclete* (masculine) to stress the personality of the Holy Spirit. Note *ekeinos* (masculine, that one) in John 16:13-14.

6.6 DISCOURSE SIX: JESUS' GOODBYE TO HIS DISCIPLES, 16:16-33

(16) A little while, and ye shall not see me: and again, a little while, and ye shall see me, because I go to the Father. (17) Then said some of his disciples among themselves, What is this that he saith unto us, A little while, and ye shall not see me: and again, a little while, and ye shall see me: and, Because I go to the Father? (18) They said therefore, What is this that he saith, A little while? we cannot tell what he saith. (19) Now Jesus knew that they were desirous to ask him, and said unto them, Do ye enquire among yourselves of that I said, A little while, and ye shall not see me: and again, a little while, and ye shall see me? (20) Verily, verily, I say unto you, That ye shall weep and lament, but the world shall rejoice: and ye shall be sorrowful, but your sorrow shall be turned into joy. (21) A woman when she is in travail hath sorrow, because her hour is come: but as soon as she is delivered of the child, she remembereth no

more the anguish, for joy that a man is born into the world. (22) And ye now therefore have sorrow: but I will see you again, and your heart shall rejoice, and your joy no man taketh from you. (23) And in that day ye shall ask me nothing. Verily, verily, I say unto you, Whatsoever ye shall ask the Father in my name, he will give it you. (24) Hitherto have ye asked nothing in my name: ask, and ye shall receive, that your joy may be full. (25) These things have I spoken unto you in proverbs: but the time cometh, when I shall no more speak unto you in proverbs, but I shall shew you plainly of the Father. (26) At that day ye shall ask in my name: and I say not unto you, that I will pray the Father for you: (27) For the Father himself loveth you, because ye have loved me, and have believed that I came out from God. (28) I came forth from the Father, and am come into the world: again, I leave the world, and go to the Father. (29) His disciples said unto him, Lo, now speakest thou plainly, and speakest no proverb. (30) Now are we sure that thou knowest all things, and needest not that any man should ask thee: by this we believe that thou camest forth from God. (31) Jesus answered them, Do ye now believe? (32) Behold, the hour cometh, yea, is now come, that ye shall be scattered, every man to his own, and shall leave me alone: and yet I am not alone, because the Father is with me. (33) These things I have spoken unto you, that in me ye might have peace. In the world ye shall have tribulation: but be of good cheer; I have overcome the world. (John 16:16-33)

This was His closing message to His disciples. In these six discourses or parts, He covered a rather wide range of truths. He spoke of His approaching death in conversational tone and form. What words for His last! How we should hang on them!

6.6.1 HIS DECLARATION, 16:16

He mentions two brief delays with opposite results. The first "little while" was the short space from then till His death; the second was the short time from His death to Pentecost. "Seek Me no more" refers to His absence from the time of His death and resurrection to Pentecost. "Shall see Me" refers to seeing Jesus by faith by the coming of the Holy Spirit on Pentecost. Recall the glorification of Jesus in His disciples through the Holy Spirit in 16:13-16. Compare with John 14:17-23.

6.6.2 THEIR PUZZLE, 16:17-18

There is no marvel that they were puzzled; we still are! The enigma was just this: "I come because I go away; come in a greater way." Minds darkened by sin slowly grasp His blessed words.

6.6.3 HIS EXPLANATION, 16:19-28

His Interest, 16:19

He anticipates their question and gives proof of His higher knowledge. He loves to explain to listening hearts. Are you listening?

Joy Through Sorrow, 16:20-22

The greatest joy will suddenly follow the greatest grief. It will be brief, like the hour of childbirth for the mother. The use of "verily, verily" makes these words emphatic. Rejoice that morning follows the night, that sunshine follows the cloud, that a calm follows the storm. We can bear the sorrows because we look forward through Jesus to the glories ahead.

Prayer In Jesus' Name, 16:23-27

An illustration: A check is cashed to a certain one because of the standing of the name signed to the check. We are heard because of Who He is with the Father, not because of what we are. We have no natural standing with God; He has infinite standing with the Father.

An illustration: During the Civil War, a man was condemned to be shot the next morning. He got away and came to the White House. The servant at the door repeatedly refused to let him see President Lincoln and pushed him away with stern words. In fact, President Lincoln had shut himself in his room for study over war problems. Lincoln's son led the man to his father and secured pardon. We get what we get in Jesus' name.

Summary of His Incarnation, 16:28

Here is much in little. This stretches from His birth to His ascension. Note two departures and two arrivals. How wonderfully He came and how beneficially He went away!

6.6.4 THEIR CONFESSION, 16:29-30

His omniscience gave them proof of His deity. (Compare with John 16:19 for His supernatural knowledge.) He knows all things. He never made a mistake in judgment. O sinless Savior!

6.6.5 HIS FARWELL, 16:31-33

Do you really believe at this critical moment? (A paraphrase, 16:31.) Let this search your heart.

There will be desertion by His disciples but fellowship from the Father (16:32). How glorious that, when all turn us down, He never does!

We do not have peace in our trials, sorrows, persecutions, etcetera, but we do have peace in Jesus (16:33). And what peace! He does not paint a rosy path for them as He leaves them. But He does promise victory. The thought is, *I overcame; through Me you may overcome*. There is no excuse for defeated Christians. Jesus wants to make us overcome. Jesus leaves a bundle of gifts for his disciples—peace, good cheer, victory.

Note "I have overcome"—while His sorest trials were ahead. This is what we call futuristic or anticipatory perfect. Such is the use of "it has been finished," another anticipatory perfect, spoken from the cross! It was not finished but would be immediately. He had not finished His overcoming the world, but such was as sure as if it were finished.

6.7 QUESTIONS ON JOHN 14–16

6.7.1 JOHN 14

1. Why not prefer "mansions" today?
2. Discuss 14:6.
3. Explain "greater" (14:12).
4. Discuss the relation of discourse two to discourse one.
5. Explain "another" comforter.
6. Explain "comforter."
7. How does Jesus explain Pentecost?
8. Discuss at length "shall be" in you, from two angles.

6.7.2 JOHN 15-16

1. What is the danger in making figures of speech "walk on all fours?"

2. How is joint witnessing specified?

3. Why did Jesus say that it was "profitable" that He should go away?

4. Why prefer "convince" over "reprove" and "convict?"

5. What limits the word "the world" in Holy Spirit conviction?

6. Discuss the three topics on which the Holy Spirit convinces men.

7. Why should we not call the Holy Spirit an "it" or an "It?"

6.8   SERMON SUGGESTIONS

6.8.1 JOHN 14

- A Prepared Place for a Prepared People (John 14:6)
- Prayer (John 14:12-15)
- The Promised Coming of the Holy Spirit
- Our Hearts as His Abode
- The Mystery of Divine Fellowship
- Christ's Bequest of Peace

6.8.2 JOHN 15–16

- Fruit Bearing
- Abiding In Jesus
- The Cleansing Word
- Jesus' Joy Within His Own (15:11; see also 17:13 and 1 John 1:4)
- Chosen to Serve (15:16)

- The World's Estimate of Believers
- Man: The Excuse Maker
- Joint Witnessing
- Why Believers Are Persecuted
- The Profit of His Going Away
- The Profit of the Spirit's Coming
- The Convicting Work of the Holy Spirit
- Joy Through Sorrow
- Praying In Jesus' Name—or, more broadly—In Jesus' Name
- His Incarnation (16:28; stretch your mind toward the compactness of Jesus' thought. We rarely correlate great but kindred truths and events.)
- Never Alone Until the Cross (16:32)
- Jesus' Legacy for His Own (16:24; see also 14:27 and 15:11)

7: Jesus' Great Intercessory Prayer, Chapter 17

(1) These words spake Jesus, and lifted up his eyes to heaven, and said, Father, the hour is come; glorify thy Son, that thy Son also may glorify thee: (2) As thou hast given him power over all flesh, that he should give eternal life to as many as thou hast given him. (3) And this is life eternal, that they might know thee the only true God, and Jesus Christ, whom thou hast sent. (4) I have glorified thee on the earth: I have finished the work which thou gavest me to do. (5) And now, O Father, glorify thou me with thine own self with the glory which I had with thee before the world was. (6) I have manifested thy name unto the men which thou gavest me out of the world: thine they were, and thou gavest them me; and they have kept thy word. (7) Now they have known that all things whatsoever thou hast given me are of thee. (8) For I have given unto them the words which thou gavest me; and they have received them, and have known surely that I came out from thee, and they have believed that thou didst send me. (9) I pray for them: I pray not for the world, but for them which thou hast given me; for they are thine. (10) And all mine are thine, and thine are mine; and I am glorified in them. (11) And now I am no more in the world, but these are in the world, and I come to thee. Holy Father, keep through thine own name those whom thou hast given me, that they may be one, as we are. (12) While I was with them in the world, I kept them in thy name: those that thou gavest me I have kept, and none of them is lost, but the son of perdition; that the scripture might be fulfilled. (13) And now come I to thee; and these things I speak in the world, that they might have my joy fulfilled in themselves. (14) I have given them thy word; and the world hath hated them, because they are not of the world, even as I am not of the world. (15) I pray not that thou shouldest take them out of the world, but that thou shouldest keep them from the evil. (16) They are not of the world, even as I am not of the world. (17) Sanctify them through thy truth: thy word is truth. (18) As thou hast sent me into the world, even so have I also sent them into the world. (19) And for their sakes I sanctify myself, that they also might be sanctified through the truth. (20) Neither pray I for these alone, but for them also which shall believe on me through their word; (21) That they all may be one; as thou, Father, art in me, and I in thee, that they also may be one in us: that the world may believe that thou hast sent me. (22) And the glory which thou gavest me I have given them;

that they may be one, even as we are one: (23) I in them, and thou in me, that they may be made perfect in one; and that the world may know that thou hast sent me, and hast loved them, as thou hast loved me. (24) Father, I will that they also, whom thou hast given me, be with me where I am; that they may behold my glory, which thou hast given me: for thou lovedst me before the foundation of the world. (25) O righteous Father, the world hath not known thee: but I have known thee, and these have known that thou hast sent me. (26) And I have declared unto them thy name, and will declare it: that the love wherewith thou hast loved me may be in them, and I in them. (John 17:1-26)

This is truly the Lord's Prayer. Matthew 6 is the disciple's prayer. This is the glorious climax to the self-revelation of Jesus to His own disciples. (Try comparing this with all the other prayers of Jesus.)

This prayer is holy ground indeed. We should not read nor study it with irreverence. We should do our best to hear our blessed Lord speaking therein. Oh, to catch the spirit of this majestic prayer. No other prayer of Jesus is just like this one; it is unique among prayers and unique among even the prayers of Jesus.

To sum up the conditions that enforce the importance of this prayer, we see that they are prayer words, they are words of our Lord, and they are words near His death.

The outline is as follows: concerning Himself (17:1-5), concerning His disciples (17:6-19), and concerning future believers (17:20-26). We have three pictures, with Jesus as the center of each: first, the cross that would take Jesus away; the crown of His work. Second, we see the disciples in consecration and in telling of Jesus. Third, there is an ever-expanding spread of the gospel.

Note the formal introduction: "These things spoke Jesus." What climactic, age-telling, and heart-probing words, specifically chapters 13-16! "And after, He lifted up His eyes toward heaven." Is "the heaven" used here perhaps suggesting the Father's presence? The words could be rendered, "Into the heaven."

The emphasis is on "said." Though posture in prayer is very important, the content and quality count more. *Spoke* and *said* seem interchangeable. In Attic Greek, *laleo* was as our *talk*, but in Koine this distinction seems to be gone. That is, usage may wear away a one-time synonymous distinction.

Jesus could lift His eyes up to heaven without a consciousness of sin; we cannot because we are sinners. We bow our heads out of reverence and close our eyes out of a sense of shame.

7.1 His Prayer Concerning Himself, 17:1-5

7.1.1 His Prayer for Glorification, 17:1

The address: Jesus did not constantly call God "Father" as some today. Our address to Him should be with deep awareness of meaning, not simply emotional ebullition (the act of bubbling). Study in what setting He used God's name and seek to imitate Him.

Note besides the appropriateness of each address to the situation in His prayers; His addressing God as "Father" reflects communion of nature, sharing in intent, and harmony of fellowship. Thus He calls Himself "Thy Son." The Greek position stresses "Thy." In His incarnation, "Son" figuratively represents the same three ideas but with the added note of obedience!

The occasion: The hour about which He had often spoken had arrived. (Collect all references to that hour and study them as a unit.) The hour of the Cross was just ahead.

The request: Note both the request itself and its purpose. "Manifest the perfection of Thy Son that Thy Son may manifest Thy perfection." He did not ask for selfish glorification but that He might glorify the Father.

7.1.2 His Plea for Glorification, 17:2-4

The Father commissioned Him in the bestowal of authority (17:2). "All flesh" means all humanity, "flesh" suggesting frailty. "All which" is neuter singular to comprise all given ones as a unit. "To them," since it is plural, regards this unit in the individuality of each one.

His fulfilling this commission brings needed knowledge (17:3). You cannot have eternal life without knowing experientially the Father and the Son. You cannot know Him without having eternal life. "The eternal life"—the article makes it the same as "life eternal" in the previous verse. "True"—better, "genuine," since all other gods are unreal. The words *Jesus Christ* are in apposition with "the One whom Thou didst send." Only an evolutionary view of Jesus' Messiahship needs to take these words away from His prayer!

The Son's accomplishment of His mission shows He is no longer needed here (17:4). His faithfulness ought to inspire us to do more. "I" is emphatic and so is "Thee" by being placed before the verb. The aorist, "glorified," not the perfect, puts His entire life "upon the earth" into one grand act.

"In that I finished the work." The particle is explanatory or epexegetic. He glorified by finishing. "The work" is emphatic before the participle. "Which Thou hast given to Me" as incarnate Redeemer.

7.1.3 His Prayer for Glorification Renewed, 17:5

Every word is precious for meditation. "Now" sums up the coming of the hour of Calvary. "Glorify" is as above.

"Me" is emphatic before "Thou, Father." Such is a very personal and very intimate moment of interchange between the Son and His Father.

The manner of the manifestation of the perfection of the Son is unique. No one else could utter truly such a request. "Alongside Thyself!" His deity made Him equal with the Father. The preposition *para* stresses both fellowship and equality in this situation.

"With the manifested perfection which I was having…alongside Thee." He turned with longings to the fellowship of eternity past. "Was having," better than "had," stresses the continuance of the eternal state. In some Greek manuscripts, the "which" is a normal accusative, but in some it is attracted to the case of its antecedent "glory." English does not have such an idiom.

In English, "alongside Thee" must be set off by a comma or placed before the infinitive phrase, "before the world was existing." This is a concrete picture and suggests the eternal state before any act of creation. His statement denies the eternity of matter.

7.2 His Prayer Concerning His Disciples, 17:6-19

This request is no longer than the first. It moves logically through four specific and related phases. Nowhere else is the intimacy between Jesus and His own more tenderly and pointedly traced.

7.2.1 Their Progress Under His Ministry, 17:6-8

He reviews what they were then about to show as their need.

The faithfulness of Jesus Christ: In 17:1-5, His performances during His earthly sojourn here concerned specifically the Fatherward aspect of His commission; now His performances concern the ones whom He had won and chosen. He used three different words to describe His actions:

1. "I manifested Your name" (17:6): This ties the two phases of prayer together. Since His "name" means His Person and work, the expression is much akin to "glorify." The definite act (the aorist tense) sums up into one all of His many efforts.

2. "I have given" (17:8, 14): The perfect implies His giving and their still having His gift. He used the plural in 17:8 and the singular in 17:14.

3. The imperfect tense in "I was keeping" (17:12) reflects the repeated and constant care of Jesus for His own. (See the same verb in 17:11, 15.) The second verb for "kept" is aorist to sum up as one act all of Jesus' guarding them. The second verb "indicates safe custody and often implies assault from without" (Thayer 1977). Their being juxtaposed shows similarity and distinction. The lesson is that He still is keeping His own.

If one seeks to make Judas a case of one's being saved and then lost, two things follow. First, one must prove that Judas was saved; spiritual perceptions and aspirations are lacking in the man (see comments on chapter 13). Second, Jesus' "no one...except" rules out any comfort for the man who would use this to disprove the eternity of salvation. Judas was an exception, a sad and terrible one.

Jesus likely referred to Psalm 41:9. Compare with John 13:18. See "the son of lostness" applied to the antichrist (2 Thessalonians 2:3), which affirms sameness of character—a shocking coincidence but most likely not sameness of person. Other factors would have to be affirmed to indicate identity of persons.

To be lost does not mean to be non-existent. To be annihilated would not be such a tragedy. To be lost means to be lost to all good, all righteousness, all joy. It is to be given over to misery and ruin. To say that it means that the ruin would be eternal but that the ruined one is non-existent is mere juggling of words. Ruin is not ruin except as attached to an individual!

Their salvation or their receiving His Word: Jesus and His disciples have often been slandered by the teaching that none of His disciples were as yet saved. Jesus shows that they were already saved. Such is too clear to be doubted. Note each of the five words which our Lord used: "Thy word they have kept" (17:6). He started with the fruit of their experience. "Now they have known experientially" (17:7). They got to know and still know. The "now" stresses the reality of their experiential knowledge. They did not get to know and then renounce as had Judas. "They got to know experientially" (17:8) is aorist of the decisive act of coming to know or getting to know.

"They received" (17:8): This definite act is linked with, "and got to know really that from beside Thee I came forth." "And believed" (17:8). The content of faith is stressed—"that You sent Me." Their faith confidently accepted Him as the One sent by the Father. "To think to be true; to be persuaded of; to credit, place confidence in" (Thayer 1977).

7.2.2 THE DISCIPLES BRING JESUS GLORY, 17:9-10

Saving faith trusts the Lord Jesus Christ as Savior; saving faith is trust in a person. It is more than acceptance of a creed, but saving faith definitively trusts Jesus in His role as Savior. Faith does not accept a colorless person; it accepts the Christ of the Bible. Definite truths are involved.

Obedience to Jesus Christ as Lord is not an integral part of saving faith but a vital fruit. The soil of saving faith produces obedience to Him as Lord. When obedience to Him does not follow, we know that the faith (1) was mere head-faith or mere feeling, (2) was a profession without possession, or (3) a wrong attitude toward Christ Jesus. He who falls out of love with sin and into love with Jesus will love Him enough to crown Jesus as Lord of his life.

"I have been glorified in them" (17:10). This is the climactic word as to the spiritual progress of His own; this is a fruit of the other verbs. However poorly they had performed, Jesus affirmed their manifesting His perfection, and He centered His request on them.

He sets the world aside for the present and prays for these only. His prayer definitely encompasses the world (see comments below on 17:20, 23). "I pray not for the world" (17:9) is not the best translation, and careless study has brought more confusion. Plummer (1902) rightly says, "Literally, I am praying concerning them; concerning the world I am not praying. . . . Of course this verse does not mean that Christ never prays for unbelievers; 17:23 and Luke 23:34 prove the contrary; but it is for the chosen few, in return for their allegiance, that He is praying now." Montgomery and the Revised Standard Version (RSV) make the translation clearer; thus, "I am praying for them; I am not praying for the world."[29] C. B. Williams' translation

---

29. Editor's Note: No citation is given for Montgomery.

(1950) best perceives the force of the Greek; thus, "I am not praying for the world now."

7.2.3 The Reason for His Petitions—The Oneness Between Him and the Father, 17:6, 10

He amplified the common oneness of what the Father possessed and what He possessed.

7.2.4 The First Petition—Negative—Keep Them from the Evil One, 17:11-15

In His attitude, the Cross is already past (17:11). He used the present tense—"no longer am I"—in anticipation of what would soon be reality. John 17:12 makes this attitude even stronger: "While I was with them."

"The evil one" (17:15) could be neuter, favoring "the evil" of the KJV, but the masculine seems better and, therefore, refers to the devil (as so in Matthew 6:13). The use of *cpo* and *ek* (here) seems to make no difference as to whether it is an evil principle or an evil person. The adjective with the article seems to refer to a person.

He asked for them the same protection that He gave them during His time with them. The Father alone could give that. John 17:15 explains why we are left here in this world after we are saved. He says "Holy Father" as an appeal to God's holiness.

Even in the negative petition there was a positive note—"that they may be having My joy fulfilled in themselves" (17:13). "My joy" is emphatic. What a precious thought! *Fulfilled* means in a state of perfect fulfillment. What an ideal for each believer!

7.2.5 The Second Petition to Consecrate them, 17:16-19

The series of ideas builds up to a grand climax.

Their Heavenly Nature, 17:16

This re-states as a basis for His plea what He had just declared. Through the new life that He gave them, their origin in its essential quality was not "out of the world," here regarded as evil or depraved. Such is a negative way of affirming for them a heavenly nature. This adds another description of the salvation of the apostles, Judas excepted.

The Plea Itself, 17:17

"Consecrate them in the truth; Thy word is truth." *Sanctify* means the same as our word *consecrate* or *dedicate*. Service is here emphasized. The aorist suggests a decisive act in view of their deep need. *In the truth* means *in the sphere of* the truth. Our consecration ceases when we step over the line of truth.

"Thy word is truth." The possessive adjective "Thy" is emphatic in position. "Truth" is both without the article and emphatically before the verb "is" to stress the nature of truth. Yes, Jesus stressed both propositional truth and experiential truth. In fact, without objective truth, the experience would be unstable and unreal.

Note incidentally that the word *sanctify* cannot mean *to make sinless*, since Jesus was always that. He could, however, consecrate or dedicate Himself. In fact, the word *sanctify* never in the Bible has the sense of freedom from sin or sinlessness.

Their Soul-Saving Mission, 17:18

Note at least three pictures: the two Senders (God and Jesus); the act of sending or commissioning; the area of labor. Jesus saves actually and meritoriously; the apostles only save instrumentally.

Jesus' Example of Consecration, 17:19

"And for their sakes" doubly (in the connective and in the phrase) ties His consecration to theirs. "I am consecrating Myself" indicates a new act and attitude with the Cross ahead. The Cross both saves and provides power for service.

His purpose was clear. "They themselves also"—they in addition to Him and in imitation of Him. "May be consecrated" expresses a completed state of dedication. What a goal for His own!

7.3 HIS PRAYER CONCERNING FUTURE BELIEVERS, 17:20-26

In John 17:1-5, Jesus prayed concerning Himself. In 17:6-19, Jesus prayed concerning disciples whom He had already won. He prayed that they might be clean and pure and busy for Him. Their mission was similar to the mission of Jesus. "As Thou hast sent Me into the world, even so have I also sent them into the world" (17:18). His mission was to save souls; ours is the same. Jesus saves actually; we can be only instruments in His hands.

The five movements reach a climax similar to the former (17:6-19)—with the dedication of our Lord in each case. He desired thereby to move His own.

7.3.1 JESUS' ENLARGING HORIZON, 17:20

Christ saw victory ahead of the darkness of the Cross. Jesus' outlook enlarges: "Neither pray I for these alone" (17:20). That explains 17:9, which means, "I am making petition for them; I am not now praying for the world." Much misunderstanding has arisen here because we do not note the three main divisions of Jesus' prayer. Jesus did pray for the world. "That the world may know that Thou hast sent Me and hast loved them as Thou hast loved Me" (17:23).

7.3.2 EACH SAVED ONE TO BE A MISSIONARY, 17:21

This is the way Jesus continues His work. It is like a relay race. One runs to another person, another to the next person, and so to the end. Jesus prayed for future believers. How were they to believe? "Shall believe on Me through their word" (17:20). That kills Hardshellism. People are not saved without the gospel. That is why it is our chief business to pray for them and send them the gospel.

He defines saving faith: "Believe on Me" (17:20). Jesus is the object of faith that saves. Literally, "into Me"—faith takes one by the hand and leads him into Christ as the genuine shelter. The present participle of *believe* represents the distributive force of linear action. Saving faith is not a process in the individual but an act. The progress lies in its spread from one to another (see above at length on 17:8). (Collect all the pictures and facets of saving faith in John; you will be enriched.)

7.3.3 THE WAY TO VICTORY: ONENESS, 17:21-23

Jesus prays for oneness or unity but not for union. You may unite things that differ. You can have unity or oneness only by uniting things that are alike. "How can two walk together except they be agreed?" (Amos 3:3). Baptists believe in and pray for unity but do not pray for nor believe in union. The standard of this oneness is "as We are one." There are no differences between the Father and the Son. Here is perfect oneness, "I in them, and Thou in Me, that they may be made perfect in one" (17:23). The source of this oneness is "one in Us" (17:21). We cannot unite with those who teach salvation by works instead of by grace, who teach infant baptism instead of believer's baptism, who teach salvation through baptism instead of salvation before baptism, etc. There can be no oneness when these differences are involved. Baptists are willing to unite upon one condition, namely, only and altogether what the Bible teaches. We will not sacrifice truth for the sake of union. Jesus does not want us to do it.

Notice that Jesus twice here brought in the world. Let our horizon expand to His!

7.3.4 THE FINAL PURPOSE FOR THE SAVED, 17:24

This is Christ's will for the believer.

The address: "Father." (See comments on 17:1.) The inner relation of the Father and the Son became the ground of His plea.

The gift: Again, the singular "that which" (neuter) and "these also" (masculine plural) interplay.

The will or desire: The will includes three items. One, being where Jesus is. Note the anticipatory or futuristic use of "am." He was not actually back with the Father, but such was His viewpoint or perspective of anticipation. Two, being with Jesus indicates fellowship with Him. Three, beholding His manifested perfection. This will be an important phase of their activity continuously in heaven.

The reason: "for You set Your affection on Me before the foundation of the world." This is similar to 17:5 but more particular. The world existed because He laid its foundation—literally, "before the casting down of the world."

7.3.5 CHRIST'S PLEDGE TO MISSIONS, 17:25-26

Note the intertwining of ideas which rushed through His soul at the climax of His intercession.

The address: "Righteous Father." This shows the prospective of Jesus' achievement as the second Adam in coming to know the Father and is similar to His appeal to the Father's holiness in 17:11.

The obligation of assurance: Three conjunctions tie together three related ideas about getting to know God—"and yet...but...and." In each instance, the verb is aorist of a definite act and is weakened by its translation by the perfect tense.

The world's failure: "and yet the world Thee did not get to know experientially." (See also 1:5, 10, 18, etc.) "The world" refers to all human beings. The emphasis is on "Thee" by position. Whatever else the world got to know, experiential knowledge of the Father was not on the list.

Jesus' achievement: "But I Thee got to know experientially." His achievement stands in loving and triumphant contrast. "I" is emphatic, but "Thee" also is emphatic before the verb. Jesus does not refer to His knowledge as deity but to His achievement as incarnate.

The achievement of His own: "and these got to know experientially that I was sent." "And" ties this clause to the two former ones. "These"— emphatic exultation on His own. This resumes all that He said previously about the progress of His own. They did get to know, but His initiatory and causal part in such is stressed immediately.

The unceasing Missionary: One, He never ceases His work in them (17:26). "Declare" tends to obscure the play on the verbs. It is a causative verb on the same root as in 17:25—"to make known." Two, He never ceases His dedication—"and I will go on making known." He is the One Who still works through the Holy Spirit and His own. Three, He never ceases His gracious purpose—"that the love with which You loved Me in them may be and I in them." What mysterious and yet assuring indwelling!

Since Christ got to know, He pledged Himself to make known. Since believers get to know, they also must be making known the Father's name. Our Lord is the unceasing Missionary. He ever duplicates this spirit in the lives of the redeemed. Are we the same persons after studying this prayer? Sad, sad the condition of the heart that is not touched by such words!

7.4   Questions on John 17

1. What three conditions enforce the importance of John 17? Fix the outline in your mind permanently.

2. What can we learn from Jesus about how to address God in prayer?

3. Did Jesus pray for the world?

4. Estimate my discussion of *sanctify*.

5. Distinguish union and unity or oneness.

6. Discriminate Jesus' reference to His own in the singular number and in the plural.

7.5   SERMON SUGGESTIONS

If you expound the whole prayer in one message, be careful to allot a balanced number of minutes to each part. Three prayer meeting talks could well follow the main divisions.

- His Hour
- How Jesus Addressed God (study each instance for its specific setting)
- Jesus' Explanation of Eternal Life (correlate John 17:3 with previous references to "eternal life")
- The Christ in Eternity Past
- The Pre-Cross Progress of Jesus' Disciples (look at both His activities and theirs)
- Saving Faith in John's Gospel
- The Believer and the World
- Prayer for Unsaved People
- The Dedicated Believer
- Christ's Legacy of Joy
- "Thy Word Is Truth"
- Sent as Jesus Was!
- Jesus as Missionary
- The Relay Race of Soul Winning
- Christ's Will for Believers
- Beholding His Glory
- Christ's Dedication to Missions or Evangelism

PART IV:

HIS SELF-REVELATION IN THE CROSS AND RESURRECTION, CHAPTERS 18-21

8: His Work as Priest on the Cross, Chapters 18-19

We now pass to the last phase of Jesus' self-revelation of Himself and the Father. His work as Prophet is seen in His showing Himself to the world in chapters 1–12 and to His disciples in chapters 13–17. We now study His work as Priest on the Cross and as King in His glorious resurrection. Phases one and two pointedly prepare for phase three.

8.1　The Betrayal and Arrest of Jesus, 18:1-11

(1) When Jesus had spoken these words, he went forth with his disciples over the brook Cedron, where was a garden, into the which he entered, and his disciples. (2) And Judas also, which betrayed him, knew the place: for Jesus ofttimes resorted thither with his disciples. (3) Judas then, having received a band of men and officers from the chief priests and Pharisees, cometh thither with lanterns and torches and weapons. (4) Jesus therefore, knowing all things that should come upon him, went forth, and said unto them, Whom seek ye? (5) They answered him, Jesus of Nazareth. Jesus saith unto them, I am he. And Judas also, which betrayed him, stood with them. (6) As soon then as he had said unto them, I am he, they went backward, and fell to the ground. (7) Then asked he them again, Whom seek ye? And they said, Jesus of Nazareth. (8) Jesus answered, I have told you that I am he: if therefore ye seek me, let these go their way: (9) That the saying might be fulfilled, which he spake, Of them which thou gavest me have I lost none. (10) Then Simon Peter having a sword drew it, and smote the high priest's servant, and cut off his right ear. The servant's name was Malchus. (11) Then said Jesus unto Peter, Put up thy sword into the sheath: the cup which my Father hath given me, shall I not drink it? (John 18:1-11)

8.1.1 JUDAS AND THE GARDEN, 18:1-3

Jesus was ever busy (18:1). He went forth from teaching and prayer to a crisis outside the city of Jerusalem. The brook Kedron rises about one and one-half miles north of the city, flows along by the east side of the city wall, and empties into the Dead Sea after a course of eighteen or twenty miles southward. The word *brook* means a winter torrent. A brook is ordinarily dry during nine months of the year. This deep ravine is about 150 feet below the garden and was 400 feet below the top of the height of the temple.

Brook is an old word, compound from *roos*, *reo*, flowing, and *cheima*, only here in the New Testament, in winter—hence, "flowing in winter" or a winter brook. "Kidron," only here in the New Testament (see also 2 Samuel 15:23; from a Hebrew root, "turbid," "dark," "dirty"). Job 6:15-16 speaks of a brook that, in the snow and thawing, cuts away dirt and draws leaves and filth (thus, one would conclude from the Hebrew, Arabic, and Sabean).

More data are to be noted. The Latin *cedrus*, cedar, comes from the Greek *kedros*. Does it come from the Sanskrit *kadru*, the Akkadian *kidru*, or the Hebrew *kadar*? Westcott and Hort (1881), Vincent (1887), and Robertson trace the root to "cedar." Thayer (1977), Gesenius,[30] Brown-Driver-Briggs (1939) and Dods (1908) follow the route of "dark," etcetera. The two meanings very likely come from the same root. The spellings point to this conclusion; the historical situations lend themselves to such contacts. Such, however, means no more than probability.

The Garden of Gethsemane lies on the slope of the Mount of Olives, and travelers are shown olive trees that the guides claim stood there in the day of Jesus. The trees are old, centuries old, but the statement of Josephus that the Romans cut the trees to aid in burning the walls of Jerusalem so that battering rams could pulverize the limestone rocks seems to make improbable that the present trees go back to the first century.

The Bible links together certain great events by their occurrence in gardens: sin brought man's fall in the Garden of Eden; Jesus wrestled with the powers of darkness in the Garden of Gethsemane; then He was crucified and buried in a garden (John 19:41). "It was fitting that the blood of the Physician should be poured out, where the disease of the sick man first commenced" (Augustine).[31]

---

30. Editor's Note: No citation is given for Gensenius, but see the bibliography for the likely source.

31. Editor's Note: No citation is given for this quotation.

Between 18:1 and 18:2 comes the agony in the garden (Matthew 26:36-46; Mark 14:32-42; Luke 22:39-46).

Jesus did not hide nor try to escape but went to the place well-known to Judas—the pluperfect used with the force of an imperfect (18:2). The "also" in "Judas also" hints how differently varied characters use things. Judas degraded the place from one of prayer and fellowship to one of heartless betrayal. How hard the heart that was so close to Jesus and yet so far away!

Judas led the band of soldiers (18:3). The Jewish officers were to arrest Jesus, and the detachment of Roman soldiers was to aid in case of trouble. The "band" or cohort, if full, consisted of six hundred men, one-tenth of a legion (6,000). Matthew 26:47 describes the group as a "great multitude." They had before attempted arrest and failed because the officers did not bring Him; at this time they feared His disciples and probably all Galileans who were in the city of Jerusalem at the Passover.

"Cometh"—better, "comes"—"dramatic historical present" is used to add movement to the story (Robertson). John re-lives the story and sees Judas approaching.

The juxtaposition of "lanterns and torches" indicates some distinction; "better: with torches and lamps" (Hovey 1885). Against Trench (1854), Thayer (1977) decided for "lamps" here (Acts 20:8; Matthew 25:1ff). This would refer to the earthenware olive oil lamp with a wick, many instances of which have come to light in a century and more.

The "torch," only here in the New Testament, would be "a link or torch, consisting of strips of resinous wood tied together" (Dods 1908). A reference to a scholium in Aristophanes Lysistratus calls this "a torch made of vine-twigs."[32] I guess that the lamps burned for a long time, so long as the olive oil lasted, and that the torches were flares which burned up more brightly but were self-consuming. They would aid in "exploring shady recesses or rock-caverns and tombs" (Hovey 1885).

Weapons, a general term, would include the two specific terms *swords* and *staves* (Mark 14:43). While the two agree admirably, the details suggest two independent witnesses: John and Peter (as reported by Mark).

They brought lights to facilitate the night travel of the arresting party—but especially to seek out Jesus as if He were hiding as a cowardly fugitive from justice—and weapons to overcome Him as if He were resisting as a dangerous criminal. How little they knew Him! The

---

32. Editor's Note: A side note made in an ancient text. No citation is given.

Passover came at the time of the full moon, but their cruelty would not leave a gap open.

8.1.2 THE COHORT AND JESUS, 18:4-9

Jesus' Voluntary Self-Surrender, 18:4-5

(See also John 10:18.) Knowing the future full well, He chose Calvary. Known sorrow adds keenness to its angry bite. Yet they, not He, were terrified. He exhibited a calm and sublime demeanor, a patient and un-resentful self-possession. He offered no resistance but even "went forth" (18:4) from the group of disciples out into the open from the shadow of the trees, or more likely, from the gates of the garden. Adam in Eden hid in cowardice.

Jesus avoided popularity and the throne in John 6:15 but went forth to welcome death. He opened the conversation. His calm and dignified bearing was not that of a criminal, though they acted as if He were such (Luke 22:52-53). Nor was His attitude one of melancholy or self-destruction. He went courageously to do a great work, to atone for the sins of men.

"Said" (18:4) and "saith" (18:5) are alike the historical present for vividness in the actions of Jesus. "Therefore since He Knew" (8:4; cf. 13:1). "He was not taken by surprise. The surrender and death of Jesus were voluntary acts, though the guilt of Judas and the rest remains" (Robertson).

Sentence three in 18:5 is somewhat a parenthesis, but what a poignant one! "But there kept on standing Judas also, who was betraying Him, with them." "Kept on standing" is a pluperfect with the force of an imperfect. "Judas also"—John could never forget that bitter tragedy and gave it a graphic touch by adding "also."

The Effect on Them, 18:6

He overwhelmed, with a sudden flash of His omnipotence and glory, those who were arresting Him. The enemy fell. How unlike Eden; there Adam fell. "He flashed upon the men who were approaching Him some evidence of His power and majesty" (Morgan 1960).

Such a quiet, unexpected announcement could surprise His arresters but not strike them with such unparalleled panic. We may not be able to explain the forthputting of divine majesty, but it is here undeniable. The "words were pronounced with majesty and seemed to fall as a threatening from heaven" (Godet 1886). "A secret invisible power, no doubt, accompanied His words" (Ryle 1860). Judas may have understood the force of the "I am" (compare Exodus 3:14 with John 6:20; 8:24, 28, 58). Here was "the calm courage of conscious innocence" (Reith 1889). (Study the majesty and meekness of Jesus.)

His Tender Care for His Disciples, 18:7-9

He illustrates John 10:12. Compare 18:9 with 17:12. He asks again to see if His power touched their hearts. He thought of others only. How different Adam in Eden! They were not ready to suffer, and Jesus protected them for a while yet [1 Corinthians 10:13). He did not want them mistreated, and His exertion of power was for them far more than for Himself. "If therefore, Me ye are seeking, let these be going."

8.1.3 Peter and Jesus, 18:10-11

These are the words of an eye-witness; John recalls which ear and the name of the servant of the high priest.

All four evangelists rate Malchus as a *dulos* (servant or bondslave) of the highpriest. Only John names him or Simon Peter. This agrees with the idea that John's later writing, when both Peter and Malchus were likely dead, would not involve them in trouble. Since Peter singled out this one man, Malchus was likely showing himself vigorous in the arrest of Jesus. "Malchus" is the Latinized form of *malchos*, the Grecized form of the Hebrew *melech* (king).

John agrees with Luke in naming the right ear. Robertson thought that this detail marked the detail of the physician. Matthew and Mark use a word which pictures "drawing from or forth" from the sheath. Robertson used "jerked out" for John's word. John's aorist pictures a single, momentary, and decisive drawing out of the sword, but I cannot see "jerking" in the Greek word. It adds a nuance not native to the Greek.

One shudders to think what the outcome might have been but for the merciful touch of Jesus. It was mercy to Malchus and to Peter, preventing Peter's indictment. Peter did not lack courage, but it was a natural and unreasoning impulse. If fighting with the sword was then wrong, how can it ever be right in His children? (Luke 22:49-51.) Learn how to act in persecution and in the spread of the gospel (John 18:36; Revelation 13:10; Matthew 26:52-53). This word of Jesus would kill all force in religion.

"The cup" is a metaphor of what was ahead for Jesus in the way of suffering. It indicates intensity and fullness of suffering. Many and bitter were the ingredients of that cup, yet He drank the last dreg for you and me. Jesus suffered at the hands of men, at the hands of the devil and the demons, but at the hand of His Father also. It was a part of the redemptive plan, and it "pleased Jehovah to bruise Him" (Isaiah 53:10). God did not enjoy seeing His Son suffer; He looked to the outcome: glorious redemption for multitudes. Jesus died as more than a martyr to the truth as He saw it; He died in fulfilment of the plan of redemption; He offered Himself as an offering to God. He had but one response to all this because He saw gleaming through the bitterness of the cup the words of His Father's will for Him. Self-will in Eden brought ruin; Jesus' submission here brought redemption.

Center these thoughts around the cup of suffering, the Father's giving the cup, and the voluntary drinking.

8.2 JESUS IN RELIGIOUS COURT; PETER'S DENIAL, 18:12-28

(12) Then the band and the captain and officers of the Jews took Jesus, and bound him, (13) And led him away to Annas first; for he was father in law to Caiaphas, which was the high priest that same year. (14) Now Caiaphas was he, which gave counsel to the Jews, that it was expedient that one man should die for the people. (15) And Simon Peter followed Jesus, and so did another disciple: that disciple was known unto the high priest, and went in with Jesus into the palace of the high priest. (16) But Peter stood at the door without. Then went out that other disciple, which was known unto the high priest, and spake unto her that kept the door, and brought in Peter. (17) Then saith the damsel that kept the door unto Peter, Art not thou also one of this man's disciples? He saith, I am not. (18) And the servants and officers stood there, who had made a fire of coals; for it was cold: and they warmed themselves: and Peter stood with them, and warmed himself. (19) The high priest then asked Jesus of his disciples, and of his doctrine. (20) Jesus answered him, I spake openly to the world; I ever taught in the synagogue, and in the temple, whither the Jews always resort; and in secret have I said nothing. (21) Why askest thou me? ask them which heard me, what I have said unto them: behold, they know what I said. (22) And when he had thus spoken, one of the officers which stood by struck Jesus with the palm of his hand, saying, Answerest thou the high priest so? (23) Jesus answered him, If I have spoken evil, bear witness of the evil: but if well, why smitest thou me? (24) Now Annas had sent him bound unto Caiaphas the high priest. (25) And Simon Peter stood and warmed himself. They said therefore unto him, Art not thou also one of his disciples? He denied it, and said, I am not. (26) One of the servants of the high priest, being his kinsman whose ear Peter cut off,

saith, Did not I see thee in the garden with him? (27) Peter then denied again: and immediately the cock crew. (28) Then led they Jesus from Caiaphas unto the hall of judgment: and it was early; and they themselves went not into the judgment hall, lest they should be defiled; but that they might eat the passover. (John 18:12-28)

The trial and the denials develop at the same time, but what a chasm of difference. How little Peter knew himself in John 13:37!

Jesus' trial was a long, drawn-out procedure. In its national aspect, it was twofold—Jewish and Roman; in its nature, it was twofold—religious and civil. There were three stages of each of these two phases of the trial. Yet the trial had, truly speaking, no legal side; it was all illegal. The greatest farce of the centuries for legality was perpetrated on the sinless Savior. The trial of Jesus was not a trial but a mistrial. Justice was on the scaffold; injustice reigned. Yet out of such injustice to Jesus, the just God so wrought that He might be just and the justifier of everyone who believes in Jesus.

8.2.1 Jesus Before Annas, the Ex-High Priest, 18:12-14

He was bound as an incontrollable criminal; He submitted with the indescribable meekness of a lamb (18:12). These picture in vivid contrast the awfulness of sin and the unfathomable love of the divine heart. Annas still exerted great influence. (Compare 18:13ff with 11:49-52 and the notes there.)

Annas and Caiaphas first appear in the Gospels at Luke 3:1 in Luke's dating of John the Baptist's ministry. Annas or Ananos (Greek forms of the Hebrew *Chanan*, to be gracious) was high priest in AD 6-15 and father-in-law of Joseph Caiaphas. In fact, he was succeeded by five sons and his son-in-law (Josephus 1984).[33] According to Josephus and the Talmud, the family was Sadducean and especially odious to the Pharisees, the "house of Annas" becoming a by-word in the Talmud. His son Eleazar came next, about 15-18 AD, though his date is a bit difficult to determine (Broadus 1886, on Matthew 26:57). As John 18:13 and 24 show, even after he was put out of office, Annas exerted great influence.

Joseph Caiaphas (high priest from 18-36 AD) appears in John 11:49-52 and at the trial of our Lord to have been "shrewd and self-seeking, and unscrupulous" (Broadus). He lost his office shortly after Pilate lost the procuratorship in 36 AD. The sons of Annas (Jonathan, Theophilus, Matthias, Annas the Younger) came after their brother-in-

---

33. *Antiquities*, XVIII, id, lf; XX, ix, 1.

law. (See Thayer 1977 on the suggested derivations of the Hebrew name "Caiaphas.")

They staged this trial with the hope of formulating a civil charge against Jesus. To this end they used the most diabolical cross-examination to catch Him in His words. Fairness was not known to them.

8.2.2 PETER'S FIRST DENIAL, 18:15-18

What a time for such an interlude! But John cannot cover up the facts. The testimony of Jesus in the trial and the shameful denial of Peter are so skillfully interwoven as to intensify both greatly. Jesus witnessed a good confession, but what of Simon (1 Timothy 6:13)?

Note three details: "Followed"—more vividly, "was following." The "other disciple" was John, the writer of this Gospel. He modestly chose veiled references to himself. The maid used "me," expecting a negative answer, and the contemptuous "this man." "She made it easy for Peter to say no" (Robertson). The world always tries to make fools of the followers of Christ.

How sad the picture! Peter's boastfulness of faithfulness to Jesus was gone or turned into shameful denial. Whatever Peter did, he did with vehemence. That is why the sins of active and useful people are so great. It takes a big man to commit a big sin. A saint warming at Satan's fire! What shame that too many Christians still imitate this picture! Are you doing it?

8.2.3 JESUS BEFORE CAIAPHAS AND THE SANHEDRIN, 18:19-24

This trial was informal and met before the legal hour for the meeting of the great religious court of the Jews, the Sanhedrin. (Compare here Matthew 26:57, 59-68; Mark 14:53, 55-65; Luke 22:54ff, 63-65.)

The cross-examination question (18:19): Had they been concerned before on these two topics—His disciples and His teaching—they could have learned all that was necessary. At this stage, one hardly needs to say that the examination lacked sincerity.

The reply of Jesus (18:20ff): Those that have been taught are a teacher's best witnesses. So is a church a pastor's best recommendation. Jesus did not fear investigation. Light does not fear light; only the darkness of sin fears the light of investigation.

Their cruel and irrational treatment (18:22): What right had they to smite Him? They probably smote Him with their hands as well as with rods. Because of the inconclusive nature of the passage, one may conclude that both may have been used.

The rebuttal of Jesus (18:23): Jesus would not refuse to suffer if they could produce a true charge. They turned from fact to abuse because they had no answer. Abuse is the tool of a defeated man. Physical persecution can never answer a spiritual problem.

Transfer of Jesus to Caiaphas (18:24): What a strange "therefore!" Although the writer shifts the scene, he could not forget the denier of Jesus, even Simon Peter.

8.2.4 Peter's Second and Third Denials, 18:25-27

Study Matthew 26:58, 69-75; Mark 14:54, 66-72; Luke 22:54-55, 62. The animal gave testimony to Jesus when His follower would not. The stones will cry out.

Note how the two denials intertwine. "Moreover, Simon Peter kept on standing and warming himself." This ties the picture to 18:18. "Consequently" or "therefore," he aroused their curiosity.

Peter had ample time to think. An hour passed (Luke 22:59).

On the form of the question, compare 18:17. There was very likely a cheap twitting of Peter by the questioners. How could he still deny? "I did, didn't I, see you in the garden with Him?"

John used "again therefore" (18:27) to show that dread settled on Peter. Peter knew that the man was present when Peter cut off the ear of Malchus. Peter added cursing and swearing or oaths (Mark 14:17; Matthew 26:73). John adds the poignant note, "immediately" (18:27).

8.2.5 Jesus Before Caiaphas and the Sanhedrin, 18:28

(Compare Luke 22:66-23:1; Matthew 27:1-2; Mark 15:1.) They met as soon as the rules would let them and formally condemned Jesus, though they had no just charge against Him. They had all crooked plans previously set for this phase of the trial and soon rushed Him to Pilate for civil judgment. Recall that the Jews had no right to put anyone to death. That is why they turned Him over to the Roman government. This finishes the stages of the religious trial.

Lessons to emphasize:

- The shame of self-confidence: Peter boasted that he would not deny the Lord. Though he most likely was utterly sincere, he shamefully boasted. Self-confidence is never fitting on the part of depraved and weak sinners. As it was with Peter, confidence in our goodness or powers always ends in shame for Him.

- The shame of denying Jesus: Confess Him; do not deny Him! Our denials are more subtle than Peter's but no less truly shameful.

- The shame of being found warming at Satan's fire: "The world is no friend to grace to hold us onward towards God" today any more than formerly.

- The farce of a trial for Jesus: The trial was mere pretense. No fairness was shown Jesus. Jesus is on trial before you. What are you doing with Him? Trust Him in your heart. Confess Him in your life. Honor Him in your home, in your church, in your community—everywhere.

8.3 JESUS BEFORE PILATE, 18:28-19:16A

(28) Then led they Jesus from Caiaphas unto the hall of judgment: and it was early; and they themselves went not into the judgment hall, lest they should be defiled; but that they might eat the passover. (29) Pilate then went out unto them, and said, What accusation bring ye against this man? (30) They answered and said unto him, If he were not a malefactor, we would not have delivered him up unto thee. (31) Then said Pilate unto them, Take ye him, and judge him according to your law. The Jews therefore said unto him, It is not lawful for us to put any man to death: (32) That the saying of Jesus might be fulfilled, which he spake, signifying what death he should die. (33) Then Pilate entered into the judgment hall again, and called Jesus, and said unto him, Art thou the King of the Jews? (34) Jesus answered him, Sayest thou this thing of thyself, or did others tell it thee of me? (35) Pilate answered, Am I a Jew? Thine own nation and the chief priests have delivered thee unto me: what hast thou done? (36) Jesus answered, My kingdom is not of this world: if my kingdom were of this world, then would my servants fight, that I should not be delivered to the Jews: but now is my kingdom not from hence. (37) Pilate therefore said unto him, Art thou a king then? Jesus answered, Thou sayest that I am a king. To this end was I born, and for this cause came I into the world, that I should bear witness unto the truth. Every one that is of the truth heareth my voice. (38) Pilate saith unto him, What is truth? And when he had said this, he went out again unto the Jews, and saith unto them, I find in him no fault at all. (39) But ye have a custom, that I should release unto you one at the passover: will ye therefore that I release unto you the King of the Jews? (40) Then cried they all again, saying, Not this man, but Barabbas. Now

Barabbas was a robber. (19:1) Then Pilate therefore took Jesus, and scourged him. (2) And the soldiers platted a crown of thorns, and put it on his head, and they put on him a purple robe, (3) And said, Hail, King of the Jews! and they smote him with their hands. (4) Pilate therefore went forth again, and saith unto them, Behold, I bring him forth to you, that ye may know that I find no fault in him. (5) Then came Jesus forth, wearing the crown of thorns, and the purple robe. And Pilate saith unto them, Behold the man! (6) When the chief priests therefore and officers saw him, they cried out, saying, Crucify him, crucify him. Pilate saith unto them, Take ye him, and crucify him: for I find no fault in him. (7) The Jews answered him, We have a law, and by our law he ought to die, because he made himself the Son of God. (8) When Pilate therefore heard that saying, he was the more afraid; (9) And went again into the judgment hall, and saith unto Jesus, Whence art thou? But Jesus gave him no answer. (10) Then saith Pilate unto him, Speakest thou not unto me? knowest thou not that I have power to crucify thee, and have power to release thee? (11) Jesus answered, Thou couldest have no power at all against me, except it were given thee from above: therefore he that delivered me unto thee hath the greater sin. (12) And from thenceforth Pilate sought to release him: but the Jews cried out, saying, If thou let this man go, thou art not Caesar's friend: whosoever maketh himself a king speaketh against Caesar. (13) When Pilate therefore heard that saying, he brought Jesus forth, and sat down in the judgment seat in a place that is called the Pavement, but in the Hebrew, Gabbatha. (14) And it was the preparation of the passover, and about the sixth hour: and he saith unto the Jews, Behold your King! (15) But they cried out, Away with him, away with him, crucify him. Pilate saith unto them, Shall I crucify your King? The chief priests answered, We have no king but Caesar. (16) Then delivered he him therefore unto them to be crucified. And they took Jesus, and led him away. (John 18:28-19:16)

How important these days were in the minds of the evangelists may be inferred from the amount of space that they gave to the narrative of them. To the three years and more of His public ministry, the four evangelists give in all fifty-five chapters; but to the eight days spoken of here, they give thirty chapters. It is most significant that, if they had told the story of his public ministry in as great detail, it would have occupied over four thousand chapters. "Again, if the story of our Lord's whole life had been told at as great length as that of the last eight days, we should have over 45,000 chapters. This would make more than thirty-seven Bibles of the size of our present Bible. This is most significant" (Schauffler 1908, 102).

Before you take up the details, note three phases of the trial before Pilate, the Roman Governor: (1) before Pilate; (2) before Herod Antipas; (3) before Pilate again.

Before Pilate (18:28-38; Matthew 27:11-14; Mark 15:2-5; Luke 23:2-5): At least three movements appear in this phase of the trial—the slimy scrupulosity of the Jews (18:28); the pertness of Pilate with the Jews (18:29-32); Pilate and Jesus (18:33-38a).

8.3.1 THE WHITEWASH OF RELIGIOUS CEREMONY, 18:28

The place: "the hall of judgment" and "the judgment hall" translate as the same Greek article and noun. The Greek *praetorion* stands for the Latin *praetorium*. A word "natural here in the atmosphere of the court and the military environment" (Robertson 1930, on Matthew 27:27). The word was used of the tent of the general, then of the official residence of the governor.

The compound is from *prae*, "before," and *eo*, "I go": hence to go before, to lead the way. With the agent ending "or," *praeeoitor* or *praeitor* was shortened to praetor—a leader. The adjective *praetorius*, in its neuter form, *praetorium*, was used substantively of the place of residence.

Herod the Great built a magnificent palace for himself, and it seems that the Roman procurator occupied it. (See reference to another in Caesarea, Acts 23:25.) "Herod's palace in Jerusalem was on the Hill of Zion in the western part of the upper city. There is something to be said for the castle of Antonia, north of the temple area, as the location of Pilate's residence in Jerusalem" (Robertson).

The time: Significantly, John reminds us of the time. "Moreover, it was early"—technically, the fourth watch of the night, 3-6 a.m. The time spelled out the farce in the trial. In fact, two violations had been made. One, the Sanhedrin court could not hold a legal meeting before sunrise, especially in capital cases. In addition, the Jewish court had no legal authority to pass a death sentence. Two, the Sanhedrin could not try and sentence the same day. According to the Hebrew computation of time, a day began at six in the evening.

The whitewash: The members of the Sanhedrin would not defile themselves ceremoniously or outwardly by entering the house of a Gentile (see also Acts 10:28; 11:3) but had no scruples against laying their slimy and illegal hands upon the spotless Son of God! John's purpose clause (*hina*) puts both the negative and the positive sides of their farce or pretense. "Be defiled" is aorist passive subjunctive of *miaino*, to stain, as with color, or to defile, as in religious profaining or unhallowing. (Vincent 1887 treats the word well.)

Robertson logically shows that reference to the Passover may be specific of the Passover meal or general of the Passover festival. The general sense here suits better the statements in the Synoptic Gospels.

8.3.2 The Concession and Pertness of Pilate, 18:29-32

"Therefore"—consequence, not time as "then" could suggest today. Right actions would have refused to concede to take any part in the Sanhedrin farce. "Outside"—likely a gallery over the pavement in front of the palace (see 19:13). "Says," not "said" (KJV, NASB); "saith" (ASV). John shifts from the narrative aorist ('went outside") to the vivid historical present to show the tragic drama of the farce.

"What accusation are ye bringing against this man?" This was a hard question for the Jews to answer. Such questions always bring uneasiness to guilt. The conversation had not yet named a formal charge. Pilate had a right to know their "legal charge" (*kategoria*, an open and formal charge before a tribunal or governor).

"This fellow"—most likely contemptuous. Emphatically, they used the periphrastic imperfect to stress Jesus' persistence in doing evil. Insolently, they posed infallibility in their judgment.

With a likely twitch in his voice, Pilate suggested their judging Jesus, a thing he well knew to be preposterous for them under Roman rule. He likely enjoyed their effort to explain their galling subjugation. "Take him—I mean, you" brings out his emphatic and shrewd insolence. He thus drew out their admission that they did not desire a fair trial but his approval to put Jesus to death (7:1, 25).

John perceived meaning in their admission: "in order that the remark of Jesus might be fulfilled which he said to be signifying be what kind of death He was about to be dying." (See John 12:32.) John regarded the statement as a prophecy (Robertson). "Crucifixion was not a Jewish punishment" (Vincent 1887).

8.3.3 Pilate and Jesus, 18:33-38A

If Pilate himself had sought the facts, what a holy moment for him! He saw the perfidy of the Jews but stood with his back toward the light. He wished to speak privately with Jesus, away from the Sanhedrin (18:33).

"You are the king of the Jews?" Both "you" and "the king" are emphatic. Pilate meant a civil king inimical to Rome.

"From yourself, You, are you saying this or did others speak to you about Me?" That is, is this a personal and sincere inquiry or a trap engendered by the Sanhedrin?

"Can it be that I am a Jew?" Pilate dodged as if Jesus spoke of racial affinity. He obviously knew that Jesus referred to his insincere connivance. His further words look in this direction. "Your [emphatic] nation and the chief priests delivered you to me." Pilate sought to whitewash the chicanery, which he knew in the Sanhedrin.

"What did you do?" Robertson rightly paraphrases this to "what is thy real crime?" Further, "John's picture of this private interview between Pilate and Jesus is told with graphic power" (Robertson). Not a word is wasted; every word deserves long and perceiving meditation.

"My [emphatic] kingdom is not out of this world." He royally claimed a kingdom but not an earthly one. (See also 17:13-18.) But Pilate had little ear for spiritual truth. "If put of this world were my kingdom, my [emphatic] assistants would be fighting in order that I might not be delivered to the Jews." Note the emphatic position of "out of this world." The source and nature of a kingdom determines the nature of the activity of a king's assistants. Jesus affirmed here the same which he affirmed when Peter smote the ear of Malchus.

Jesus saw the outcome. He expected wobbly Pilate to surrender Him to the cruelty of the Jews. Jesus perceived the politician better than Pilate understood himself.

"But now my kingdom is not from here." Jesus persisted to refer to his kingdom as unearthly since this was the charge of the Sanhedrin and the only one properly to concern Pilate.

"Are you not therefore a king?" (18:27). The compound interrogative particle (*ouk* and *oun*) expected an affirmative answer. It is used only here in the New Testament "and in LXX only in a text in II Kings 5:23" (Robertson). Pilate was caviling or ironical, not sincere. Pilate urged that the nature of Jesus' kingdom was inconsequential. He wished to win a shadowy argument to salve his scheming conscience.[34]

"You, you are saying that a king am I." Whatever be the exact meaning of this sentence, the rest leaves no indecision and should have won even Pilate.

"I for this purpose have been born and for this purpose have come into the world in order that I might bear witness to the truth." The emphatic "I" stresses Christ's Person and destiny. The repeated "For this purpose" is emphatic. It is *eis* with the accusative case of extension for purpose. What a declaration of Jesus' mission! The two perfects explain His incarnation and advent into the world. Paul refers to this confession (1 Timothy 6:13). His kingdom is the kingdom of truth.

---

34. Editor's Note: LXX or Septuagint is a Greek translation of the Old Testament: *Septuaginta: Id est Vetus Testamentum graece iuxta LXX interpretes,* edidit Alfred Ralfs. (Deutsche Bibelgesellschaft, 1935).

"Everyone who is out of the truth is hearing my voice." Jesus reached out to enclasp Pilate, if he desired. Its inclusiveness—"everyone," even Pilate. Its characterization—"out of" or "sprung from: whose life and words issue from the truth" (Vincent 1887). Its fruit—"is hearing my voice." The position of "my" before "voice" is emphatic.

"Says to him Pilate, 'what is truth?'" John made dramatic Pilate's saying such more than who said it. Pilate dodged by omitting "the" with truth, meaning "truth in any particular case" (Vincent 1887). In the very presence of Incarnate Truth, Absolute Truth (John 14:6), Pilate sneered, showed indifference, and dodged the issue.

"Pilate's exclamation is neither the expression of an ardent thirst for truth, nor that of the despair of a soul which has long sought it in vain; it is the profession of a frivolous skepticism, such as is frequently met with in the man of the world, and especially in the statesman" (Godet 1886).

Jesus did not attempt to answer Pilate. This he had done already in John 17:17, "Thy word is truth." If one does not answer this as Jesus did, he charts himself into the raging sea with all of its dangers.

Before Herod Antipas (Luke 23:6-12): The Westcott-Hort Greek New Testament (1881) indicates a paragraph within John 18:38 (see ASV). John did not propose to tell every detail, but one needs the fuller story in mind in a full study.

8.3.4 Before Pilate Again, 18:38b–19:16a

(For the parallels, see Matthew 27:15-30; Mark 15:6-19; Luke 22:13-25. The movements so intertwine as to make analysis difficult. The main pictures are as follows.)

Pilate's Report to the Sanhedrin Leaders, 18:38b

"I no crime at all find in him." "I" stresses his official verdict; "no crime at all" emphasizes the innocence of Jesus. "Fault"—better, "cause of accusation" or "crime" (ASV). Pilate, therefore, should have set Jesus free at once.

Barabbas or Jesus, 18:39-40

"But," a custom trapped the wobbly Pilate. Perhaps Pilate hoped that he could get Jesus released because of the intense evil of Barabbas. His use of "the king of the Jews," however, seems to say such hope is too mild. Perhaps more doubts and dreads seized Pilate than he could discern.

Their depravity comes out in their choosing Barabbas instead of Jesus. John accented the evilness of the man: a robber. Since the verb from which "robber" is derived means "to plunder," this man was a brigand, an insurgent, and a murderer (Luke 23:19, 25). "Barabbas" is Aramaic for "son" (*bar*; cognate with Hebrew *ben*) of a father.

Strange irony! The worst escaped because the best died in the place of the worst. Did Barabbas ever wake to see his good fortune? "They cried out"—the intensity of wrong. "Not this man"—a contemptuous utterance. Wickedness imposes some fierce options.

Pilate's Scourging of Jesus, 19:1

"Then therefore"—a strange time and conclusion. "Scourged"—a verb built on the noun *mastix*: whip. The scourge was a Roman whip with pieces of metal or bone with which to take out plugs of flesh.

The ending on *mastigoo* is causative—to cause to whip. Pilate did not actually scourge Jesus. He simply ordered it done, perhaps to see if the mob would be satisfied with this penalty on the alleged pretender to royalty (Luke 13:22) whom Pilate has pronounced "innocent" (Robertson). This therefore was another illegal act.

The Mockery of the Soldiers, 19:2-3

There were three similar mockings of Jesus: the previous mocking perpetrated by the Sanhedrin (Mark 14:65; Matthew 26:67ff; Luke 22:64ff); this incident; and by the soldiers later, after His condemnation (Mark 15:16-19; Matthew 27:27-30). None were just; none were essential parts of crucifixion. They were abusive extras, each part of which was inexcusable. In the light of man's wickedness, there is nothing improbable against repetition of the mockery.

John described four acts. Each was meant to mock and insult:

1. The crown of thorns: "And the soldiers, after they plotted a crown of thorns, placed it upon his head." *Pleko*, an old verb, only here, Mark 15:17, and Matthew 27:19 in the New Testament, means "to weave."

2. "And a purple garment they cast around Him." They obviously took from Him His *himation* (outer garment), possibly before

the scourging. The purple suggested royalty. They wished for it to appear that He was dressed as a king.

3. The mockery reached its climax in hailing Him as king. Note two imperfect tenses: "they kept coming" and "kept saying." One heaping of mockery and derision did not satisfy their cruelty. Cheapness knows not to do other than repeat itself.

4. "They repeatedly gave Him vicious strokes." Notice the imperfect again. The plural of the noun indicates intensity. The noun *rhapisma* is from the verb *rhapizo*, which is in turn from a noun *rhapis*. Thayer (1977) cited instances from the second and third centuries about this word. In the later years, the word usually meant a strike with the hand. Moulton and Milligan (1915) supply one instance from a first-century papyrus in which "knuckles" was used. In the case of Jesus, one cannot be certain whether the strokes were with rods or with palms of the hands. In any case, the act was most insulting.

Pilate's Second Report, 19:4-5

In three acts, one sees the empty effort of Pilate to release Jesus. One: same as before, no fault or crime in Jesus. Two: presentation of Jesus in the caricatured and abused form. "Then"—better, "therefore" (ASV, NASB)—in consequence of Pilate's brutal effort to have Jesus released. Three: Pilate's salute to Jesus—"Behold, the man!" As Hovey (1885) observed, "behold!" is not a verb but an interjection. "The man" is nominative, not accusative.

Whatever Pilate's exact intention, the principle of "Lo! The Man" becomes a great meditation for lovers of Jesus. We have rightly made much of the words of Jesus from the cross. The words of men, on the other hand, toward the cross bring much revealing light to the earnest student of them. Christ speaking from Calvary—we cannot preach this too much. Man speaking toward Calvary—this theme may profitably engage our attention.

"'The man, whom you have asked me to crucify; the man, scourged, mocked, abused, yet gentle, silent, enduring! Lo, there he stands, an object of pity, rather than of fear.' These words of half-contemptuous pity were designed to change the fierceness of the spectators into compassion" (Westcott and Hort 1881).

"A man who allows himself to be treated thus, is surely a harmless fanatic, whom there is no reason for killing" (Meyer 1891). "See this man who submits to and has suffered these indignities—how can he ever stir up the people, or set himself up for a king? Now cease to persecute him! Your malice surely ought to be satisfied" (Alford 1859). "Would they let the scourging and mockery suffice after all?" (Geikie 1879).[35]

The Scream for Crucifixion, 19:6-7

There are three movements:

1. Their clamorous scream: What a strange "Therefore" again! Sin never stumbles upon logic! "Assistants" of the Sanhedrin, not of Pilate. "Crucify! Crucify." In their frenzy of madness, they needed no object. "Him"—after their cruel outcry. The hatred of the Sanhedrin could not be reduced. "They had sworn to compass his death, and they were determined to make it as painful and ignominious as possible" (Hovey 1885).

2. Pilate's answer: His answer is desperate, and John used the historical present for tragic vividness. Even the King James saw this ("saith"—retained by ASV but not by the NASB).
    "Take him, I mean, You." Same as John 18:31, which see "and crucify." "For" expressing a reason—but what reason? Why taunt a mad group of politicians? If he meant "to their peril," he knew not the depths of their chicanery. Anyway, Pilate's refusal "led them to bring forth a new charge against the Savior" (Hovey 1885).

3. Their wily answer (John 19:7): "We a law have, and according to this law he ought to die because God's Son himself he made." The "we" is empathic, but their seeing Pilate's vacillations gave them a ray of hope of winning Jesus' death. "This"— deictic force of the article to refer to the same "law"—"that" (ASV and NASB) and "our" (KJV).

They likely had Leviticus 24:16 in mind. Although "Son of God" is without the article, the entire proceedings show that "they used the expression to signify a special divine Sonship, based upon a special union of Christ with God" (Hovey 1885). If Jesus had not claimed such

---

35. Editor's Note: John Cunningham Geikie was a Scottish-born minister who wrote extensively upon biblical themes. There no specific citation is given for this quote; however, see the bibliography for the likely source.

uniqueness, He could have been released by explaining that He had been misunderstood. Recantation lured Him not at all since He came to drink the bitter cup.

Pilate and Jesus Again, 19:8-11

Fear drove Pilate to seek more evidence. Had not the dream of his wife troubled him (Matthew 27:19)? Had not the claim of Jesus to deity made Pilate more fearful? That Pilate's fear "was not a fear of the Jews, nor of acting unjustly, but of the person of Jesus, is evident from what follows" (Alford 1859).

"From what source are you; I mean you?" Pilate meant more than mere place. Jesus had already answered Pilate's question. Hovey (1885) suggests several reasons for Jesus' silence but does not touch the real reason, as I see it. For the moment, temperamental and harassed Pilate regarded Jesus' silence as disrespectful.

"To me, you are not speaking, are you?" The pronoun *me* is put first to indicate Pilate's wounded grandeur of office. He boasted of his civil authority or legal authority.

The answer of Jesus showed calmness, not dread like what distressed Pilate. "You were not having"—imperfect to stress not one instance but the continuous possession of civil right. "Civil right against me at all"—every phase of civil right, including the mentioned option. Jesus stressed for Pilate that he boasted too much and regarded his responsibility too little. "Unless it had been given to you"—periphrastic pluperfect. The participle is neuter and more general than the feminine, agreeing with the Greek *exousia.* "From above"—in "precise answer" to Pilate's "whence" (19:10). Equivalent to "out of God" or "out of My Father," "but this Pilate would not have understood" (Schaff, in Lange's *Commentary*, 1870).

"Therefore" (KJV, ASV)—on this account, for this reason. "He who betrays me to you"—Caiaphas representing the Sanhedrin. (See John 6:71 and 13:21 for this sense of "delivered.") "The greater sin has"—Caiaphas than Pilate. There are degrees of sin and degrees of punishment of sin. Jesus' calm word to Pilate in no wise excused him.

Pilate's Yielding to the Mad Clamor, 19:12-16a

Rapidly does John turn from the actions of Pilate to the Jews in these fatal minutes.

"Upon this" (see also John 6:66)—the same construction, both casual and temporal (Dods 1908)—the reason or occasion for Pilate's conduct and the influence of Jesus' remarks upon Pilate (Hovey 1885). "Thenceforth" weakly limits the idea to time. "Was seeking"—the persistent efforts of Pilate to release Jesus. The efforts are not narrated, but John stressed the continuing struggle of the puppet Pilate.

"If this fellow you release"—a contemptuous and emphatic (by position) taunt at Jesus. "Not a friend of Caesar." The Sanhedrin would report the slimy story to Caesar in such a way as to cause Pilate to lose his job. Sadly, the Jews had played their winning card. Sadly, it became with the wobbly politician a question of his job or Jesus. He shook with indecision, with urges to do what he knew was right, but yielded to the lures of popularity, to the lures of a job. To hand in such indecision is dangerous. To choose against Jesus is fatal. Your job or Jesus, which is it?

"Therefore" (19:13)—because he could not resist the threat of the Sanhedrin, he "led outside Jesus" or had his soldiers do it—outside the praetorium. "Every word for Pilate was an arrow" (Hengstenberg 1865).

"Sat down on"—for the official farce. *Bema* was used during the time of Homer (variously dated from the 12th to the 8th century BC) and later—from *bao* or *baino*, "to go," "to make a step"—hence a raised place mounted by steps (a platform, tribune: the raised platform outside the palace).

It bore two names. "The mention of these names is in harmony with the general minuteness and accuracy of the narrative proving that it must have been written by an eye-witness of the events recorded" (Hovey 1885). "Pavement" is a Greek compound: *lithostroton—lithos +* stone—and the verbal adjective *strotos*, from *stronnumi*, "to spread"—hence a mosaic or tessellated pavement, spread with stones. A late word but found in 2 Chronicles 7:3, Josephus, Epictetus, Suetonius, Pliny, and the papyri. *Gabbatha*, Hebrew or Aramaic, for a raised place—an elevation; likely, from "height." "The tribunal was raised as a symbol of authority and in order that the judge might see and be seen" (Dods 1908).

The time is doubly marked. "The preparation of the Passover"—Friday, or the preparation day belonging to the Passover. "About the sixth hour"—if Hebrew time, such would cause conflict between John and the Synoptic Gospels. "Why should John give Jewish time writing at the close of the first century when Jerusalem and the Jewish state passed away in AD 70? He is writing for Greek and Roman readers. The time would be something after 6 a.m. The actual crucifixion got under way about 9 a.m. (15:25, the third hour of Jewish time).

"Behold, your king." As John 1:29 and 19:5, not an imperative but an exclamation. In sarcasm toward the Jews, Pilate called Jesus the king of the Jews. "Then therefore"—as John 19:1. "Delivered"—the same word for the Sanhedrin's handing Jesus over to Pilate (18:30, 35). "To be crucified"—the clear purpose. (See also Matthew 27:24ff for Pilate's hypocritical act.)

Lessons to emphasize:

1. They would not defile themselves ceremoniously or outwardly, but they had no scruples against laying their slimy hands upon the spotless Son of God (18:28).

2. The Kingdom of Truth (18:36-38): The kingdom of Jesus is a spiritual reign of grace in the heart. Truth, not error, leads men into the kingdom. When men are sincere and yet hold to error, that cannot lead them into the kingdom of Jesus.

3. Barabbas or Jesus? Barabbas was the John Dillinger or Hitler of that day. He was a cutthroat. What is your Barabbas? Is it sinful pleasure? A woman saw a beautiful flower on a rock at Niagara Falls. She attempted to get it. Though her friends warned her against trying, she made her way over one rock after another and through the shallow water until she clasped the flower in her hand. She slipped in returning and went over the falls. What is your Barabbas?

4. "Behold, the man!" (19:5). "Behold, your king!" (19:14). Look until you learn What and Who He is and until you learn Him as your Savior. Jesus alone can save. Behold, the Lamb of God!

8.4 Jesus On The Cross, 19:17-30

(17) And he bearing his cross went forth into a place called the place of a skull, which is called in the Hebrew Golgotha: (18) Where they crucified him, and two other with him, on either side one, and Jesus in the midst. (19) And Pilate wrote a title, and put it on the cross. And the writing was Jesus Of Nazareth The King Of The Jews. (20) This title then read many of the Jews: for the place where Jesus was crucified was nigh to the city: and it was written in Hebrew, and Greek, and Latin. (21) Then said the chief priests of the Jews to Pilate, Write not, The King of the Jews; but that he said, I am King of the Jews. (22)

Pilate answered, What I have written I have written. (23) Then the soldiers, when they had crucified Jesus, took his garments, and made four parts, to every soldier a part; and also his coat: now the coat was without seam, woven from the top throughout. (24) They said therefore among themselves, Let us not rend it, but cast lots for it, whose it shall be: that the scripture might be fulfilled, which saith, They parted my raiment among them, and for my vesture they did cast lots. These things therefore the soldiers did. (25) Now there stood by the cross of Jesus his mother, and his mother's sister, Mary the wife of Cleophas, and Mary Magdalene. (26) When Jesus therefore saw his mother, and the disciple standing by, whom he loved, he saith unto his mother, Woman, behold thy son! (27) Then saith he to the disciple, Behold thy mother! And from that hour that disciple took her unto his own home. (28) After this, Jesus knowing that all things were now accomplished, that the scripture might be fulfilled, saith, I thirst. (29) Now there was set a vessel full of vinegar: and they filled a spunge with vinegar, and put it upon hyssop, and put it to his mouth. (30) When Jesus therefore had received the vinegar, he said, It is finished: and he bowed his head, and gave up the ghost. (John 19:17-30)

"Standing before that cross one can but tremble at sin and at love" (Morgan 1960). Oh, for that double feeling! There is no detailed description, no editorial note, no effort to color it with the writer's impressions, no effort to touch it up. They felt too deeply to add their own words. The words of Jesus and the facts themselves speak eloquently to believing hearts.

8.4.1 THE CRUCIFIXION ITSELF, 19:16B-22

The Place of Crucifixion, 19:16b-17

"Therefore"—in consequence of what had just transpired. "They therefore took Jesus"—in itself, the verb "does not point to any particular way of taking or receiving" (Hovey 1885). (See the same in "received" in 1:11.) The context shows that they took Jesus from Pilate into their own control. "They had cast Him from the Temple, the City, and the Nation" (Morgan 1960). The words, "and led him away," while not supported by the stronger textual witnesses, seem implied in "took" or "took along."

"And"—This word turns the eye to Jesus and away from His crucifiers. "Bearing for Himself the cross." The present participle *bearing* expresses the attendant circumstance. "For Himself" is the dative of the reflexive pronoun. Roman custom required that the victim carry his own cross. Because of the strain of the night and the anguish of His heart, Jesus fell under the burden, and Simon of Cyrene was conscripted to carry Jesus' cross the remainder of the way (Mark 15:21ff; Matthew 27:32ff; Luke 23:26).

"Went out"—or went forth from the palace of Pilate—"into the place which was customarily called Skull's Place" (19:7). Two reasons have been assigned for the name: its actual appearance or the many skulls of those crucified there. The former is more likely.

"In Hebrew"—We used to say that first-century Hebrew meant Aramaic. Since most of the approximately six hundred manuscripts of the Dead Sea Scrolls are in Hebrew, one hesitates today. Besides, "Golgotha," the Greek spelling, is not exactly Hebrew *Gulgoleth*, nor Aramaic *Gulgalta*. The word came from *galal*, "to roll"—hence from its round shape or resemblance to a skull (Judges 5:53; 2 Kings 9:35). The Greek *kranion*, through the Latin *cranium*, gives us our word *cranium*. The Latin *calvaria*, skull, gives us our word *Calvary*.

The Act of Crucifixion, 19:18

"Where Him they crucified and with Him." John stresses the One Who was crucified.

The method of crucifixion is quite clear. Either before putting the cross into its socket or thereafter, they stretched Jesus on the cross. Each hand was nailed. Then His feet were nailed together with one spike or more to the sides of the upright beam and with two spikes to prevent Him from wrenching Himself from the cross because of His intense sufferings. If the former method was used, when the cross was raised, it went into its socket with a thud and tore the hands and feet.

To crucify was to put on a cross—a causative verb built on the word *cross* (*stauros*). It comes from the root *sta*, "to stand," as in *histemi* and many words and as in the English "staff" (Skeat 1878). Hence *stauros* in Homer, Herodotus (Rawlinson 1859), Thucydides, and Xenophon means an upright stake, especially a pointed one.

At least two, therefore, concluded that Jesus was impaled because they stopped with etymology. To study a word, one notes three steps: etymology, general usage, and context. Haman in Esther was clearly impaled. (See Davies 1910 in *The Century Bible* and Paton 1907 in *A Critical and Exegetical Commentary on the Book of Esther*.) Davies demonstrates impaling for Haman.

Three reasons prove that Jesus was crucified, not impaled. One, the nail prints in His hands and feet. Two, the placard above Him on the cross (see below). Three, the historical and contextual use of the word *crucify*. Thayer (1977) rightly states the late meaning: "The well-known instrument of most cruel and ignominious punishment, borrowed by the Greeks and Romans from the Phoenicians; to it were affixed among the Romans, down to the time of Constantine the Great, the guiltiest criminals, particularly the basest slaves, robbers, the authors and abettors of insurrections, and occasionally in the provinces, at the arbitrary pleasure of the governors, upright and peaceable men also, even Roman citizens themselves." Moulton and Milligan (1915) cite an instance of this late meaning in Polybius (I. 86. 4) of the second century BC.

The shame of crucifixion was always present. (See Philippians 2:8.) Josephus called it "the most wretched of deaths" and Cicero "a most cruel and terrible penalty."

The following from Broadus (1886) on Matthew 16:24 is still significant:

> The Jews had long been familiar with the punishment of crucifixion, which was used in Egypt and all Western Asia, and from early time in Italy. More than a hundred years before our Lord's ministry, King Alexander Jannaeus crucified eight hundred rebels at Jerusalem, while he was feasting in public (Josephus, Antiquities: 13, 14, 2), and even under Antiochus Epiphanes, many Jews were crucified (Josephus 13, 5, 4). For a revolt which followed the death of Herod the Great, the Procounsul Varus crucified two thousand Jews. And yet a Jewish Rabbi of today has said that the saying here ascribed to Jesus is an anachronism, for the disciples could not have understood an allusion to cross-bearing till after his crucifixion.

"With him two other men, one on either side, and Jesus in between" (NASB). For John, it sufficed to say that Jesus was between these. He made no comment on their character. Luke called them evil-doers or "malefactors" (Luke 23:32); this would name them as especially evil. Mark 15:27 and Matthew 27:38 called them robbers. "Thief" in the KJV (1611), when the King James Version was translated, meant the underhand thief and the rapacious robber (see a large English dictionary for more information). (See the weaker and stronger Greek words together in John 10:1, the latter in Matthew and Mark.) Isaiah 53:12 declared that "He was numbered with the transgressors." They meant to classify Him as the worst of criminals.

"The whole of humanity was represented there: the sinless savior, the saved penitent, the condemned impenitent" (Plummer 1902). One died for sin, one to sin, and one in sin. What a world of difference between those on the three crosses. Here one has an epitome of the destinies of men!

The Title of Crucifixion, 19:18-22

There are four movements:

1. The writing of the title: Only John assigns the writing to Pilate. He either did it or had one write it; in any case it was under his direction. "Pilate himself, meaning to insult the Jews, ordered the precise terms of the inscription" (Dods 1908).

    "A title also"—in addition to other insults to the Jews. "The Bill, or placard, showing who the condemned person was, and why he was punished" (Plummer 1902). "The board was whitened with gypsum" (Dods).

    Only John used the technical Latin term *titulus*, Greek *titles*, or *title*, used of a bill or notice of sale in varied situations (see Vincent 1887; also Moulton and Milligan 1915). Luke has an "epigraph [inscription] of the accusation."

    "Put it upon the cross"—most likely "above the head of Jesus, on the upright shaft" (Hovey 1885). This would determine the type of cross used. Three types were most prominent: the X cross—in the shape of an X, a very painful instrument; the T cross—with the upright shaft not extending above the cross beam; and the traditional cross— with the upright shaft extending above the horizontal beam sufficiently for the title.

    "And it had been written"—The ASV has "and there was written," and the NASB has "And it was written"—take the pluperfect periphrastic to be the imperfect tense. The pluperfect seems to stress that it had previously been written by Pilate's planning. It was not an afterthought with him.

    John's Gospel "is the fullest of the four" (Robertson). "No one of them added anything to what was written; no one omitted any word of the accusation. Historians of perfect veracity are doing the same thing continually. To say that this or that was said, is not, ordinarily, to affirm that this or that is all that was said. If nothing is omitted which changes the meaning of what is repeated, there is often no reason for saying that anything is omitted. We regard, therefore, such differences as appear in the several copies of this title made by the Evangelists as entirely consistent with the doctrine of plenary inspiration" (Hovey 1885). "In the sense of the man Pilate, it meant: Jesus, the King of the Jewish fanatics, crucified in the midst of Jews, Who should all thus be executed; in the sense of the Jews: Jesus, the seditionary, the King of rebels; in the sense of the political judge: Jesus, for whose execution the Jews, with their ambiguous accusation, may answer; in the sense of the diving irony which ruled over the expression: Jesus, the Messiah, by the crucifixion became in very truth the King of the people of God" (Lange 1870).

2. The reading of the title: Only John has this item. The nearness of the place of crucifixion to the city made it easy for many Jews of the city and of those attending the Passover to read it.

   The sign was meant to be read by all who passed by. It had been written in the three most prominent languages that are broadly considered: Hebrew, especially for the Jews; Latin, the legal and official language; Greek, the popular language of the Greco-Roman world.

   Such gave it worldwide significance. How true was what Pilate had written! And how prophetic that inscription!

3. The objection to the title (19:21): Pilate wrote the title as declaring the kingship of "Jesus the Nazarene." The chief priests wanted it to be merely the claim of Jesus because they "were uneasy for fear that the joke in the mock title was on them instead of on Jesus. They were right in their fear" (Robertson). The imperfect *elegon* (they were saying) is about as our "they begged piteously."

4. The unchanged title: The conscience of Pilate was smarting under what he had done in giving Jesus over to be crucified, and he tenaciously and impatiently declined to change what he had written. "That which I have written I have written."

8.4.2 THE ONLOOKERS AT THE CRUCIFIXION, 19:23-27

The Soldiers, 19:23-24

Roman custom gave, as a perquisite or reward to the crucifying soldiers, the individual effects of the One crucified. His seamless robe or tunic excited their covetous desire.

This was commonplace gambling. Their one intent was gain. What shame! Their "brutal ignorance fulfilled ancient prophecy." They gambled for gain beneath the cross.

John saw a hand watching over this too: "in order that the scripture might be fulfilled." The Broadus (1886), ASV, and NIV translations, along with Westcott and Hort (1881) and Aland (1966)[36] rightly arrange the citation from Psalm 22:18 as a repetitive couplet of Hebrew poetry. Note the earliness of Broadus!

"On the one hand, therefore, the soldiers did these things, but. . ." The NIV and KJV weaken *oun* (therefore) to "so." John sees the providential hand of God over all "because they were predicted in Scripture, or, looking a little more deeply, because they were included in the purpose (of) God as made known in part by the Holy Scriptures" (Hovey 1885). The soldiers did not intend such, but John saw beyond the reckless soldiers.

The Woman, 19:25-26

"Men" (on the one hand) and *de* (but) vividly contrast the onlookers. "But there had been standing alongside the cross of Jesus His mother, etc." Emphatically John drew his contrast. The verb is pluperfect in form, but ordinarily in John's Gospel a pluperfect functions as an imperfect (Thayer 1977). Thus "were standing" could be preferred.

Were there three or four women? "Mary the wife of Clopas" may stand in apposition with "the sister of His mother." Since *kai* (and) does not stand between them, three seems quite likely. It is possible that they are named in two groups with the "and" tying each group together. I agree with Robertson that we cannot be sure. The KJV and the ASV did not supply the "and." The NIV cuts the Gordian knot by disregarding the problem and by omitting the earlier "and"!

"Jesus, therefore, because he saw His mother," etc. KJV and ASV make the participle temporal: *when*, etc. Mary is mentioned as the center of the women. The fiercest sword was then piercing her soul (Luke 2:35). How tender Jesus was amidst this cruelty! He stopped dying long enough to provide for her. "Woman, look, your son!" He was thus committing her to John's care.

Although there is no disrespect in the title "woman" (see John 2:4 also), this is against the Catholic worship of Mary. They call her "the mother of God." She mothered only His humanity; His deity was eternal.

---

36. Kurt Aland, Matthew Black, Bruce Metzger & Allen Wikrem, *The Greek New Testament* [also known as the *Nestle-Aland Novum Testamentum Graece*] (Stuttgart: United Bible Societies, 1966).

John, 19:27

John 19:26 had mentioned John's presence. Only John from the apostles is mentioned as courageous enough to take his stand with the women at the cross.

"The disciple . . . whom He was loving"—John could never forget the constancy (imperfect tense) of Jesus' love. The adverb *then* may simply mean "next" in an enumeration or may stress the nature of what is added. The vivid, historical present ("says") inclines me toward the latter meaning.

"Look, your mother!"—Note the tender care of Jesus. He so cared for John alone of the apostles. How Jesus trusted him! John acted immediately. John alone of the apostles had a home in Jerusalem.

Two words of tradition may be added. Joseph had died some years previously. John and Mary died and were buried at Ephesus.

8.4.3 Two Words from the Cross as He Faced Death, 19:28-30

Much else appears in the other Gospels. John concentrated his attention on two sayings not elsewhere mentioned.

The Thirst of Flesh, 19:28-29

"After this"—a logical sequence but not a temporal sequence as if nothing intervened. "Since Jesus has been knowing"—the perfect participle thus fits the historical present: *says.* Jesus remained to that moment fully conscious of the meaning of His atoning death (See also 13:1).

"That there may be made perfect the Scripture"—John saw Jesus as conscious of accomplishing the Scripture predictions. The two verbs *teleo* and *teleioo* come from the same root, the latter being causative. It may, therefore, stress a little more the causation or accomplishment, while the other marks the finished state. The two verbs are quite close from Herodotus onward, the shorter form going back to Homer's time.

"I am thirsting" (see Psalm 69:21-22)—With no food since the past evening, with the heat of that land, and with the blood lost in crucifixion, this was a cry of severe physical agony. He was being perfected as our Mediator (Hebrews 2:10; 5:7ff).

He had previously refused the drink which was drugged with myrrh (Mark 15:23) and gall (Matthew 27:34). The former would have been stupefying; this tended to revive Him.

The sponge would hold the vinegar. The "reed" of Matthew and Mark is called here a reed of the hyssop bush. Its stalks are not long (say about three feet) but would easily reach since the feet of the crucified were not far from the ground. (Our words *sponge* and *hyssop* are both Anglicized from the Greek.)

His Word of Victory, 19:30

"Therefore" seems to refer to the stimulant that He had just received.

"It is finished" or "It has been finished" both translate the Greek perfect. The latter stresses the past act and the present result. The former emphasizes only the present result. It means that "all was accomplished that would give such value to His death as should be available for the redemption of man" (Morgan 1960). Here we have what the Greeks sought, a sea of matter in a drop of language. It is only one word in the Greek.

Let us learn this lesson well. Salvation is not offered to us to do or perform. It is a gift; God does not come seeking that we give to Him but that we receive from Him. It is the height of blasphemy for us to add any of our puny works to His spotless and finished righteousness. Let us not attempt it. God has accepted His finished work; let us accept it. The more we see the perfection of His finished work, the least shall we think of trying to add ours. O spotless, perfect, eternal righteousness wrought out for me on the Cross!

(As to the Greek, see the same word in 19:28 and comments there. See 16:33, "I have overcome.") If He were to utter the word of victory, He had to utter it in anticipation for what would be completed fact, in every sense, very shortly.

As to separating two types of death, Jesus paid our penalty in full. One cannot separate physical death from the penalty of sin (Genesis 2:17; Ezekiel 18:4; Romans 6:23; Hebrews 9:27). It is not a question of spiritual suffering or physical suffering; His paying our sin debt includes both.

"And as He reclined His head, He gave up the spirit"—The bowing of His head was a forerunner of His last physical gasp. Note the phrase "He gave" and study 10:17-18 on the voluntariness of His death. The word *ghost* of the KJV in 1611 no longer means "spirit" in our English. The article *the* with "spirit" (*pneuma*) could well be translated, "His spirit"—ASV has "his spirit." NIV paraphrases "his life" but is better than current connotations of "ghost."

8.5 THE BURIAL OF JESUS, 19:31-42

(See also Matthew 27:57-61; Mark 15:42-47; Luke 23:50-60.)

The importance of His burial: Some claim that Jesus merely fainted, swooned, or became insensible for three days. If His death was not real, His atonement was not beneficial. If He was not really dead, His resurrection was mere make-believe. The unique sign or type of the three days of Jonah in the grave was fulfilled. Reasons for believing He was really dead: First, the soldiers saw He was dead. Second, the spear pierce proved no life whatsoever was left. Three, the grave cloths and the napkin would have tended to suffocate Him if any life remained. Together these factors are convincing.

In defining the gospel, Paul gave two events as essential and meritorious—His death and resurrection—and two as evidential— His burial and the appearances (1 Corinthians 15:3ff). Only those who would weaken the saving meaning of His death and resurrection have problems with the reality of His death and burial.

8.5.1 WHAT HIS ENEMIES DID, 19:31-37

(31) The Jews therefore, because it was the preparation, that the bodies should not remain upon the cross on the sabbath day, (for that sabbath day was an high day,) besought Pilate that their legs might be broken, and that they might be taken away. (32) Then came the soldiers, and brake the legs of the first, and of the other which was crucified with him. (33) But when they came to Jesus, and saw that he was dead already, they brake not his legs: (34) But one of the soldiers with a spear pierced his side, and forthwith came there out blood and water. (35) And he that saw it bare record, and his record is true: and he knoweth that he saith true, that ye might believe. (36) For these things were done, that the scripture should be fulfilled, A bone of him shall not be broken. (37) And again another scripture saith, They shall look on him whom they pierced. (John 19:31-37)

The Request of the Jews, 19:31

"The Jews"—likely the Sanhedrin. "Therefore"—in consequence of Jesus' death as just narrated.

"Since it was the preparation" (see 18:28)—The Romans often left unburied those who were crucified. This posed a problem for the Jews. Deuteronomy 21:22-23 forbade Israel to leave bodies overnight on a tree. How dead the conscience to be so meticulously scrupulous about a ceremonial regulation but so monstrously cruel as to crucify the Innocent One.

"Besought Pilate"—in recognition of their enslavement. "Might be broken"—from Homer's time down. In the New Testament only here and Matthew 12:20. As is common in later Greek, the augment is retained in both passages. A peculiar spelling but still Greek! A heavy mallet was used and would hasten death. "Legs"—from Homer's time down; "from the hip to the toes inclusive" (Thayer 1977). Only found here in the New Testament.

The Roughness of the Soldiers, 19:32-34

"Therefore"—in consequence of Pilate's order. The penitent robber was not spared the breaking of his legs; salvation does not free us from bodily pain.

"Men" (on the one hand, with "of the first"—not translated by KJV or ASV) and "but" (de) in 19:33, used correlatively, accent the contrast between the lingering life of the robbers and the death of Jesus.

"Already dead"—The adverb ede (already) and the perfect participle accent the quickness of Jesus' death. Tacitus and Cicero (Church & Brodribb 1872) state that dying on a cross in twenty hours was unusual and that surviving beyond thirty to thirty-six hours was unusually long. Jesus had lived only about six hours.[37]

John 19:34, "But"—the strong adversative. "One of the soldiers with a spear"—the piercing was a rough, hasty act of a careless soldier. It was needless. He had proof already. Probably it appeared to him as a capital joke. Some today so treat the Savior.

"Spear"—only here in the New Testament. Used first of the iron head or point of a spear (so Herodotus 1859; see citation in Vincent 1887). By extension, used as here of the spear itself—a lance or a spear.

"His side"—the pronoun of Him precedes to emphasize whose side. Again, the entire object precedes the verb for emphasis. Side (pleuran, from which our "pleurisy" comes) is an old word but in the New Testament found only here and in 20:20, 25, 27.

"Pierced"—aorist as if one stroke drove deep. The verb nusso occurs only here in the New Testament. The liberal contention that the word pierced means that the spear wounded only slightly the side of Jesus has been answered in many technical commentaries since Strauss put forth his quibble before 1850 (see Hovey 1885 and Vincent 1887).

---

37. Editor's Note: No citation is given for these statements from Tacitus and Cicero, but it is likely from John Albert Church and William Jackson Brodribb, *The Annals of Tacitus: Translated into English with Notes and Maps* (London: Macmillan and Co., 1872).

"And there came out immediately blood and water." Dr. William Stroud (1847) wrote a book in defense of the probable theory that a factor in Jesus' death was a broken or ruptured heart.[38] The load of sin was heavy enough to do it. The spear pierced the pericardium, the tough sac which surrounds the heart. This brought a coagulation of blood, which came out as blood and water. One great Greek scholar refused to enjoy the song about His dying of a broken heart. I tried to suggest that many factors caused His death and that this is a valid cause, among many.

The Testimony of John, 19:35

"He who has seen"—John's substantival perfect participle tells of what he saw at the cross and what was at this writing a living reality. Why is this not history? "Has borne witness"—throughout his ministry and in writing his Gospel. "And genuine is His witness"—Was John deceived? He was better qualified to know than any of the apostles since he stood closer to the cross than any of them. "And that one knows that a true thing is he saying"—He used both adjectives for "true": "genuine," not a pretense but reality, and "true," not a lie or misrepresentation as critics generally take John's Gospel to be.

This personal witness answered effectively the Gnostics who denied the reality of Jesus' humanity. Now, men deny His deity but with no more cogency.

The Fulfillment of Scripture, 19:36-37

"For"—assigning a reason. John saw the picture of the Messiah in the Old Testament and in Jesus' ministry and death as one and the same. Yes, John was theological but knew why he believed such. He rested on the Scriptures. That is, he was not a speculative theologian but a biblical one.

John applied Exodus 12:46 about the paschal lamb to Jesus. The verb *suntribo* means "to crush together." John saw the Passover lamb as prefiguring the Lamb of God pointed out to him by John the Baptist.

John 19:37—John went behind the LXX and translated the Hebrew of Zechariah 12:10 (Hovey 1885; Robertson; Dods 1908). "The same rendering is adopted in the Greek versions of Aquila, Theodotion, and Symmachus, and is also found in Ignatius," as well as Justin Martyr, and Barnabas (Dods 1908).

---

38. Editor's Note: Stroud's article from 1847 may have been referenced from Lange's (1870) *Commentary*.

John saw Zechariah 12:10 as describing the Messiah. The guilt of Israel in our Lord's death is implied. The pierced side speaks of the open fountain of cleansing (Zechariah 13:1). This is now true of the penitent who looks on Him by faith and will be true of the conversion of Israel when Jesus returns (Zechariah 12:10 and Revelation 1:7).

8.5.2 What His Friends Did; Or the Actual Burial of Jesus, 19:38-42

(38) And after this Joseph of Arimathaea, being a disciple of Jesus, but secretly for fear of the Jews, besought Pilate that he might take away the body of Jesus: and Pilate gave him leave. He came therefore, and took the body of Jesus. (39) And there came also Nicodemus, which at the first came to Jesus by night, and brought a mixture of myrrh and aloes, about an hundred pound weight. (40) Then took they the body of Jesus, and wound it in linen clothes with the spices, as the manner of the Jews is to bury. (41) Now in the place where he was crucified there was a garden; and in the garden a new sepulchre, wherein was never man yet laid. (42) There laid they Jesus therefore because of the Jews' preparation day; for the sepulchre was nigh at hand. (John 19:38-42)

Two secret disciples became tenderly courageous. The three movements center around each individually and then their teamwork of devotion to Jesus. The dead body of Jesus was magnetic; it called out two fearful disciples.

Joseph's Securing Jesus' Body, 19:38

"Moreover, after these things"—John thus keeps us aware of new developments. "Asked"—the verb comes early to emphasize it. Then Pilate is mentioned next as the one with civil authority. Then John identifies Joseph and characterizes his discipleship. "From Arimathea"—in Judea, but a more definite location is debatable (Adams 1938, 347-8).

"Because he was a disciple of Jesus but a secret one on account of fear toward the Jews"—the participle *being* could be "who was," merely descriptive, but the casual force gives the reason. Discipleship which does not result in something done for Jesus is a farce or emptiness. "A secret one" hews to the Greek more than "secretly." Dods (1908), too, has "a hidden one."

Joseph of Arimethea appears nowhere in the Bible except in the Gospels. Matthew 27:57 calls him "a rich man," which fulfills the Messiah's making his grave with the rich (Isaiah 53:9). Mark 15:43 calls him "an honorable counsellor"—"a councilor, not in the provincial town,

Arimathaea, which would have been mentioned, but in the grand council in Jerusalem" (see Bruce 1897, *Expositor's Greek Testament*). So, others hold Joseph as a member of the Sanhedrin. ASV translates "a councilor of honorable estate"; NASV and NIV paraphrase a bit: "a prominent member of the council." Luke 23:50 adds to "councilor" the adjectives "good and righteous."

Only John plays up "a secret one." His flaw was lack of courage. The obstacle was real; but the circumstance brought his true worth to the light. Some genuine believers are little known for a while. Recall the 7000 in Elijah's time. Although the apostles fled, Joseph honored the Messiah at great danger to himself. What one does in the pinch indexes his worth! Besser (1862) remarked that this rich Joseph ministered at the last as the poor Joseph at the first.

"And Pilate permitted"—Joseph's securing the body was in two steps: legal (gaining the right) and physical (the actual removal of the body, either by means of a ladder or by raising the cross out of its hole). John adds no color; the simple facts spoke for themselves: "he came, therefore, and took away His body."

Nicodemus' Bringing Embalming Spices, 19:39

"Moreover there came Nicodemus also." "Moreover"—continuative *de*; not adversative here. The word *also* knits together in lasting fame the souls of two famous Sanhedrists. "Thus Jesus, by being lifted up, is already drawing men unto Him. These Jewish aristocrats first confess Him in His hour of deepest degradation" (Plummer 1902).

"Who came to Him at night time at the first"—(See chapter 3.) Ah! The victor over the people (Nicodemus, the Greek name, so signifies) here became victor over himself! By his coming at night time (genitive case to define the kind of time), does John thus identify Nicodemus or thus contrast his boldness with a less bold attitude? I incline to see no opprobrium here and prefer the former; Dods (1908) and Vincent (1887) saw a contrast.

"Bringing" (ASV; NASV)—The KJV and NIV make it a main verb, "brought"—the NIV even making a new sentence. Translations should leave the ideas in the same correlation as in the original, insofar as the idioms of the two languages allow. John put first emphasis on the coming of Nicodemus: so should each translation. I want the ideas as they tumbled out of John's mind rather than the rearrangement of any translator.

The participle is best taken as attendant circumstance, though it may express purpose: bringing or bearing or carrying.

"A mixture"—*magma*, from *mignumi*, to mix, to mingle. Only here in the New Testament; used generally in Greek for a mixture (compound or confection) of medicines and of colors. The spelling "smigma" (see the Aland 1966 *Greek New Testament*) in some manuscripts follows a somewhat common custom in Greek of prefixing the spirant sigma before *m*; the prefixing of zeta in some papyri (see Moulton and Milligan 1915) is simply another dialectal variant. The *smegma*, a late reading in Aland, may be itacism or confusion of iota and eta.

Almost as strong an array of Greek New Testament manuscripts has *heligma*, a wrapping, from *helisso*, to roll. Largely because the Codex Vaticanus has this reading, Westcott and Hort (1881) favored this reading.

Both of these readings made good sense. No doctrine is at stake, and new discoveries may settle the matter. P66 (a Greek papyrus fragment) of 175-200 AD appears to favor *migma*.

The use of sweet-smelling spice in burial goes back a long time (Asa in 2 Chronicles 16:14). Three purposes are clear: one, the love of the provider of the expensive spices; two, to offset odors of decay or be an aromatic; and three, to slow the process of decay or be an antiseptic.

"Myrrh"—Myrrh was similarly used by the Egyptians (Rawlinson 1859).[39] Showing the official price, a Tebtunis papyrus of 111 BC says, "For the myrrh distributed in the villages, no one shall exact more than forty drachmae of silver for a minaweight." (See Moulton and Milligan 1915).[40]

The Greek dialects spelled "myrrh" in different ways: Aeolic, *murra*; Attic, *smurna*; Ionic, *smurne*; the city Smyrna has the name. The word is Semitic-Hebrew, *mor*; Arabic, *murr*; Phoenician, *morah*; Ugaritic, *mr* (see Gordon 1915);[41] Akkadian, *murru*. The Arabic and Hebrew clearly mean "bitter," connected with Hebrew *marah*, bitterness. It is the balsamic juice or resinous gum exuding from the bark of the Arabian myrtle. It is yellow to reddish brown in color. It was used for embalming, burnt as an incense, used for anointing, and a salve for ulcers.

"Aloe"—Greek, *aloe*: Hebrew, *ahalim* and *ahaloth*, in plural with singular meaning (Numbers 24:6; Psalm 45:9; Proverbs 7:17; Song of

---

39. *The History of Herodotus*, II, 83.
40. Editor's Note: Tebtunis was a city in ancient Egypt. No citation is given for this quote.
41. No. 1217, page 247.

Solomon 4:14). These last three using myrrh and aloes together; not in Gordon (1915); from Sanskrit *agaru, aguru*, akin to Hindi *aghil* and Tamil *akil*, with the liquid "r" softened to the liquid consonant "1." The name of a fragrant tree which grows in India and Conchinchina (modern Vietnam). The soft wood was used in fumigation and in embalming the dead. Here of the resin from the quick-drying, aromatic sap or juice. Through confusion later, it was identified as a bitter drug. (See the Oxford English Dictionary for more details.)

"About one hundred pounds"—*litra* (pound) of twelve ounces—hence about seventy-five pounds avoirdupois.[42] The NIV has "about seventy-five pounds." "The word *litra* seems to have been merely a Sicelo-Greek form of the Roman *libra*." (See also Freund on the Latin origin of *litra*.)

The large amount would serve at least three purposes: (1) the lavish and deep love of a rich man; (2) ample for spreading over the bandages with which He was wrapped; and (3) some may have been designed for the couch of the body in the tomb (see Dods 1908).

His Burial By the Two, 19:40-42

"Therefore"—in consequence of the two disciples, as related. "And bound it"—*deo*, to bind, to swathe, used of Lazarus too (11:44).

The body of Jesus was bound with linen binding strips to encase it with the mass of spices used (19:40). The word is plural here as in all the four other instances (Luke 24:12; John 20:5, 6, 7). Besides, the word is a diminutive, "a piece of linen, small linen cloth" (Thayer 1977). This word was used by Greek writers for ships' sails, bandages for wounds, and other articles made of linen; the regular word (*othone*, not the diminutive) is thus used twice in Acts (10:11; 12:5). Thus, in all five instances in the New Testament, the diminutive *othonion* describes the strips of linen cloth used for swathing the body of Jesus.

Webster clearly discriminates between "cloths" and "clothes." This was not true when the KJV was made in 1611. An extra "e" often appeared then, which is redundant, obsolete, or incorrect today, the case differing according to the word involved. In any case, the Greek shows no ambiguity. The ASV and RSV "linen cloths" and the KJV "linen clothes" point up the change suffered by English in three centuries and less. The ASV change of KJV "clothes" to "garments" (*himation*) is in point (Mark 5:28). NIV translates, "in strips of linen"; NASB translates, "in linen wrappings."

---

42. Editor's Note: Avoirdupois is a system of weights used in English-speaking countries based on a pound consisting of sixteen ounces.

One is forced to the conclusion, therefore, that the Turin Shroud cannot be genuine. Catholics (some, at least; a priest from Tampa made a trip to Italy while I lived in Tampa and wrote a book on the matter) claim that this is a genuine relic from the body of Jesus. It is claimed that the stains have the contour of a body. Note these indisputable counts against the Turin Shroud: first, its possession can be traced no further back than the Middle Ages; second, popes have decreed differently about it; third, it utterly fails to meet the specifications of the Scriptures already elucidated, especially several pieces with no mention whatsoever of a "robe." Lloyd C. Douglas' historical novel *The Robe*, written in 1942, is built on wholly unsupported tradition. Besides, the pattern or style of the Turin Shroud is medieval or even Italian, not Greco-Roman or Hebrew.

Besides, the term used by the Synoptic Gospels is instructive. Matthew 27:59—wrapped "in a clean linen cloth," *en* (in) with the locative case; Mark 15:46—"with the linen cloth" (instrumental case) that had been bought for the purpose (ASV: "in the linen cloth"); Luke 23:53—"with a linen cloth" with no mention of buying; "in a linen cloth" (ASV). The tomb of King Tut had faded and tattered pieces of linen but pieces also as beautiful as one would buy in the store today.

In these three instances, the word is *sindon*. Andrews-Freund[43] marks the Latin *sindon* as from the Greek, "a kind of fine cotton stuff, muslin."

The word is very likely Semitic. The Hebrew *sadin*, from the verb *sadan*, to loosen, to hang as a loose garment; so Gesenius, but Crawford H. Toy in the *International Critical Commentary* (1899) doubted this. Arabic, *sidn*, and Akkadian, *sudinnu*; the Syriac *sudna* "appears to be a loan-word from the Greek" Toy argued that the Greek *sindon* seems to be derived from the Semitic word and correlates "linen cloth." (See Toy 1899 on Proverbs 31:24. See also Hebrews 9:42 with *sindon*, Mark 14:51-52, and Herodotus in Rawlinson 1859.)

Sindon stands in the LXX (Greek Old Testament) of Judges 14:12-13, Proverbs 31:24, and Isaiah 3:23. Only Toy (1899) discusses the etymology in *The International Critical Commentary*; Moore (1966) on Judges and Gray (1912) on Isaiah do not. Gill (1810) cited medieval comments of reference to linen but nothing on the derivation. The Egyptian *schentic* likely interchanged "t" and "d." Toy objected to correlation of the root with the Sanskrit *sindhu* because the earlier Greek form was *indos*, not *sindos*. Knowing the tendency to prefix the spirant sigma, I doubt Toy's objection.

---

43. Editor's Note: This refers to Lewis, Short, Andrews, and Freund's, *A Latin Dictionary Founded on Andrews' Edition of Freund's Latin Dictionary*. Revised and Enlarged Edition (Oxford: Oxford University Press, 1956).

In the writings of Roman historian Herodotus (c. 484–c. 425 BC), this word designates especially a mummy cloth or a surgeon's bandages. I cite three instances from George Rawlinson's (1859) translation.[44] Herodotus 2:86 speaks of embalming "with bandages of fine linen cloth." Herodotus 7:181 speaks, "dressed his wounds with myrrh, and bound them up with bandages of cotton." Herodotus 2:95 refers to a statement against gnats, of a man's rolling himself "in his dress or in a piece of muslin."

A translation as "linen cloth" varies too much in using "linen clothes" and "linens." Confraternity is better with "linen cloth." These men knew their Greek too well to favor the Catholic tradition about a robe.

"With the spices," including both the myrrh and aloes. *Aroma*, a late word, spices or perfumes, is general enough for the perfumes brought by the women (Mark 16:1; Luke 24:1).

John speaks of the burial-manner of the Jews. This may have been consciously to contrast it with the Egyptian or the Roman method. The Roman custom was to burn the bodies. Had this method been followed, the proof of a bodily resurrection would have been weakened. The Egyptian method, according to Herodotus (Rawlinson 1859),[45] drew out the brains through the nostrils by means of a crooked piece of iron; then the cavity was rinsed with drugs. The abdomen, upon being emptied, was washed with palm wine and cleansed with aromatics; then the cavity was filled with various spices and the body placed in subcarbonate of soda for seventy days. Thereafter, the body was washed and wrapped around with bandages of fine linen, smeared over with gum. Tacitus says of the Jews, "The bodies of the deceased they choose rather to bury than burn, following in this the Egyptian custom; with whom also they agree in their attention to the dead" (Church & Brodribb 1872).[46]

"To bury"—*entaphiazo,* the compound from *entaphia,* which in turn is from *en* and *taphos* (of which the verb *thapto* is a strengthened form). Thayer (1977), Vincent (1887), and Robertson rightly insist that it means "to prepare for burial." Arndt and Gingrich hesitate between this meaning and the KJV, "to bury."

Thus, three processes are to be observed in the preparation of Jesus' body for burial. One, the *sindon,* the linen cloth which was the

---

44. Editor's Note: George Rawlinson's (1859) translation of *The History of Herodotus,* (440 BCE).

45. *The History of Herodotus,* ii, 86.

46. History, v. 5.

main part of the burial bandages, lying underneath the body. Two, the spices which were spread under the body. When one application of spices had been made, the body was rolled or turned and thus until the entire seventy-five pounds were used. Three, to secure these in place, the strips of linen were applied.

John 19:41—"A garden"—*kepos*, from Homer's time down; only here and 18:1, 26, and Luke 13:19. The root is *kepouros*, a garden keeper, 20:15. Note other garden experiences. Proof of His poverty: manger for birth, no stone for His head, a cross for death, a borrowed tomb for burial. What condescension? What love? Yet He never complained that His lot was hard. Let us be like Him. Do the tests for Jesus bring us out on His side like it did Nicodemus and Joseph? Do we love Him enough to stand up for Him even when it costs?

"A new tomb"—hewn from limestone, common in that area; hence, there was no secret passage through which He might be stolen. "New or unused"—hence, no possibility of one's saying that another than Jesus had been raised. John's habit of expressing a matter both negatively and positively comes out: "in which at no time whatsoever any one had been placed" (pluperfect periphrastic). "Therefore" in 19:42 seems to refer to the unused quality of the sepulcher.

"Tomb"—*mnemeion*, in general: any visible object for preserving or recalling the memory of any person or thing—hence, a memorial or monument. Specifically, to give the loving purpose of a tomb or sepulcher; it is a memorial. The word comes from the *mrnea*, from the verb *mnaomai*, to remember. The meaning is more beautiful than the Hebrew noun for "tomb" whose verbal origin means "to heap up"— hence to heap up stones.

Some pointers on the location of the garden are clear: (1) outside the city; (2) near a road as the cross was; and (3) within a garden. Many feel that the Garden Tomb is far more likely than "the Holy Sepulcher" in the present city. This preference is bound up with the place of the trial, the identification of the walls of Jerusalem, the location of Golgotha, and the entire Catholic tradition respecting the Church of the Holy Sepulcher (see Adams 1938, *Biblical Backgrounds*, 370-375, 390-399).

8.6 QUESTIONS ON JOHN 18–19

8.6.1 JOHN 18:1-27

Fix in mind the physical picture of the garden of Gethsemane:

1. What likely spells out that the present olive trees do not date to the first century?
2. Why does John add "Judas also"?
3. Discriminate "torches" and "lamps."
4. Why at full moon did the police band bring lights and weapons?
5. What made the men fall backwards?
6. Why did Jesus call Calvary a cup?
7. What were the two phases of Jesus' trial?
8. What were the stages under each phase?
9. Discuss the form of the questions asked Peter respecting his denials.

8.6.2 JOHN 18:28–19:42

1. What are the three phases of the trial before Pilate?
2. What was the praetorium?
3. Name two civil violations of the Sanhedrin.
4. What kind of kingdom did Jesus claim?
5. How did Jesus explain His incarnation?
6. What was Pilate's verdict about Jesus?
7. Why was Jesus scourged?
8. What trick of the Sanhedrin persuaded Pilate finally?
9. How did the place of Jesus' crucifixion get its name?
10. How would you prove that Jesus was crucified, not impaled?
11. Explain the word *thief*.
12. Name the three more common types of crosses.
13. How does one determine which of the three was the type of Jesus' cross?

14. Why did Jesus refuse one drink and accept another?

15. In what sense was the perfect, "it has been finished," used?

16. Why was the burial of Jesus important?

17. Was Jesus buried in a robe or shroud?

18. Why such a large amount of spices for preparing Jesus for burial?

19. What are the three processes in the preparation of His body for burial?

20. Why was a "new" tomb significant?

21. What is the meaning of the Greek word for "tomb"?

22. What indications do the Gospels give as to the location of our Lord's tomb?

8.7 Sermon Suggestions

8.7.1 John 18:1-27

- Grace in Three Gardens, or Three Gardens in the Bible
- Jesus' Surrender of Himself
- His Majesty at Arrest
- His Mercy Overreaching Our Wild Acts
- A Dilemma: Sheath, or Perish by the Sword
- My Master's Cup
- Warming by Satan's Fire
- The Kingdom of Jesus
- The Kingdom of Truth

8.7.2 John 18:28–19:42

Work up more sermons on the Cross. Your best can merely touch the edge of its grandeurs.

- Christ Speaks from Calvary (on His seven utterances from the cross)
- Man Speaks toward Calvary (I gave two radio series of six each, as the Centurion, etc.)
- The Doings of God at Calvary
- As the Rent Veil
- Firstfruits of Christ's Resurrection
- Darkness Enshrouded the Cross
- Persons Around the Cross (the Sanhedrin and the two high priests, Pilate, Barabbas, etc.)
- The Nature of Christ's Kingdom
- The Kingdom of Truth
- My Part in Christ's Crucifixion
- The Story of His Crucifixion (for children and others)
- The Doings of Men at the Cross
- The Burial of Jesus (correlate His burial with both the Cross and the Resurrection)

9: His Work as King in Resurrection, Chapters 20-21

9.1 The Empty Tomb and the Living Lord, 20:1-18

(1) The first day of the week cometh Mary Magdalene early, when it was yet dark, unto the sepulchre, and seeth the stone taken away from the sepulchre. (2) Then she runneth, and cometh to Simon Peter, and to the other disciple, whom Jesus loved, and saith unto them, They have taken away the Lord out of the sepulchre, and we know not where they have laid him. (3) Peter therefore went forth, and that other disciple, and came to the sepulchre. (4) So they ran both together: and the other disciple did outrun Peter, and came first to the sepulchre. (5) And he stooping down, and looking in, saw the linen clothes lying; yet went he not in. (6) Then cometh Simon Peter following him, and went into the sepulchre, and seeth the linen clothes lie, (7) And the napkin, that was about his head, not lying with the linen clothes, but wrapped together in a place by itself. (8) Then went in also that other disciple, which came first to the sepulchre, and he saw, and believed. (9) For as yet they knew not the scripture, that he must rise again from the dead. (10) Then the disciples went away again unto their own home. (11) But Mary stood without at the sepulchre weeping: and as she wept, she stooped down, and looked into the sepulchre, (12) And seeth two angels in white sitting, the one at the head, and the other at the feet, where the body of Jesus had lain. (13) And they say unto her, Woman, why weepest thou? She saith unto them, Because they have taken away my Lord, and I know not where they have laid him. (14) And when she had thus said, she turned herself back, and saw Jesus standing, and knew not that it was Jesus. (15) Jesus saith unto her, Woman, why weepest thou? whom seekest thou? She, supposing him to be the gardener, saith unto him, Sir, if thou have borne him hence, tell me where thou hast laid him, and I will take him away. (16) Jesus saith unto her, Mary. She turned herself, and saith unto him, Rabboni; which is to say, Master. (17) Jesus saith unto her, Touch me not; for I am not yet ascended to my Father: but go to my brethren, and say unto them, I ascend unto my Father, and your Father; and to my God, and your God. (18) Mary Magdalene came and told the disciples that she had seen the Lord, and that he had spoken these things unto her. (John 20:1-18)

9.1.1 THE EMPTY TOMB, 20:1-10

A dark morning and a lost Master are turned into the glorious light of the Risen Christ. What is it worth to know that the tomb was emptied if we do not know that He lived and still lives? Assuredly none.

The story centers around three disciples: Mary Magdalene, Peter, and John. Of course, Jesus is the center of their thoughts and must be of ours. Each one is mentioned as running. The story reads as pretense or that of an eye-witness. The good qualities of the writer argue against insincerity. Oh, the mingled sadness and darkness, surprise and excitement, light and joy of the first Sunday, the first Lord's Day. The words of Mary show how keenly they felt the loss (20:13). Their darkness is the sign of what Christianity would be without the Risen Christ: hopes disappointed, love bereft, and faith vanquished.

Mary's Finding the Stone Rolled Away, 20:1-2

The time (20:1): The time is doubly named—the day of the week and the time of the day. Moreover: continuative, after the burial of Jesus. John would urge us onward beyond the Cross to its sequel.

"On the first day"—locative of time when, a common extension from place to time, even with the preposition *en* (in), as in 1:1. "Day," as the most prominent division of the week, is easily supplied. As in Mark 16:2 and Luke 24:1, the cardinal numeral "one" is used for the ordinal numeral "first." Both Moulton (1908, 95ff) and Robertson (1934, 671ff) show this idiom in both the papyri and Modern Greek. It is more than a Hebraism.

"Of the week"—literally, "of the sabbaths." Add Acts 20:7 to the three instances on "first." (See the singular in Luke 18:12 and Mark 16:9.) The genitive of definition explains "first"—the first moving from the sabbath as the climax, the first after the sabbath. "The first day" holds this rank if a series is meant or one is considered. The Hebrew "shabbath" means rest and has cognates in Arabic, Aramaic, and Akkadian (*shabatu*, "probably cease, be completed," Brown-Driver-Briggs 1939, not in Gordon 1915).

"Is coming"—vivid historical present.

"Early while it was yet dark"—genitive absolute with two adverbs. Some have seen a contradiction with Mark 16:2, "when the sun was risen" or "after the sun arose." Several factors must be weighed. One, Mark's full statement is, "very early ... when the sun was risen." Obviously, Mark did not contradict himself and easily refers to the first appearance of the sun. Two, note the historical present: "is coming" (John) and "are coming" (Mark). Three, the distance from Bethany around the southern tip of the Mount of Olives (the frequented way) to Calvary would be about two miles. The change in the light along such a distance removes all possibility of a contradiction.

"Mary Magdalene"—Mary of Magdala, a place on the northwest shore of the Sea of Galilee; a few miles south of Capernaum or about three miles north of Tiberias; in the tribe of Naphtali (Joshua 19:38); in Jerusalem Talmud, *Magdal* or *Migdal*; today, Mejdel; the variant spelling "Magadan" rests on the interchange of the liquids "l" and "n"—meaning "tower" (a fortified city, Joshua 19:35, 38).

The evidence: "The stone taken away out of the tomb." John's general word merely asserts the fact of removal. Matthew (28:2) used a specific word, "to roll away"; Mark (16:4) used the same verb with another preposition, "to roll back." Therefore, it was a rolling stone. "Out of" or out of its place in front of the opening of the tomb. "Taken away" is a perfect participle describing the completed state of the stone as removed from obstructing Mary. The watching soldiers, after having been struck as if dead, had fled (Matthew 28:4). What convincing facts these are! Robertson (on Matthew 28:2) phrases McNeile (1929) thus: "the stone was rolled away not to let the Lord out, but to let the women in to prove the fact of the empty tomb."

The wavering testimony: Not at all did Mary expect His resurrection. Therefore, she did not stand still with no opinion. Her eagerness is shown by two historical presents: "she is running" and "is coming." She wished to share with Simon Peter and John (see his self-description in 19:26). John used the stronger and more volitional word *agapao* in 19:26 but the more emotional, more humanly warm word *phileo* here. They may be interchanged, but their overtone of meaning richly differs. Both are strong in the facet of love, which is stressed.

She thinks of men as removing Jesus' body. "We know not"—the plural may reflect the other women. If we do not have a risen Savior, this sad testimony must still be ours. If we do not know where He is, such futility still overcomes us! What a wrong conclusion she made!

John and Peter's Finding the Grave Cloths Lying, 20:3-7

"Therefore"—her statement moved John and Peter to investigate. "There went out therefore Peter"—the aorist speaks of the event of departure. "And the other disciple [went out]"—a case of ellipsis of the verb. "And they were going on their part toward the tomb." The imperfect gives a time exposure of their dramatic going.

John 20:4: "And they were running, the two together" in their eager race. "And [yet] the other disciple ran ahead more swiftly than Peter." Aorist of *protrecho*, from Xenophon on down it means to run ahead, to outrun; only here and Luke 19:4 in the New Testament; *dramo*, to run, not in the New Testament but second aorist of *treche*; see the simple verb in the first of the verse. "More swiftly"—comparative degree of adverb. "Than Peter"—ablative of comparison. First: or, as the first one; adjective, not adverb *proton*. Superlative used where only two were involved. "To the tomb"—*eis* or *pros*, translated as "to," not here "into" since John did not yet enter the tomb.

John 20:5: "And as he stooped down, he sees." In 20:11, *parakupto* means simply peeping or glancing into the tomb. The LXX and a second century Oxyrhynchus papyrus (see Moulton and Milligan 1915) thus used the word. That is, the purpose of the stooping was so obvious that the meaning was transferred from the act of stooping to its purpose, to take a peek or glance. Some think the same meaning appropriate here. In any case, the dramatic historical present "sees" puts the emphasis here.[47]

"He sees lying the linen cloths"—The emphasis is on the predicative accusative or actual perception participle more than on the grave cloths. On "grave cloths" or "linen cloths." John saw the fact, but his cautious and/or timid nature made him pause.

John 20:6: "Therefore"—in consequence of Peter's running. "Also"—in addition to John. "Following him"—already implied but spelled out by John; participle of attendant circumstance or identical with "comes." "And sees"—Although Peter impulsively entered, he "sees" a bit differently. John gave the linen cloths "a mere glance" (*blepo*) but Peter a "careful notice" (*theoreo*; so Robertson).

John 20:7: "And the napkin"—Peter saw more. The Greek word for napkin occurs four times in the NT and is a loan-word from the Latin *sudarium*, from *sudor*, "sweat." It was naturalized in Aramaic also, hence a sweat cloth, a handkerchief. Two New Testament instances refer to a cloth for wiping the perspiration from the face and for cleaning the nose (Luke 19:20; Acts 19:12). It is used twice by John for a cloth swathing the head of a corpse (John 11:44; 20:7). (See papyrus instances in Moulton and Milligan 1915, 581.)

"Not with the linen cloths but apart rolled up into one place"—Not a scene of robber's violence. Not a scene of theft at all. If the body had been removed, the grave cloths also would have been taken. Not a

---

47. Editor's Note: Oxyrhynchus was a city in Egypt where archaeologically significant written records were found.

scene of haste but one so left in an orderly fashion as to accent a lesson. A scene strangely undisturbed. "Rolled up" is singular and refers to no more than the napkins about the head. The apartness was as if clearly intended. What small details God used to convince all of the resurrection of Christ!

John's Finding Meaning in the Situation, 20:8-10

"Then therefore"—*tote* for time and *oun* for consequence. "Also"—noting the "unconscious influence" of Peter upon John. Peter's zeal, fervor, and boldness urged John to enter. Perhaps, but for Peter's impulsiveness, John would not have gone in to have perceived the evidences. Different temperaments can bless each other.

"And he saw and believed"—Despite Peter's very close scrutiny, he saw facts but without their deep meaning. John saw to the bottom of the situation: Jesus had risen and left behind these cloths as evidence. "Peter saw more after he entered than John did in his first glance, but John saw into the meaning of it all better than Peter. Peter had more sight, John more insight" (Robertson).

John 20:9: John was thus the first believer in the bodily resurrection of Jesus. John perceived that the little circumstances, those casual features in the story, clinch the truth of the resurrection story beyond any possibility of dispute. With confident faith and deep humility, John wished others to follow his example of faith.

The sad story of unbelief has to be told. "For"—explanatory use of *gar*. He had called himself the first one to believe. Now, he offered the proof. "Not yet had they known"—pluperfect tense. Knowing in the sense of perception or recognition. "The Scripture"—as Psalm 16:10. "Jesus had repeatedly foretold his resurrection, but that was all forgotten in the great sorrow on their hearts" (Robertson). Even though with stealth, the chief priests and Pharisees exceeded the apostles (Matthew 27:63).

"That He must"—death could not hold Him. Wherein the necessity? The Scripture could not be broken. Jesus' Word as the always dependable prophet could not prove to be an impostor. Once the sin debt was paid, the Father's covenant mercies demanded that Jesus rise again. "From among (the) dead ones" or dead bodies. Jesus' resurrection was physical or mockery. This prepositional phrase demands such.

John 20:10 is transitional. "Therefore" looks back, but *de* (but) in 20:11 stands in contrast with "the disciples" They went away without seeing the Risen Lord. Luke (24:12) described Peter as still "wondering" or "marveling." Peter saw strangeness and wonder but just could not yet see through the maze. At Pentecost he had put two and two together to make four.

9.1.2 The Living Lord, 20:11-18

There are three movements in which Mary Magdalene is prominent. From where she had met Peter and John, she obviously returned to the tomb more slowly than they. Anyway, after they left, she tarried, and what a blessing for tarrying.

Mary and the Angels, 20:11-13

John left us three glimpses of her: weeping, seeing the angels, and talking with them.

Her weeping: She was standing or kept on standing. Pluperfect used as imperfect. Her stronger emotions and lingering nature disclosed to her what Peter and John did not get to see. "At the tomb"—*pros* (near) with the locative case; *para* (alongside of or by the side of) in 19:25; not very different but richly varied.

"Outside" is in contrast with Peter and John's entering the tomb. "Weeping"—attendant circumstance participle. (See in 11:31 and 35, for the outward weeping or wailing in the verb *klaio*; see Thayer 1977 under this word and Trench 1854.)

Her Seeing Two Angels, 20:11b-12

"While therefore she kept on weeping audibly"—"therefore" is a conclusion from the former sentence. Her weeping would obscure her peep (see above on 20:5) into the tomb. "And observes"—see 20:6 on *theoreo*. "Two angels"—heavenly messengers; "two" is the number of witness. Peter and John left too soon to observe the angels. "In white [garments]"—since *white* is a plural adjective, the word *garments* is implied. Luke 24:4 has "in dazzling apparel" (ASV). Mark 16:5 has a young man in "a white stole" or robe, "a loose outer garment for men which extended to the feet" (Thayer 1977; see English word *stole*). The whiteness is a symbol of purity, consecration, and heavenly origin. (See John elsewhere on angels, 1:51.) Note details of their posture of alertness, watchfulness, and helpfulness. "Where was lying"—verb emphatically before the subject; imperfect tense, but since the body was not there, the context gives the sense of "used to be lying" or even "had been lying."

Their Conversation, 20:13

"And they say to her, that is, these [angels]"—dramatic historical present with subject at the last. "Woman" (see also 19:26). "Why are you audibly weeping?" (See 20:11.) "She says"—same dramatic historical present. *Hoti* is equivalent to our quotation marks. "Men took away"—in the Greek idiom, the third person may be somewhat indefinite and equivalent to our "men" (see also 15:6). "My Lord"—my depth and personal attachment. She had not even a vague idea that He could be alive.

Mary and Her Lord, 20:14-17

Until one sees Jesus in the story, he almost wishes that the angels had given an explanation. They were but messengers until the Messenger could take over! What personal touches between Mary and her Lord!

Mary is unique in that she was the first actually to see the Risen Savior. John's uniqueness lies in his being the first one to believe that Jesus was actually alive. Each was unique in a different area.

Her Lack of Recognition, 20:14

"After she said these things, she turned herself back"—On the voice of the verb, see Robertson. Completely overwhelmed with sorrow, she turned away from the angels. Did she hear the footsteps of Jesus as He approached her? "Instinctively Mary felt the presence of someone behind her" (Robertson). "And observes or beholds"—see 20:12, "an observant look" (Hovey 1885), "not a merely casual glance." The tragedy of too many tears and too much turning inward in grief can obscure the presence of Jesus, blessedly near. "As the causes of non-recognition were entirely natural, so likewise were the means employed to secure recognition" (Hovey).

Her False Impression, 20:15

Beyond the question of the angels, Jesus added, "Whom are you seeking?" Her suffusion of sorrow failed to catch His question. If she had only said, "My Lord ..." "That One"—emphatic reference to Mary. "Since she is supposing that the gardener is he, she says"—causal use of the participle of *dokeo*, to be of opinion, to suppose, to think, which "refers to the subjective judgment, which may or may not conform to the fact" (Thayer 1977). Grief may, as here, warp the judgment so that we miss the grandest. "The" with gardener means the one in charge; proleptic. "Gardener" is a compound of *kepos* (see on 19:41), garden and *ouros*, keeper, watcher, from the same root as *horao*, to see; strictly, digamma and *or*; from Homer down; a garden-watcher; in the New Testament used only here. A gardener alone would be expected there this early. How preciously near He may be when we do not recognize Him!

"Sir"—the context tells whether a human Lord or the divine Lord. "If you"—emphatic pronoun; condition of first class. "Took"—aorist of definite act, from *bastago*, to take up with the hands (10:31), to take up in order to carry (19:17), to bear away or to pilfer (12:6), to bear away (here, and this meaning often in the papyri, see Moulton and Milligan 1915).

HIS REVEALING HIMSELF, 20:16

The way in which He pronounced her name was the needed cue. He gave it a familiar turn. He knows His own personally.

"In Hebrew"—Since "*Rabboni*" is given an Aramaic turn, "Hebrew" here may mean Aramaic. John translated "*Rabboni*" here and "*Rabbi*" in 1:38 by the same Greek word *didaskalos*, "teacher" (see also 3:2; 11:28; 13:13; the longer form is thought to have shown more respect). The root of the word is "great" and came to mean one with great respect as an instructor. Thayer (1977) translated it by "my"—therefore literally, "my teacher." Popular usage tends to wear away emphatic expressions, as often in the case of diminutives. A clear parallel is the word *Adonai*, my Lord, but common usage has worn it down to "Lord," simply. This longer form occurs in the New Testament only here and in Mark 10:51 (see Swete 1913). "This was used from the era of Gamaliel I in addressing the president of the Sanhedrin if he were a descendant of the great Hillel (50 BC to 10 AD)" (Miller 1952; see the article *rabboni*).

JESUS' WORDS OF CORRECTION AND COMMAND, 20:17

A few ancient Greek manuscripts add, "And she ran to touch Him." Such is implied in 20:17, but it would be difficult to explain the absence from the larger number of witnesses to the text. Absence makes 20:17 more crisp, more vibrant. Do we recognize Jesus when He calls us?

"Stop touching Me" or "Do not be touching Me"—In her emotional delight, she thought of Him mainly or altogether as a man, as a resuscitated man. Hers was not the highest style of faith. He wished to lift her to higher concepts of Himself. This is clear from the concrete reason which He named—*gar* (for) introduces the reason. "Jesus checks Mary's impulsive eagerness" (Robertson).

"Not yet have I ascended"—He does not refer to the going of His spirit at death (19:30) but to His ascension as triumphant, Risen Lord.

In Luke 24:39, His disciples were frightened and doubted His identity and reality as risen. Mary doubted this not at all, but Jesus saw that she needed a higher faith even then. The difference in the need that Jesus met explains the action that He invited and the action that He prohibited.

"To the Father"—He distinctly explained this phrase. "But be departing"—The general meaning of the verb is "to go" more than "to come." "To my brothers"—What a precious assurance of love for the apostles! He held a closer relation to His Father and His God than any believer does. This too accented the uniqueness of His personality and unique relation to God. He is the Only Begotten Son; we are adopted and regenerated children. Many have misconstrued Jesus' meaning because of their slowness at perceiving the force of concrete language.

Mary and the Disciples, 20:18

This is a grand sequel to all of the hesitancies and doubts of Mary. She obeyed His command.

"There comes Mary"—The historical present is emphatic but so is the order, putting the emphasis on her coming. "Magdalene"—see on 20:1; John thus identified her at the beginning and at the ending of her story.

"Announcing"—present participle of attendant circumstance. "I have seen"—the perfect tense. She saw, but her seeing had a living reality the moments she was announcing or telling the disciples. Tell me not of your former experience so much as tell me if it is as real now as ever. "The Lord"—she carried ever her new picture of the Risen Christ.

"And [that] these things He said to her"—Her report is not detailed. *Hoti* is recitative, and one must supply the ellipsis by "that" (as above) or by "how that" (so Robertson).

New Testament preachers made much of the resurrection of Jesus. Emphasis on His resurrection is too nearly a lost note in modern day preaching. I think that explains why they were more victorious than we. They lived day by day with a conscious inflow into their lives of the resurrection power of Jesus. His power is just as sufficient today as it was then. To tell the truth, we do not have much faith in the Risen Christ. He lives. Believe it, and let His power into your heart!

9.2 JESUS' APPEARANCE TO HIS DISCIPLES, 20:19-29

(19) Then the same day at evening, being the first day of the week, when the doors were shut where the disciples were assembled for fear of the Jews, came Jesus and stood in the midst, and saith unto them, Peace be unto you. (20) And when he had so said, he shewed unto them his hands and his side. Then were the disciples glad, when they saw the Lord. (21) Then said Jesus to them again, Peace be unto you: as my Father hath sent me, even so send I you. (22) And when he had said this, he breathed on them, and saith unto them, Receive ye the Holy Ghost: (23) Whose soever sins ye remit, they are remitted unto them; and whose soever sins ye retain, they are retained. (24) But Thomas, one of the twelve, called Didymus, was not with them when Jesus came. (25) The other disciples therefore said unto him, We have seen the Lord. But he said unto them, Except I shall see in his hands the print of the nails, and put my finger into the print of the nails, and thrust my hand into his side, I will not believe. (26) And after eight days again his disciples were within, and Thomas with them: then came Jesus, the doors being shut, and stood in the midst, and said, Peace be unto you. (27) Then saith he to Thomas, Reach hither thy finger, and behold my hands; and reach hither thy hand, and thrust it into my side: and be not faithless, but believing. (28) And Thomas answered and said unto him, My Lord and my God. (29) Jesus saith unto him, Thomas, because thou hast seen me, thou hast believed: blessed are they that have not seen, and yet have believed. (John 20:19-29)

The first Lord's Day was a busy one for Jesus. He appeared to His disciples five times: to Mary Magdalene, to the women, to Simon Peter, to two on the way to Emmaus, and to ten at the close of the day.

9.2.1 JESUS' APPEARANCE TO THE DISCIPLES WITHOUT THOMAS, 20:19-23

The Fear of the Disciples, 20:19a

(See also Luke 24:36-49.)

The time of His coming was one of fear toward the Jews. His disciples feared that the Jews might put them to death for efforts to carry on the work of Jesus which He left for them to continue. Two genitive absolutes occur before the main clause.

"When it was evening"—genitive absolute with no structural connection with anything in the main clause. "On that day"—locative of time. "The first [day] of the week." (See also 20:1.) Here John follows Roman time since "evening follows day instead of preceding it" (Robertson). "When the doors had been shut"—second genitive absolute—perfect participle to bring the time up to when Jesus came.

Jesus' Message of Peace, 20:19b-20a

"Took His stand"—aorist of His assuming His posture in their midst. "Says"—vivid historical present. "Peace [be] to you"—common oriental salutation (also 21, 26, and Luke 24:36) and more. He was meeting their need; He was bringing a renewal of His legacy of peace (14:27). Both His words and His actions were combined to drive away fears. Since they doubted His physical presence, He therefore invited them to touch Him, and He ate in their presence (Luke 24:39-43). Mary was too much attached to Him in a physical sense or relation (on both, see above on 20:17).

"And after He said this, He showed"—pantomime of the most genuine sort backed up His words. "His hands and His side"—His body signs were "signs of ransom and resurrection." Luke (24:39ff) adds the feet to the hands and side. These proved His body was no seeming body. They proved His resurrection was genuine. Except that His body was glorified that it could not die, it was the same, a genuinely real body.

If they looked back, the signs told of the blood shed for their redemption. If they looked on Him, the signs declared that He was truly a man and that it was the identical body, except for glorification so as not to die again, which was placed on the Cross. If they looked ahead, the signs were calls for missionary service.

The Disciples' Vision of Joy, 20:20b

"Therefore"—Their joy was in consequence of what He had said and had done. "Rejoiced"—a second aorist passive in form, but Thayer (1977) rates it as used as an active. Robertson so handled it at 14:28. "The disciples"—after the verb for emphasis on the verb. "Because they saw the Lord"—Causal use of the participle makes fuller sense than the temporal use. (Compare "the vision which begets joy" with "the vision which begets worship, Matthew 28:17.) Luke (24:41) had, "They disbelieved from joy." Terror seized them at first, but unbelief gave way to faith, and belief drove out dreads and let gladness into their hearts!

Jesus' Program of Peace 20:21

"Therefore"—Whatever factors enter into this consequential word, the joy of His own is there. Missionary programs are not launched by doubters. They may dissipate much of the evangelistic fervor of others. Missionary programs are launched by those who live the joy of Jesus Christ day by day. "Again"—we never learn too well His assuring message of peace in Him, whatever tribulations the world continues to heap upon us.

Compare Mark and Luke. Note the statements which link together His commission and ours. One, "according as . . . even so." Any similarity between the two brings encouragement to us. Two, the commissioners: "My Father sent . . . I am sending." He was sent as the Embassy or Representative of His Father; we are sent as servants of the Representative. Three, the one sent: "Me . . . you." His mission was to seek and to save the lost personally and actually; ours is to seek them with the gospel that we save by becoming the means of salvation, the agents getting the saving message to perishing men.

"The first 'Peace unto you' was His answer to their fear, and the argument was Himself, wounded and yet living. The second 'Peace unto you' was preparation for their service, and the argument was His authority to send, demonstrated by His victory over death" (Morgan 1960).

Empowerment of the Spirit Breathed On Them, 20:22-23

"And after He said"—John's way of passing to a new phase. When we wrangle about this passage, we have forgotten the missionary context. We have forgotten that it is Christ's way of empowering His own for missionary service.

"He breathed on [them]"—Although the object is not expressed, it is naturally implied in the compound verb. The preposition suggests the direction of His breathing: on them. *Emphuao*, "late verb, here only in the New Testament though eleven times in the LXX (Septuagint) and in the papyri" (Robertson). He pantomimed His words; this takes the art of gesture to a meaningful height. The "breath" represents life-living power.

"And says"—John transfers to the dramatic historical present to make the words more pungent and striking. "Receive ye"—second aorist imperative of *lambano*, to receive. "He gives"—we receive. They received the Holy Spirit for empowerment and enlightenment.

Luke showed that Jesus opened the understanding of His own and opened the Scriptures.

This was a genuine experience, not just a symbolic promise pointing to Pentecost. This was individual. Pentecost was the public coming of the Holy Spirit, His inaugural day to assume the work of the Lord absent in glory. The imperative refers to the present or the immediate future unless some projection into the future is inserted as a qualifier. "The Holy Spirit"—they already had the indwelling Spirit. This was simply a new empowerment set in a richly meaningful background or situation.

John 20:23: The omission of the conjunction makes the two statements stand in vivid contrast (see also 1:17). The role of the disciples is both negative and positive, and what will help us understand one will help us understand the other. Sins are retained by our not telling them of Jesus' power to release them. Our silence adds nothing to their guilt, but what a solemn responsibility for us as His witnesses. On the other hand, we cannot actually remit sins, but—how wonderful!—we can remit them by giving them the gospel.

Several reasons confirm this view. One, whatever right was conferred by Jesus was conferred to all alike. Peter had no more authority than any other. Whatever Matthew 16:19 means, the others were included in Matthew 18:18. Two, Peter never understood Jesus as giving him supreme power. He was a "fellow-elder" (1 Peter 5:1). Three, making us but instruments in giving the word of salvation gives all of the glory to God and accords with all other Scriptures. The Catholic view sets this verse and Matthew 16:19 against all other Scriptures. "This glorious promise applies to all believers who will tell the story of Christ's love for men" (Robertson).

The word *remit* (KJV) or *forgive* (ASV), twice here, is a rich one. The word is a compound *aphiemi*, from *apo*, away, away from, and *iemi*, to send—hence, to send away. It paints at least three pictures: the fact of sin and man's need to be forgiven; the nature of forgiveness or remission, a sending away or removal of the penalty; the act of remission, which we cannot perform. Only the Lord can meritoriously send our sins away. The perfect, a Doric form, means that the forgiven are in a state of complete forgiveness (Romans 8:33-34).

9.2.2 Jesus' Appearance to His Disciples With Thomas, 20:24-29

The absentee got more attention than the ten who were present (see also Luke 15:2ff). The two movements center around (1) the disciples and Thomas and (2) Jesus and Thomas.

The Testimony of the Disciples, 20:24-25

There are three actions.

THE ABSENCE OF THOMAS, 20:24

"But"—if *de* is adversative, it goes back to the earlier part, as 20:19. "Thomas"—twin, double; Hebrew and/or Aramaic; in Phoenician inscriptions also (see Gesenius' entry on "Thomas"). "One of the twelve"—an official designation although Judas was dead. Not only does the title identify Thomas, it accents the tragedy of his absence. "Didymus"—*diduomos*, Greek equivalent, twin, double, twofold, twain, reduplicated from *duo*, meaning "two" from Homer onward.

"Was not with them when Jesus came"—to John the significant feature. Although coming in spirit as the Risen Lord, should not this be the chief mark which we remember about our services? How much we miss by non-attendance (Hebrews 10:25)!

THE WISDOM OF THE TEN, 20:25A

How wisely they dealt with Thomas; they simply told what they had seen. From this we may learn how to deal with absentees. Do not chide; be positive. "Therefore"—the fact of Thomas's absence led them to concern. "Were saying"—imperfect: repeatedly or enthusiastically said. "We have seen"—more than "we saw" the untellable glow was still theirs. "The Lord"—spoken with a new conviction; it began to break upon them with new significance.

THE DOUBTS OF THOMAS, 20:25FF

A desire to know is commendable; we term it curiosity. Doubt is persistent uncertainty in the face of evidence. Thomas's unbelief was unreasonable. "Unless I may see . . . I will not at all believe." Testimony was not enough. Physical sight and physical feeling alone would be convincing. The double negative ("not at all") bespeaks the stubborn determination of Thomas. Had they mentioned to Thomas the prints which He showed to them? I take "we have seen the Lord" as but the central point or epitome of their witness.

Jesus' Revelation to Thomas, 20:26-29

ALL PRESENT THIS TIME, 20:26

"And"—a delightful continuance. "After eight days"—the second Lord's Day. "Again"—stressing the repeated appearance of Christ to them. "Were inside"—apparently the very same place. "And Thomas with them"—his presence particularly noted.

Jesus' Coming and Message of Peace, 20:26b

Much like 20:19. The varying tenses reflect the moods of emphasis which John gave. How did Jesus enter? His resurrection body had capacities beyond our comprehension. Material doors were no hindrances to Him, but we must not tone down the supernatural to the point of denying the reality of His resurrection body. If we make the problem too simple, we remove the ground of adoration. Let us prostrate ourselves in adoration instead of being plagued with an unbelief worse than that of Thomas at the first.

Jesus Meeting Thomas's Challenge, 20:27-29

There are three striking movements:

1. The challenge of Jesus (20:27): "Then"—a particular moment. "He is saying"—vivid historical present. "To Thomas"—the very man who had doubted most and talked too much. How merciful indeed is Jesus! There was no chiding (see also James 1:5). How did He know what Thomas had said? His answer is too specific to be reasoned away. Since He knew all things, He knew the fact and all of the details. Jesus met every specification precisely.

    "And"—an added caution of importance. "Stop becoming"—negative with present imperative. Jesus knew that doubts might arise again. He would tenderly forestall them. "Unbelieving"—so NASB; "faithless" (ASV) and "stop doubting" (NIV) weaken the contract of *apistos* and *pistos*. The "a" is simply the negative corresponding to "un" in our "unbelieving" in contrast with "believing." Jesus put both the negative and the positive but between them the stronger "but" (*alla*). An effective way to see the beauty of faith is to set it over against the ugliness of unbelief.

2. The confession of Thomas (20:28): Note that Thomas needed not to touch Jesus' hands and side; sight was convincing. No word is said of a change of posture. The nobility of the confession sufficed without any color from John. Thomas rose from the valley of doubt to the plateau of faith in the deity of Christ. "Answered"—replied. Thomas's exclamation and affirmation of faith were a direct response to the earnest plea of Jesus. A personal meeting with Jesus cures more doubts than all of our cogent arguments.

275

The content of his confession is notable. Mary Magdalene (20:18) and the ten (20:25) had used the title "the Lord." Thomas joined them and went beyond them. I have ever felt that my heart should join Thomas rather than my trying to weaken what he said. Two objections or rationalizations have been raised.

One writer claimed that Thomas was unduly excited and used language loosely. Nothing in the context justifies such. John has said just the same (1:1 and 14).

Another claimed that Thomas meant no more than that Jesus was God's representative or ambassador. Such a statement twists the words from their normal meaning. Perhaps the real clue lies in the repeated "my"—when people have an experience equal to that of Thomas.

3. The beatitude of Jesus (20:29): "Says"—a dramatic historical present placed first to stress the fact and content of Jesus' answer. "Because you have seen Me, you have believed"—two facts and a reason. The Greek texts of Westcott and Hort (1881) and Aland and Nestle (1966)[48] make the second clause a question; so also does ASV margin, RSV, and NASB. KJV, ASV, BV,[49] NEB (New English Bible), and NIV make it a statement. Jesus commended the faith of Thomas. Such should settle all quibblings. Unless Jesus was God as well as man, His commendation would be insincere or ignorant. If Thomas became overenthusiastic, why did not Jesus correct Thomas as He did Simon Peter (13:8)?

"Happy"—"blessed" in the sense of happy. One of the truly great beatitudes of Jesus (see also 13:17; Revelation 1:3; 14:13). (Are)—necessary in our idiom; implied in the Greek. "The ones who do not see"—those who lack the material evidence that Jesus graciously gave to Thomas. "And (yet) do believe"—both participles under the same article because they refer to the same persons. Both too are aorist of a definite event. Participles get their time from the main verb—here

---

48. Kurt Aland, Matthew Black, Bruce Metzger & Allen Wikrem, *The Greek New Testament* [also known as the *Nestle-Aland Novum Testamentum Graece*] (Stuttgart: United Bible Societies, 1966).

49. Editor's Note: "BV" may refer to Dr. Beaman's own translation of the Gospel of John, "Beaman Version."

the implied "are." Jesus looked across the centuries, even to us, who have not the evidences of Jesus' and Paul's day, and pronounced a blessing on each. The general use of the perfect here (KJV, ASV, Broadus, NIV) and the NASB's simple past do not stress the nature of the acts as do the simple present or my choice of the emphatic present. Jesus was not contrasting Thomas and someone in that day but providing for and encouraging us. Jesus announced a higher principle of faith than material or physical confirmation. Since, if I may speak for myself alone, I met Jesus who took away my burden and ever puts a fresh song in my heart, I require no bolstering of faith. Faith disclosed Him, the only confirmation that I need. This principle is involved in the present demand for outward signs. Such is a lower type of faith than what Jesus commended!

9.2.3 An Interlude: John's Purpose for Writing, 20:30-31

(30) And many other signs truly did Jesus in the presence of his disciples, which are not written in this book: (31) But these are written, that ye might believe that Jesus is the Christ, the Son of God; and that believing ye might have life through his name. (John 20:30-31)

Is this meant to be the end of the book? Such forgets the strong analogy with 19:35. Such minimizes the logical connection between chapter 20 and chapter 21. Such weakens the singular nature of the epilogue (21:24-25). These three reasons stress rather the logical position of 20:30-31 after four remarkable instances of faith: John (20:8); Mary Magdalene (20:18); the ten, including John (20:20); and Thomas (20:28). Thus the resurrection of Jesus gained believers in His unexampled resurrection and Messiahship.

The Number of Jesus' Signs, 20:30

We have a mere tithe of what He did. "Also"—in addition to the ones narrated. "Therefore"—a general inference from what has preceded. "In the presence of His disciples"—since they would be His prepared witnesses. "Which have not been written in this book"—there was purpose in rejection as well as in selection. The correlatives *men* and *de*—"on the one hand," "but," or "on the other hand"—contrast vividly the signs not selected and the signs selected.

A Purposeful Selection from Jesus' Signs, 20:31

The fact of selection: "but these [things] have been written." A few signs were picked out with a definite design. This is selection with purpose—history through selection. Such is all history. Selection itself is neither a praise nor a mishandling. The quality of selective history lies in what one selects and the way he handles the selected item or items. In "other signs," John used *allos*, like signs, not *heteros*, a different kind of signs. If he had written all that Jesus did, there would be no difference in the nature of the signs.

Whether or not John handled his selected signs reliably depends on three factors: his proximity to the events, the quality of John's character, and the touch of the Holy Spirit. As to the first, John had incalculable advantages over his critics today who count his words unhistorical. As to point two, no one has ever been able to question fairly the character of John as a witness. As to the third, the believing heart has no trouble with believing that the Holy Spirit marvelously guided John in the selection and in the recording of his book.

The purpose of selection: In the beginning of this work, in a practical way, I listed three purposes. More strictly, the purpose is twofold. The first concerns the content of saving faith: the Messiahship and the deity of the Lord Jesus Christ. The second concerns the effect of saving faith: "and that, by means of believing, life you may have in His Name." And ties the two purposes together. One without some intellectual knowledge of Jesus is an empty, colorless, and ineffective faith. "That"—the purpose still kept distinct.

"By means of believing"—predicate or adverbial participle expressing means. Its present tense expresses the distributive force of linear action. That is, each instance of saving faith is an act or event in which one trusts Jesus Christ alone as Savior, but this spreads from one to another. It is not a process. Once one has truly believed into Jesus, he enters upon a life of faith.

"Life"—emphatic position. The gospel was written that men without life might obtain what they do not have. It was written specifically to lost men. "You may have"—again, the distributive force of linear action. The word *have* means "to possess" or "to have as one's possession." The nature of *have* or *possess* is such that one possesses or does not possess life in Christ. The present participle *believing* stresses that one has life the moment the sinner exercises faith. The aorist participle often stresses what is prior to the main verb. The present participle shows, therefore, a closer correlation of saving faith and possessing life.

"In His name"—*En* (in) with the locative tells upon what or where one's faith reposes. *Name* stands for what the Lord Jesus Christ is and does. His is the secret love of all who have trusted Him. No other rivals Him. He is unique, indispensable, and incomparable!

Lessons to emphasize:

- Christ's message of peace

- Signs of ransom and resurrection

- Our missionary commission

- The power of the Holy Spirit (20:22)

- The great responsibility of retaining sins by not being a missionary (20:23)

- How to deal with absentees (20:25)

- A noble confession (20:28)

- The blessing of believing even though we cannot see with the human eye (20:29)

- The gracious purpose of the Scriptures: to lead lost ones to Christ for salvation

---

9.3 Jesus' Breakfast with His Disciples By the Sea, 21:1-14

(1) After these things Jesus shewed himself again to the disciples at the sea of Tiberias; and on this wise shewed he himself. (2) There were together Simon Peter, and Thomas called Didymus, and Nathanael of Cana in Galilee, and the sons of Zebedee, and two other of his disciples. (3) Simon Peter saith unto them, I go a fishing. They say unto him, We also go with thee. They went forth, and entered into a ship immediately; and that night they caught nothing. (4) But when the morning was now come, Jesus stood on the shore: but the disciples knew not that it was Jesus. (5) Then Jesus saith unto them, Children, have ye any meat? They answered him, No. (6) And he said unto them, Cast the net on the right side of the ship, and ye shall find. They cast therefore, and now they were not able to draw it for the multitude of fishes. (7) Therefore that disciple whom Jesus loved saith unto Peter, It is the Lord. Now when Simon Peter heard that it was the Lord, he girt his fisher's coat unto him, (for he was naked,) and did cast himself into the sea. (8) And the other disciples came in a little ship; (for they were not far from land, but as it were two

hundred cubits,) dragging the net with fishes. (9) As soon then as they were come to land, they saw a fire of coals there, and fish laid thereon, and bread. (10) Jesus saith unto them, Bring of the fish which ye have now caught. (11) Simon Peter went up, and drew the net to land full of great fishes, an hundred and fifty and three: and for all there were so many, yet was not the net broken. (12) Jesus saith unto them, Come and dine. And none of the disciples durst ask him, Who art thou? knowing that it was the Lord. (13) Jesus then cometh, and taketh bread, and giveth them, and fish likewise. (14) This is now the third time that Jesus shewed himself to his disciples, after that he was risen from the dead. (John 21:1-14)

The personal overtones of chapter 21 have made it a gem to believing hearts. How Jesus wrought with these men has incalculable lessons for us.

There is no reason why this chapter of John should be ascribed to a different hand. The style is the same as that of the rest of John's Gospel, and although the Gospel closed at the end of chapter 20, this supplementary chapter must have become an integral part of the Gospel at a very early period. No trace exists of John's Gospel without it (Dods 1956, 667).

9.3.1 THE FRUITLESS NIGHT OF FISHING, 21:1-3

John set forth four pictures.

An Explanatory Preface, 21:1

"After these things"—often for a logical turning to a new phase of the writer's topic. "There manifested Himself again"—in addition to other instances in John and elsewhere (the Synoptic Gospels and Paul). It was by decision on Jesus' part that He made Himself known. He was apparently unknown except when He chose to appear. "Upon the sea of Tiberias"—This sea had four names (two more common and two less common). Tiberias, the capital city of Galilee on the west side of the sea, gave the epithet the Sea of Tiberias. The town of Tiberias was built by Herod Antipas about 20 AD on older foundations in honor of the Emperor Tiberius Caesar (Josephus 1984).[50] The present Arabic name is *Bahr Tabiriyeh*. It was a popular winter resort and a great place for fishing, even as I have witnessed today. John 6:1 puts in apposition with one another the two more common names.

They were back in their old haunts in Galilee, but Robertson rightly says this is not the appearance in Galilee prearranged by Jesus (Mark 16:7,

---

50. *Antiquities*, XVIII, ii, 3. And in *Wars* II, x, 1.

Matthew 28:7, 16). Theirs is a defection from the appearances of Jesus on the first and second Lord's Days.

"And Jesus manifested (Himself) in this manner." John seems thus to call attention to the spiritual lessons to be learned. Each appearance disclosed the same Risen Lord, but in a different manner, to prepare the hearts of His own for their mission of witnessing.

A Group of Seven, 21:2

One wonders where the four other apostles were. Even if previous situations be forgotten, Peter's prominence here naturally puts him at the top of the list. The double name recalls the two sides of Simon Peter. "Thomas"—see the notes on chapter 20. "Nathaniel"—the same as Bartholomew, is identified by his town (see the notes on chapter 1). John used the usual reserve about himself. He and James are simply "the sons of Zebedee" and are placed near the last. John later returned to his favorite designation for himself (21:7, 20). The two others were likely only disciples, not apostles.

"It seems to me to be crass criticism in spite of Harnak and Bernard to identify the incident here with that in Luke 5:1-11. There are a few points of similarity but the differences are too great for such identification even with a hypothetical common source" (Robertson, on 21:2).

The Bad Example of Peter, 21:3a

"Says"—vivid historical present for John after decades had passed. Peter was leader again but what leadership! "A fishing" (ASV) stands for the present infinitive. He was going back to his old trade. "I'm going out to fish" (NIV) poorly catches the situation. "I am going fishing" (NASB) is much better. Restless hesitancy of faith was the evident cause of their going back to their former occupation. They were poor and hard-working men, and the marvel is that Christianity survived with such men. Success ever resides in the Risen One. Jesus had called them from fishing for fish to fishing for men (Luke 5:1ff).

The power of a silent example. Peter did not persuade them to go back. He kept his doubts within himself. They became "me too" men. John especially surprises us. "We also are coming with you."

The Unrewarding Night, 21:3b

"They went out"—from wherever they were. "And embarked into a boat"—nothing is said of how they obtained the "little boat." Diminutives (*ploion*, little boat) often wear away the diminutive force. In any case, it was large enough for seven men. And in that night one sees much effort to succeed. "They caught not even one thing" (on the adjective see 1:1). *Piazo*, Doric form of *piezo*, from Homer on down, is in general, "to lay hold of"—as by the hand (Acts 3:7). Specifically, to take hold of in arrest (John 7:30, 32, 44, 10:30, 11:57, Acts 12:4, 2 Corinthians 11:32); to take or seize the beast and the lying prophet. Revelation 19:20, here and 21:10: to catch fish for the striking papyrus instances and the etymology (see Moulton and Milligan 1915 under both verbs, 512).

They learned their lessons. Earthly tasks are fruitless when we are out of duty. One serves men best when he serves God best.

9.3.2 THE SUCCESSFUL CATCH, MAKING JESUS KNOWN, 21:4-6

Jesus Present But Unrecognized, 21:4

"But"—*de*, but, introducing a very different story. There are three movements:

1. The time "while day was already coming to be"—"Coming to be" translates the present participle of *ginomai*, "to become." ASV and NASB turned the verb to the context, "was now breaking," "was now dawning" (Broadus 1886). So, too, have Vincent (1887) and Robertson. KJV, Aland (1966) Greek text, and Dods (1908) follow the aorist participle, one letter of difference (on the data, see Dods). The aorist, strictly "when the day had already come," does not agree so well with the fact that Jesus was not at once recognized by the disciples, owing in part, perhaps, to the imperfect light" (Vincent).

2. The appearance of Jesus: "Took His stand"—(see 20:11, 19 and comments). A definite if not a sudden posture of Jesus. They were evidently not far away upon the water. "Upon the shore" or beach. Some ancient Greek manuscripts have *epi* (upon), not *eis*, toward or to, as if He came to the beach and took His stand there. "Beach"—*aigialos*, the latter half almost surely from *hals*, sea. Thayer (1977) lists three conjectures about the former part.

3. Their unawareness: "However"—in spite of His standing there. "Kept on not knowing"—pluperfect in form but

functioning as an imperfect. "Knew not" (quite common) and "did not know" (ASV) poorly accent John's point of the persistence of their lack of recognition or their unawareness. The imperfect is a time exposure more than a snapshot.

"That it was Jesus"—for vividness the Greek retained, as nearly as the idiom would allow, the tense in indirect discourse that would be used in direct discourse. The Greek has "is"; our idiom requires "was."

His Question and Their Answer, 21:5

"Therefore"—because of the continued lack of recognition; but He chose thus to reveal Himself. "Children"—better, "lads" or "boys," "little children" (Broadus 1886). "Friends" (NIV) is unjustifiable. It is diminutive of *pais* and used here alone by Jesus in addressing His disciples. It is a colloquial expression like "my boys." The aged Apostle John used it in 1 John 2:13, 10 (Robertson). It would be a common term of address for a stranger to men at work.

"You do not, do you, have anything to eat?" The adverb *me* (not) expects a negative answer. Robertson calls this a polite inquiry. I almost dare to call it a "jovial inquiry." Their folly in their self-planned resumption of the occupation was nearly a capital joke! His own do not win apart from Him, do they? "The rare and late word *prosphagion* from the root *phag* (*esthio*, to eat) and *pros* (in addition) was used for a relish with bread and then for fish as here. So, too, in the papyri. Nowhere else in the New Testament" (Robertson). "They answered Him"—thinking some stranger was seeking to buy some fish. A plain "no" was their reply. If they could have known, they would have exclaimed, "Lord."

His Advice and Their Success, 21:6

"And He"—the article with *de* (and) is a common Greek substitute for the personal pronoun; emphatic. Before sunrise and after sunset were considered the best times to fish. In their desperation, they were willing to try any expedient to catch fish. "Man's extremity is God's opportunity." If He had come early in the fruitless night, they would not have welcomed advice. He advised and promised.

"They cast therefore"—His word, their fruitlessness, and perhaps other factors in their minds brought immediate action. "And no longer"— sudden success. "It"—the net, before the verb for emphasis.

"Able or strong enough"—as they had been previously. "The imperfect active picturing the disciples tugging at the net:" (Robertson). "To draw"—draw over the side of the boat so as to secure the fish (Dods 1908). "Because of"—so NASB *apo* (from) with the ablative for cause as "for" (KJV, Broadus, ASV) means here in English. "The multitude of fish"—fish is plural in the Greek idiom.

9.3.3 JOHN'S PERCEPTION OF THE DUPLICATE MIRACLE, 21:7-8

"Therefore"—John perceived the parallels between Luke 5:1ff and their situation. They toiled in vain both times. Jesus became master of the situation each time. They caught many fish both times. John reasoned that it was like Jesus to do it and reasoned that only Jesus could produce such an effect. His meditative nature bore fruit.

"The Lord, it is He." Compare the perception of John in 20:3. John had quicker understanding; Peter acted impulsively. John was the first to recognize the Lord; Peter was the first to reach Him. Each man showed his love in his own way.

I must not pass by this gem from Chrysostom: "When they recognized the Lord, again do the disciples display the peculiarities of their individual characters. The one, for instance, was more ardent, but the other more elevated; the one more eager, but the other endued with finer perception. On which account John was the first to recognize the Lord, before Peter came to him" (Broadus 1886, III, 412).

"Therefore Simon Peter"—better than "now." "Because he heard"—causal participle. Peter put on his coat out of respect to Jesus. "Apparently Peter threw on the upper garment or linen blouse (*ependuten*) worn by fishers over his waistcloth and tucked it under his girdle" (Robertson). God called it "the blouse of a workman." The word is a double compound: *epi*, upon, *en*, in, and *duo* or *duno*, to get into, to go into of clothes and armor, to put on. The Latin borrowed *enduo* as *induo* and built as post-Augustan words *indumentum* and *superindumentum* from *superinduo*, "to put on over other clothes" (Andrews-Freund in Lewis 1956). How similar is Tertullian's *superindumentum* to the Greek *epindutes*.

Since some have cited this to favor nudity, more on this can be said. In the language of that day, "naked" meant "clad in the undergarment only" (Thayer 1977). Trench took the word to mean "stripped for toil" (1854, 185). The most definite illustration is a boy in a papyrus who wrote, "I am going about in rags. I am naked."

"And cast himself"—not middle voice but active with the reflexive pronoun. "Into the sea"—so that he could reach Jesus more quickly (Bengel, 1862).[51]

John 21:8: "But the other disciples"—other than Peter. "In the little boat"—locative case, the article makes "boat" definite, the little one anchored at the edge of the shallows or taken along with the larger boat. A double diminutive *ploiarion* requiring that *ploion* (21:3, 6) be larger. The larger "could come no closer to shore" (Robertson).

Most translations (KJV, ASV, Broadus; not NASB) indicate a parenthesis. NIV rearranges the clauses; I do not call such work translation. "Not far"—at the point of exchange to the smaller boat or where Peter left them. "Observe the unconscious exactness of the eyewitness" (Dods 1908).

"But about"—*hos* and *apo*, an anticipatory use of *apo* (from) with the ablative case. Thayer (1977) and others called this Latin influence, but Moulton (1908, 101) cited both Ionic and Doric warrant for the Koine construction,[52] citing Hippocrates of the fifth century BC.

"Two hundred cubits"—about one hundred yards since a cubit was "a measure of length equal to the distance from the joint of the elbow to the tip of the middle finger" (Thayer 1977). This would mean about eighteen inches, the variance indicated in "about" being debated but less than formerly. *Pechus*, cubit, is genitive plural *pechon*, but the Attic spelling would be *pecheon*. At first men debated. Phrynicus, Atticist of the second century promoting the return to Atticlistic forms, would have none of it. Even the LXX, generally quite strongly Koine, voted for the Attic. Matthew 6:27 and Luke 12:25 have the singular: here and Revelation 21:17, the only other New Testament instances, both have the un-Attic plural. *Pechon* is a contraction of the Ionic *pecheon*. Moulton and Milligan (1915) cite two papyri that give evidence of this, one of the third century BC and one of 127 BC, along with later ones. Xenephon and Plutarch often have *pechon* (Robertson 1934, 263).[53]

Some ask, "Did inspiration save the writers from misspellings in the autographs?" When we answer "yes," we must survey the entire

---

51. John Albert Bengel, *The Critical English Testament: being an Adaptation of Bengel's Gnomon, with Numerous Notes, Showing the Precise Results of Modern Criticism and Exegesis*. Edited by William Lewery Blackley and James Hawes. 3 vols. (Philadelphia: N.P., 1862).

52. Footnote 2 from *Prolegomena*. Of Robertson, see *A Grammar of the Greek New Testament in the Light of Historical Research* (Nashville, TN: Broadman Press, 1934), 110.

53. Footnote 3 from Robertson.

picture. When two spellings were current, neither was wrong. In this case, John followed the popular Koine and not the more erudite Attic.

Although others had a measurement similar to the Hebrew cubit (Latins, Egyptians, and Babylonians), cognates to *pechus* can be cited in only a few languages. Compare Sanskrit *bahu*, Avestan (an Indo-European language found in eastern Iran) *bazu* (arm), and Old Norse *bogr* (shoulder).

"Dragging"—present participle of attendant circumstance going back beyond the parenthesis to "the other disciples." (See also Acts 8:3, "haling" or dragging forcibly.) From Homer down. On the difference between *suro* (here) and *helkuo*, to draw, see 21:6. "With fishes"—KJV, Broadus; better, "full of fishes" (ASV) or "full of fish" (NASB), well phrasing the genitive of content.

The central spiritual lesson here is this: "I am interested in your commonplace affairs. When you obey My voice, My orders, I can make you successful. Get back to My call, and I will give you triumph in winning souls!"

9.3.4 THE MORNING MEAL WITH JESUS, 21:9-14

Five movements characterize the story of fellowship. How could Jesus more pointedly prepare them to be witnesses of His resurrection? The marks of eye-witnessing stand out in more than one detail.

A Meal Ready Prepared, 21:9

"Then"—*oun*; better, "therefore." This was Jesus' initial contribution to the fellowship, an unforgettable proof that His resources could meet all emergencies. "When they embarked to the land"—article with "land," the "land" previously mentioned. "They see"—vivid historical present. "A heap of burning coals"—"a heap of charcoal hot embers." *Anthrakia*, from Homer down, was the source of our "anthracite." In the LXX it is found only here and 18:18 in the New Testament, but anthrax, charcoal, from which it is derived, in Romans 12:20. About twenty-five derivatives exist; they mark "root unknown." Perhaps this is akin to Aramaic *ant'el*, "glowing coal."

"Lying"—present participle of *keimai*, to lie. "Already lying in place"—"lying as placed" (Robertson)—better than NASB, "already laid" as if it were a perfect. Bernard (1929) listed some Old Latin manuscripts as reading *carbones incensos* as if the Greek were *anthrakian kaiomenen*, "a heap of coals burning" or flaming. Bernard, like some others, seems eager to find that the great line of Greek transmission had gone astray. New discoveries point strongly against such looseness. Dr. William Hersey Davis (1942) often warned us against following a stray variant that would overthrow the great and often confirmed mass of Greek manuscripts. It is a peccadillo type of mind against which Davis wisely warned us.[54]

"And a little fish lying upon [it]"—"Lying upon" is simply a compound of the former "lying" by prefixing the preposition *epi* (upon). In our idiom, we have to add the object *it*. By its likely derivation from *pesso, opson,* meant "properly cooked meat, or generally meat." "Fish" was a specialized application, especially at Athens. The diminutive ending *arion* made *opson* into *opsarion,* "little fish." *Ichthus* is the regular word for fish. Is "little fish" collective here, as it may be in certain contexts? The singular stresses His miraculous provision but invites their catch to be added! "And a loaf of bread [lying upon it]"—supply the ellipsis "lying upon it." *Artos* (loaf), from Homer down but with the root dubious, may be collective, though I prefer the singular force.

Sharing Their Catch, 21:10

"Bring"—aorist imperative. "From the fishes"—partitive ablative strengthened by *apo* (from). "Which"—ordinarily accusative but ablative by attraction to the case of "fishes." "You have caught now"—caught by His direction, a solemn fact to be lovingly remembered. "Now" (*nun*) requires in the English idiom that an aorist be rendered by our perfect. Such does not make the tenses interchangeable. (See 21:3 on the verb *to catch.*)

Peter Bringing in the Full Net, 21:11

"Therefore"—encouraged by Jesus' invitation or command. "Went aboard"—see Broadus (1886), ASV margin (1901), Bernard (1929), and Robertson. *Went up* is literal for *anabaino,* but the context refers to Peter's getting on the little boat or dinghy to finish what the others had not done. "Drew"—see 21:6. "Full"—implied above; stated here. "Of large fishes"—*ichtus,* mentioned under *opsarion* in 21:9. "153"—by count and recalled vividly by John. No symbolism needed: the abundant catch showing Jesus' power to make them fruitful is lesson enough. "And"—a remark in contrast to Luke 5:6 where the net was breaking.

---

54. Editor's Note: This may recount a personal conversation between Dr. Roy Beaman and Dr. William Hersey Davis.

"Although there were so many"—genitive absolute. "Was not torn"—
schizo, to split; divide by tearing (19:24) from Homer and Hesiod down:
root of our "schism."

Dining Together, 21:12-13

"Come"—breakfast. From Homer down: at first, "to breakfast,"
"to take breakfast." The verb *aristao,* from *ariston*—the morning meal.
There are two instances in Homer where it is taken at sunrise (so in
Aeschylus). By the time of Thucydides, this refers to the midday meal, as
in Luke 11:37, the only other New Testament instance of the verb.

"No one of the disciples"—simple partitive ablative without *apo,*
as 21:10, so 13:28; *ek* (out of) in 1:40, 7:19. "Was daring"—imperfect of
tolmao, "to dare"—from Homer down. Reason for continued silence later.
"To inquire of"—absolutely, to make inquiry—in LXX, Matthew 2:11 and
10:11 (the only other New Testament instances), often from Thucydides'
time down, in which its specific meanings developed as to inspect troops,
to scrutinize, to cross-examine. Wholly out of tune with the situation,
Bernard (1929) offers only one definition: "to cross-examine." The
disciples never did that in their most careless days during His ministry.
The context is the final arbiter: among the multiple meanings that a
word develops, the task of the exegete is to choose which meaning suits
the context. This, Bernard did not do. A compound; the simple verb not
common; on possible etymology, see *eteos* and *azomai.*

"You who are you?" Since they knew—causal participle. There was
no need for an inquiry. They had special proof of His bodily resurrection.
Note Peter's testimony (Acts 10:40-41). They saw Him standing, sitting,
talking, drinking, and eating. He acted as Host. How compassionate and
kind He was: He wanted their friendly, spiritual fellowship. They needed
spiritual food and strength that He alone could give. He told them to bring
of what they had caught. What glorious cooperation of the human and
the divine. They must learn that He is interested in their physical wants.
He built a fire and prepared breakfast. They must learn that He supplied
their need and would always supply all their needs. The supreme lesson
is: "Success will follow you as long and as far as you follow My direction.
Follow at My command; obey My Word, and success will be yours."

God calls all His children to fish for men (Mark 1:17). Are you
fishing for men or fishing for fish? Are you leading somebody astray
as Peter led his fellow apostles? You stay away from church; someone
sees you and stays away. You go to a show or dance; someone sees you

and is encouraged to sin. Which way does your influence point? How often Jesus is near, and we do not recognize Him! He is near the sinner in the gospel call. He is near the Christian in trouble and sorrow. Are you feasting in fellowship with Jesus?

Numbering the Appearance, 21:14

"This is already the third [time]"—see 20:19 and 26 for the two others on succeeding Sunday evenings. "Was manifested"—active in 21:1-2. "After He was raised"—again, passive.

9.4 Jesus' Outline of Peter's Future, 21:15-25

(15) So when they had dined, Jesus saith to Simon Peter, Simon, son of Jonas, lovest thou me more than these? He saith unto him, Yea, Lord; thou knowest that I love thee. He saith unto him, Feed my lambs. (16) He saith to him again the second time, Simon, son of Jonas, lovest thou me? He saith unto him, Yea, Lord; thou knowest that I love thee. He saith unto him, Feed my sheep. (17) He saith unto him the third time, Simon, son of Jonas, lovest thou me? Peter was grieved because he said unto him the third time, Lovest thou me? And he said unto him, Lord, thou knowest all things; thou knowest that I love thee. Jesus saith unto him, Feed my sheep. (18) Verily, verily, I say unto thee, When thou wast young, thou girdest thyself, and walkedst whither thou wouldest: but when thou shalt be old, thou shalt stretch forth thy hands, and another shall gird thee, and carry thee whither thou wouldest not. (19) This spake he, signifying by what death he should glorify God. And when he had spoken this, he saith unto him, Follow me. (20) Then Peter, turning about, seeth the disciple whom Jesus loved following; which also leaned on his breast at supper, and said, Lord, which is he that betrayeth thee? (21) Peter seeing him saith to Jesus, Lord, and what shall this man do? (22) Jesus saith unto him, If I will that he tarry till I come, what is that to thee? follow thou me. (23) Then went this saying abroad among the brethren, that that disciple should not die: yet Jesus said not unto him, He shall not die; but, If I will that he tarry till I come, what is that to thee? (24) This is the disciple which testifieth of these things, and wrote these things. and we know that his testimony is true. (25) And there are also many other things which Jesus did, the which, if they should be written every one, I suppose that even the world itself could not contain the books that should be written. Amen. (John 21:15-25)

Although Peter and John intertwine somewhat in this story, Peter is the one to whom Jesus directed His words. In fact, where my outline mentions "the work of John," Peter is the one who occasioned such.

9.4.1 THE WORK OF PETER, 21:15-19

Jesus had a special message for Peter. Note the patience of Jesus with Peter. Jesus determined not to let Peter fail to do what He called him to do. Note three questions, three answers, three charges. His restoration needed to be as direct and definite, as clear and public, as his denial had been. The two experiences were never forgotten.

> Peter had denied his Lord by the side of a fire built by His foes. He must now confess Him by the side of a fire built by Himself. Thrice was the denial repeated, and thrice must the confession be made. The contrasts are as striking as are the similarities. The denial was in the darkness of the night, the confession is the dawning glow of the morning. The denial was the answer of cowardice to the sarcasm of hatred; the confession was the answer of courage to the strength of love. The confession, moreover, was of such a nature as to go far beyond the denial. He had denied knowledge of Christ. He now confessed love to Christ. (Morgan 1960)

The First Series of Question, Answer, and Commission, 21:15

The Question: "Therefore"—as a consequence of the recent fellowship and miraculous catch of fish in such a context of desertion. "When they breakfasted"—see 21:12. The ASV and Broadus (1886) chose the pluperfect. "Says"—vivid historical present, very often in John as well as Mark. "To Simon Peter"—both names as a preface to the address of Jesus. "Simon [son of] John"—the genitive is equivalent to our "son of." The fuller idea with "the son" appears at 1:42. "Simon" is still too much a hearer and not sufficiently a rock.

"John"—Hebrew, "to whom Jehovah is gracious." *Jona* (KJV) means "dove." "Do you love Me more than these?"—Grammatically, either more than the disciples (see Mark 14:29) or more than boat, tackle, etc. Both tugged at Peter's heart on occasion. Compare John 13:37 and Matthew 26:33. Luke 24:34 (see also 1 Corinthians 15:5) seems to say that His special appearance to Simon had already occurred. If we could know what passed between them. . . . Anyway, "here Christ probes the inmost recesses of Peter's heart to secure the humility necessary for service" (Robertson).

The Answer: 21:15b. "He says to him"—still vivid narrative to John. "Yes, Lord, You know"—the pronoun is emphatic. "That I am fond of You"—Peter used the humbler and weaker word for love. At long last, he had no desire to assert himself, as on other occasions, since the shame of this desertion pinched his heart. He rather cast himself on Jesus' infallible judgment of his erring heart.

A few stumble at which is the higher and more devoted of the two synonyms for "love." Though I may not cut the Gordian knot here, a little probing may help. Each is stronger in its frame of reference, but which frame of reference is higher and nobler? Jesus' word *agapao* expresses more volition, more conscious attachment, more unswerving devotion in a trying moment. Peter's word *phileo* expresses more emotion, more attachment to a friend. In the light of Peter's temperamental choice to go back to fishing, Jesus sought the stronger and more determined volition.

Bernard (1929) entered two specious objections. One, he argued that a discrimination would make Peter's "yes" mean "no." This would be true if they were antonyms, not if synonyms with only a shade of difference. Two, he urged that John's numbering "second" and "third" "seems to make it plain that the verbs are to be taken as identical in meaning"[55] Fifty years ago I answered a student on this: "Greek has no quotation marks, but such may well be understood." Bernard's argument splits hairs more than it seeks meaning. (His supposition about an Aramaic original has been answered by archaeology. His argument from translations begins at the wrong end.)

The Commissions: 21:15c or charge. Jesus trusted Peter. One qualification for trust and service is love for the Lord Jesus. "Be feeding My fodder"—root of our "botany." The present imperative calls for a continued feeding. This is the work of a genuine pastor, but recall that fishing for men came before feeding sheep (see Luke 5:10 and the former story here). We are to neglect neither. One is not to be set against the other.

"My little lambs"—Both the fact that they are Christ's and that they are little "stresses more strongly the appeal to care" (Dods 1908). *Arnos* has the digamma in Homer. The vernacular multiplied diminutives, urging "a complete absence of diminutive force" in this word, though John followed such a "tendency much earlier than our papyrus writers did in the case of this word." (See Moulton and Milligan 1915.) Until a fuller survey of the papyri appears, I incline toward a diminutive force here.

---

55. *A Critical and Exegetical commentary on the Gospel According to St. John*, additional note, pages 702-4.

The Second Series of Question, Answer, and Commission, 21:16

The Question: Jesus left out all comparisons, made it definitely personal, and kept Peter to the supreme test or issue of love to Him. John however marked it as "again, a second time."

The Answer: Peter left out an appeal to Jesus' knowledge but kept to his lower word for "love." As Jesus showed more tenderness, Peter grew in humility.

The Commission: "Be shepherding My sheep"—Put "little sheep" into the text, a still more endearing term. The task is broader than feeding; it includes all the activities of a shepherd.

The Third Series of Question, Answer, and Commission, 21:17

The Question: John marked this as "the third [time]." Jesus made a concession and used Peter's weaker word. Robertson maintained that a distinction is preserved here. The new question therefore means, "Are you really fond of Me?"

The Answer: Since Jesus challenged Peter's use of the weaker word, Peter was cut to the heart. "Was grieved"—to cause grief, to plunge into grief, to throw into sorrow from Hesiod down. Thayer (1977) calls *lupeo* "the most comprehensive word for grief, "designating every species of pain of body or soul" (see also Trench 1854).[56] Compare Sanskrit *lup*: if interchange between liquids "1" and "r," perhaps Latin *rumpo*, Old Norse *ryf*, and Lithuanian *rupestis*.

"Because He said to him the third [time]"—what a reason! How Peter's mind ran back to his third denial. Jesus did not chide, but Peter's conscience had not died. Peter may have thought that Jesus deemed Peter to be insincere. Why should He not be? Peter's denials grieved Jesus. Love wounds Peter to draw him closer.

"Lord"—more eager than before. "All things do You know"— This is the order of emphasis. *Eter* means "to keep back nothing." "You know"—the pronoun is emphatic. Peter's change from *oida*, "to know," to *ginosko*, "to know by personal experience," lays a tender request upon Jesus. Peter added to his confession and cast himself upon Jesus' full and warm knowledge. The synonyms are discriminated.

The Commission: "Be feeding My little sheep"—see above. Jesus went back to "feed" but kept "sheep." Thayer (1977) discriminated "to feed" and "to shepherd" or "to tend." "The narrower" and "the wider" "denotes nourishment" and "includes oversight."

---

56. Section LXV.

9.4.2 A Trusting Sequel, 21:18-19

Jesus forgave Peter and gave him a responsible task.

Jesus' Prediction, 21:18

The twenty-fifth "verily, verily" in John. All, as I said before, deserve earnest study. "I am saying to you"—marking Jesus' authority. Jesus drew a terrific contrast between Peter's liberty of youth and bondage for the sake of Christ in old age. Once such would have irked Peter's spirit of independence. Christ had stood by Simon in more than one mellowing stage.

"Younger"—comparative degree. "Peter was apparently of middle age" (Vincent 1887). "You customarily girded yourself"—imperfect; from Homer down; *zonnuo*, only here and Acts 12:3 in the New Testament used by women and girls; men, used of girding around the loins of a wrestler or pugilist (see technical word *zone* from this). "Were walking wherever you were desiring"—two imperfects of customary action. "The free activity of vigorous manhood" (Vincent). Indefinite relative adverb of place (*hopou*). "But whenever you become old"—adversative *de* (but). *When* is an indefinite, temporal, relative adverb. *Gerasko*, to grow old, is from Homer down only here and in Acts 12:8 in the New Testament, but the noun *geras* occurs later (the root in our *geriatrics*).

"You will stretch out your hands"—whether we are to read crucifixion here or not is not as important as Jesus' keeping to His metaphor throughout. Bernard's (1929) claim of ambiguity demanded that the metaphor be changed. Dods (1908) and Vincent (1887) are much more likely. "The helpless lifting up of an old man's hands to let another gird him" (Dods). "Here an expression for the helplessness of age" (Vincent). "Another will gird you"—a further amplification of the former idea. "And will carry [you]"—to carry, to bear, to lead, to conduct; *oisei*, future of *phero*, which verb brings in two roots for its second aorist (*enek* or *enegk*) and its future (*oi*). Since these occur in Homer, our earliest remains of Phoenician-like Greek writing, *phero* had to have a long history for such changes or adaptations. This, in my opinion, does much to explain the gap of a century between Mycenaean (c. 1450–c. 1000 BC) materials and Homeric materials. Both futures gave Bernard trouble. They placed the narrator back in the scene described. Who fits this better than John? "Wherever"—earlier in verse. "You are not desiring"—present with negative adverb.

John's Explanation, 21:19a

The following sentence (21:19b) shows that John's explanation is a parenthesis. "Moreover"—*de*. "This thing"—equivalent to this crisp saying. "He said to be signifying"—Purpose may be implied in the attendant circumstance participle of the current translations: "signifying." Perhaps epexegetic is better: "in that He was signifying" (see also 12:33). "By what manner of"—so ASV—better than "by what" (KJV). The word *poios* thus indicates the quality or nature of Peter's death (see also 12:33 and 18:32). "He would glorify"—Bernard (1929) found special difficulty in the future indicative. It "places the narrator back in the scene described, when the martyrdom of Peter was still in the future." Why not accept the historical accuracy of the account? The subjunctive *would* is the English idiom, the Greek future indicative was retained out of respect to the speaker when direct discourse was turned into indirect discourse. On "glorify," see previous discussions. "God"— the article with "God" indicates the true God in contradistinction from false gods, to whom men have sacrificed themselves in meaningless rites. If Peter's martyrdom glorified God, why do I cringe at smaller sacrifices?

Jesus' Command, 21:19b

Broadus (1886) strangely begins a new paragraph. Not so Westcott-Hort (1881) and ASV, but ASV just as strangely does not begin a paragraph with 21:20. "And after He said this thing" ties the new statement to 21:13 and requires that John's explanation be parenthetic. "Says"—again the dramatic historical present.

"Be following Me"—Whom one follows makes all the difference. I often pray, "Lord, if I stumble, let me fall with my face toward You, toward Calvary."

Some make following Jesus a picture of saving faith. The verb *akoloutheo*, to follow, is a compound from the adjective *akolouthos*, on, following, attending on mostly as substantive, follower, attendant, footman, fellow roadman, which is in turn from *a* (alpha copulative). This is "indicating community and fellowship" (Thayer 1977). *Keleuthos*, road, way, path, track, from Homer down by transference, is traveling a journey, a voyage. Curtius (1882) compared the root with Latin *callis* and Lithuanian *kelias* (way) and the verb *keliauju* (to travel). Hence properly, "walking the same road"—a beautiful metaphor from our Lord.[57]

---

57. Georg Curtius, *A Student's Greek Grammar: A Grammar of the Greek Language.* Edited by William Smith. (London: John Murray, 1882).

The metaphor has striking lessons. One, one leads ahead: ours is followership. Two, faithfulness in following is our only vote. Ways which we devise turn aside to detours, swamps, entanglement. There can be no running back. Three, ours is fellowship: sweet, close, rewarding. Sometimes we seem to be not advancing but pausing even in sickness and sorrow for deeper glimpses of His face. Even then, no face, no smile is half so important as His. Four, continuance qualifies the other pictures. Following Jesus is more than a spurt. A road is more than a parking lot. Following Him is an ever-lengthening way or road.

With this agrees the verb each time Jesus asked someone to follow Him. In none of these did Jesus use the aorist imperative, a decisive and definite act of following. I found only the present imperative: *be following, keep on following, make it the custom of your life to follow Me.* Note specific individuals: Jesus to Philip (John 1:43), Jesus to Matthew and Levi [Matthew 9:9, Mark 2:14, Luke 5:27), Jesus to the young, rich ruler (John 19:21), and here to Peter (21:19). The saying about taking one's cross and following Jesus speaks of continuance (Matthew 10:33, 16:38; Mark 3:34). Luke 9:23 adds the word *daily.* John 12:26 speaks of serving Jesus. These beautifully depict the continued following of discipleship. Salvation or saving faith is a decisive experience. Besides and very importantly, if continued followership is a picture of salvation, then one cannot have assurance that he is God's child. He must, on this supposition, follow to the end. We should never misapply to lost people the beautiful metaphor of following Jesus. Peter had no difficulty in knowing what Jesus meant.

9.4.3 The Work of John, 21:20-23

The Question of Peter, 21:20-21

"On turning around"—locative of time force for adverbial participle compound verb, *epi,* on, about, around, and *strepho,* as in 20:14, 16. "Sees"—back to his vivid historical present. Following on verb, see 21:19: actual perception participle after "sees." This verb shows that Jesus and Peter were walking away and that John felt free to follow. How far they had walked is not hinted. "The elaborate description of John in this verse is, perhaps almost unconsciously, introduced to justify his following without invitation" (Dods 1908).

"Who leaned back also"—"also" adds this to "who Jesus was loving." *Anapipto,* to fall up, to recline, to lean back. "Always in the New Testament describes a change of position. It is used of a rower bending

back for a fresh stroke" (Vincent 1887 on 13:25). "At the supper"—
The article directs us to a special meal (John 13 and parallels). "Upon
His breast"—"the breast proper" (see Vincent on 13:25); *stethos* from
Homer down in our "stethoscope." From the common root *sta*, as in
histemi, "to stand." What turn one gives the etymology is sometimes a
subjective matter. Note the following contrast: "That which stands out
is prominent" (Thayer 1977), "implying firmness and strength": "that
which stands out" (Vincent).

"And said"—John lengthens yet more his designation of himself.
Does the question about betrayal remind John of Peter's denials?

John 21:21: "Therefore because he saw this one"—John was the
occasion of Peter's question. Who else could have so reported except John?
"Lord"—Peter meant to be reverent. But this one...what? "The abrupt
ellipsis is intelligible" (Robertson). Jesus fully perceived Peter's staccato
utterance. Compare Jesus' own: "But the nine . . . where?" (Luke 17:17).

The Answer of Jesus, 21:22

"If him I desire"—condition of third class: emphasis on "him" (John)
by position. Jesus was conscious of the right to determine John's destiny.
Each man has his mission: he should be content with it. It was the concern
of John and Jesus alone as to what John was to do. Mind your own business.
Jesus' will is the supreme task for His disciple. His will is that each one follow
individually. "To go on remaining"—infinitive of *meno*, to remain, with stress
on linear action. "Until I come"—*come* obviously a vivid futuristic present
(cf. 14:3). Vincent (1887) and Robertson's "while I am coming" seems to
take for granted that *erchomai* (come) must be linear. Jesus was, I think,
referring to His return after ascension. "To apply it to the coming of Christ at
a disciple's death is a desperate expedient of exegesis: and thus interpreted,
the saying is meaningless, for every one "tarries" until Christ comes in that
sense" (Bernard 1929). "What [is it] to You?" "A sharp rebuke to Peter's keen
curiosity" (Robertson). Peter's impulsiveness again turns out wrong. Simon
Peter was more interested in his future destiny than in his present duty.
Emphatically does Jesus stress the lesson for Peter.

The Correction by John, 21:23

Broadus (1886) wrote a paragraph of this verse. "Therefore"—in
consequence of this statement. "There went out"—means the same as our
"circulated" or "went abroad" (see Broadus). "This word"—The word *logos*
in used in the sense of "report" or "rumor" (see the ASV and the NASB). This

shows us that not all rumors belong to our modern times. Rumors were a part of the ancient culture as well. "To the brothers"—This refers to brother believers. "That"—conjunction introducing the content of the misinformation. "That disciple"—The word *ekeinos* used here by John often is equivalent to our "this" (so strikingly demonstrated by Abbott 1905, *Johannine Vocabulary*). A much abbreviated self-designation of John. "Was not going to die"—obvious stress on present tense of *apothnesko*, "to die." Jesus was rebuking Peter's curiosity, not affirming that John would live on till the Master returned. John is anxious to set the matter straight (see Robertson).

"But Jesus did not say to him that he was not going to die but 'If him I desire to go on remaining until I come, what [is it] to you?'" This clear statement should squelch dame rumor! John's discrimination proves death and the Second Coming are not the same. Even Jesus' words were misunderstood; no need to marvel about ours being misunderstood. John corrected their false ideas, not Jesus' statement.

9.4.4 Epilogue: Jesus' Unrecorded Deeds, 21:24-25

The epilogue falls into two parts centering around the persons included.

A Certificate of Accreditation, 21:24

Any guess that it was added later is no more than a guess. It is just as likely that John was present and added 21:25 immediately.

The identification of John: "This one"—the one just mentioned in 21:20 and often before. "The disciple who is testifying concerning these things"—Note the explicitness. John is identified as is his testimony. "And who wrote these things"—two participles with one article because the reference is to the same person. A third item of identification.

Certification of truthfulness: "And we know"—why the plural? In John 19:35, a quite similar construction is used but with the singular. Is it the editorial "we"? Hardly. Does John include the apostles? He did in 1:14 but with reference to a past incident. Does he include a group of elders in Ephesus? Quite likely. Does he include himself with them? Many think not, but I see no certainty either way.

"True"—for emphasis, the predicate adjective is first. Negatively, they deny untruthfulness and deception. Positively, they affirm credibility and sincerity. The pronoun for our adjective *hids* is likewise emphatic. "His testimony" denies that the writing was by a younger man of their day and affirms that the writer was an eye-witness, for a witness is one who sees, feels, and experiences what he says.

The Fullness of Jesus' Deeds, 21:25

"Moreover"—continuative, most likely to what precedes 21:24 or even quite general. "There are"—This is a Greek idiom which has a singular verb with a neuter plural subject in emphatic position. "Many other incidents also"—literally "things," but the verb *do* implies our "incidents." In addition to what are here selected, see also 20:30-31. "Which He did"—this refers to Jesus. The word order puts the emphasis upon His deeds. "Which"—indefinite relative, but the *Koine* Greek tended to use the indefinite relative for the simple relative. "If"—third class conditional sentence. "Should be written"—present passive subjunctive of *possibility.* "One by one"—literal, "according to one" for completeness. "Not even the world itself"—a hyperbole, an overstatement to stress vastness. A common figure of speech. There is no untruthfulness in it. "I suppose"—Change back to the first person occurs here. We see a discourse verb with accusative of general reference (world) with the infinitive. "Would contain"—hold, have room enough. "The written books"—"How little I have written," John confesses. Selection had been strictly followed, but such selection in no wise invalidated the historical trustworthiness of what was selected. "Records can never express all the facts," stated Morgan (1960). All of the divine life cannot be put in human records. "The greatest of all books produced by man" (Robertson) merely touched the fringes of Christ's vastness! Oh, the sweep and the reach of John's Gospel. John began with the wonder of the eternal Word and climaxed with the infinitudes in Jesus, the God-Man!

9.5 QUESTIONS ON JOHN 20–21

9.5.1 JOHN 20

1. Who was the first believer in the resurrection?

2. What convinced him?

3. To whom did Jesus make His first appearance?

4. How did Jesus reveal Himself to Mary Magdalene?

5. Explain the difference between Jesus' prohibition of Mary's touching Him and His invitation that the apostles touch Him.

6. What is the threefold significance of the signs in Jesus' body?

7. How do Jesus' words to Thomas affect us?

9.5.2 JOHN 21

1. What did Peter mean by "I am going fishing?"

2. How did John recognize that Jesus had appeared?

3. How do these two instances (20:3 and 21:7) index the dispositions or characters of Peter and John?

4. In what sense was Peter "naked" while fishing?

5. Why did the disciples not inquire of Jesus who He was?

6. Wherein do the two words for "love" differ?

7. Is "following Jesus" a picture of saving faith?

8. What is hyperbole?

9.6 SERMON SUGGESTIONS

9.6.1 JOHN 20

[None given.]

9.6.2 JOHN 21

- The Power of Example
- We Can Catch Men for Jesus
- Feed Christ's Sheep
- Following Jesus

SELECTED BIBLIOGRAPHY[58]

Abbott, Edwin. *Johannine Vocabulary: A Comparison of the Words of the Fourth Gospel with Those of the Three.* London: Adam and Charles Black, 1905.

Adams, J. McKee. *Biblical Backgrounds,* 347–399. Nashville: Broadman Press, 1938.

Aland, Kurt, Matthew Black, Bruce Metzger, Allen Wikrem. *The Greek New Testament.* [Also known as the *Nestle-Aland Novum Testamentum Graece*]. Stuttgart: United Bible Societies, 1966.

Alford, H. *The Greek Testament, Critical and Exegetical Commentary.* New York: Harper Publishing, 1859.

Lewis, Charles T., Charles Short, E. A. Andrews, & William Freund. *A Latin Dictionary Founded on Andrews' Edition of Freund's Latin Dictionary.* Revised and Enlarged Edition. Oxford: Oxford University Press, 1956.

Aristophanes Lysistratus. [No citation given.]

Augustine. [No citation given.]

Bengel, John Albert. *The Critical English Testament: being an Adaptation of Bengel's Gnomon, with Numerous Notes, Showing the Precise Results of Modern Criticism and Exegesis.* Edited by William Lewery Blackley and James Hawes 3 vols. Philadelphia: N.P., 1862.

Bernard, J. H. *A Critical and Exegetical Commentary on the Gospel According to St. John,* 702-704. New York: Charles Scribner's Sons, 1929.

Besser, Rudolph. *Besser's Biblical Studies on St. John's Gospel.* This may have been originally entitled: *Christ, the Life of the World: Biblical Studies on the Eleventh to the Twenty-first Chapters of St. John's Gospel.* Edinburgh: T & T Clark, 1862.

---

58. See the Editor's Preface regarding the lack of bibliography sources in the original commentary manuscripts.

Bible, The. [Information listed on the copyright page for all versions used in this commentary.]

Broadus, John A. *Commentary on the Gospel of Matthew*. In *An American Commentary on the New Testament*, ed. Alvah Hovey, 412. Philadelphia: The American Baptist Publication Society, 1886.

Brown, Francis, S. R. Driver and Charles A. Briggs. *A Hebrew and English Lexicon of the Old Testament*. Oxford: Clarendon Press, 1939.

Bruce, Alexander B. *Expositor's Greek Testament*. Grand Rapids: Wm. B. Eerdmans Publishing Company, 1897.

Bucer, Martin. [No citation given.]

Burgon, John: Dean of Chichester Cathedral. [No citation given.]

Burkitt, William. *Expository Notes with Practical Observations on the New Testament*. Philadelphia: Sorin and Ball, 1844.

Carroll, Benajah H. *The Four Gospels*. In *An Interpretation of the English Bible*, 241. Nashville: Broadman Press, 1948.

Century Bible, The. London: Caxton Publishing, 1910.

Church, John Albert and William Jackson Brodribb. *The Annals of Tacitus: Translated into English with Notes and Maps*. London: Macmillan and Co., 1872.

Clark, George W. and J. M. Pendleton. *Brief Notes on the New Testament: The Gospels*, 53. Philadelphia: American Baptist Publication Society, 1884.

Curtius, Georg. *A Student's Greek Grammar: A Grammar of the Greek Language*. Edited by William Smith. London: John Murray, 1882.

Davies, Witton. In *The Century Bible*. London: Caxton Publishing, 1910.

Davis, William Hersey. *Beginner's Grammar of the Greek New Testament*. New York: Harper & Row, Publishers, 1942.

Dods, Marcus. *The Gospel of St. John*. In *The Expositor's Bible*, 2 vols, 164. New York: A. C. Armstrong and Son, 1908.

Dods, Marcus. *The Gospel of St. John.* In *The Expositors Greek Testament.* Edited by W. Robertson Nicoll. Grand Rapids: Wm. B. Eerdmans, 1956.

Douglas, Lloyd C. *The Robe.* Boston: Houghton Mifflin Harcourt, 1942.

Erdman, Charles R. *The Gospel of John: An Exposition.* 35–50. Philadelphia: Westminster Press, 1916.

Geikie, John Cunningham. *The Life and Words of Christ.* 2 vols. New York: D. Appleton and Company, 1879.

Gesenius, H.W.F. *Gesenius' Hebrew-Chaldee Lexicon to the Old Testament Scriptures with Additions and Corrections from the Author's Thesaurus and Other Works.* Translated by Samuel Prideaux Tregelles. Grand Rapids: Wm. B. Eerdmans Publishing Company, 1949.

Gill, John. *Exposition of the New Testament.* London: Matthew & Leigh, 1810.

Godet, Frederic Louis. *Commentary on John's Gospel.* New York: Funk and Wagnalls, 1886.

Gordon, Samuel D. *Quiet Talks on John's Gospel,* 143. New York: Fleming H. Revell Company, 1915.

Gray, George Buchanan. *A Critical and Exegetical Commentary on Book of Isaiah.* New York: Charles Scribner's Sons, 1912.

Hengstenberg, E. W. *Commentary on the Gospel of St. John.* Translated from the German. Edinburgh: T & T Clark, 1865.

Hovey, Alvah. *Commentary on the Gospel of John.* In *An American Commentary on the New Testament.* Philadelphia: American Baptist Publication Society, 1885.

Ingersoll, Col. Robert G. as quoted in *Australasian Record and Advent World Survey,* 15. Vol. 65, 45. Warburton: Victoria, 1961.

Josephus. *Josephus Complete Works.* Translated by William Whiston. Foreword by William Sanford LaSor. Grand Rapids: Kregel Publications, 1984.

Lange, John Peter. *Commentary on the Holy Scriptures: Critical, Doctrinal and Homiletical,* 63 vols. Translated from the German, and edited, with additions, by Philip Schaff. Grand Rapids: Zondervan Publishing House, 1870.

McClymont, John. *Gospel of John.* In *The New Century Bible.* Edinburgh: T C and E C Jack, Ltd., 1901.

McNeile, A. H., ed. *A Critical and Exegetical Commentary on the Gospel According to St. John.* New York: Charles Scribner's Sons, 1929.

Meyer, Heinrich August Wilhelm. *Critical and Exegetical Hand-Book to the Gospel of John.* Translated, revised, and edited by Frederick Crombie. With a preface and supplementary notes to the American Edition by A. C. Kendrick. New York: Funk and Wagnalls, Publishers, 1891.

Miller, Madeleine S. and J. L. Miller. *Harper's Bible Dictionary.* New York: Harper, 1952.

Montaigne. [No citation given.]

Montgomery. [No citation given.]

Moore, G. F. *Judges.* In *The International Critical Commentary.* Edinburgh: T & T Clark, 1966.

Morgan, G. Campbell. *The Gospel According to John,* 47. Grand Rapids: Fleming H. Revell, 1960.

Moulton, James Hope. *A Grammar of New Testament* Greek. Vol. 1: *Prolegomena,* 95–101. Edinburgh: T & T Clark, 1908.

Moulton, J. H. and G. Milligan. *The Vocabulary of the Greek Testament: Illustrated from the Papyri and Other Non-Literary Sources,* 512–581. London: Hodder and Stoughton, 1915.

Norris, John Pilkington. *A Key to the Narrative of the Four Gospels.* London: Rivingtons, 1871.

Paton, Lewis Bayless. *A Critical and Exegetical Commentary on the Book of Esther.* New York: Charles Scribner's Sons, 1907.

Plummer, Alfred. *A Critical and Exegetical Commentary on the Gospel According to St. Luke.* In *The International Critical Commentary.* Edinburgh: T & T Clark, 1902.

Rawlinson, George. *The History of Herodotus.* 4 vols. London: John Murray, 1859.

Reith, George. *The Gospel According to St. John.* In *Handbooks for Bible Classes and Private Students*, 39. Edinburgh: T & T Clark, 1889.

Robertson, Archibald Thomas. *A Grammar of the Greek New Testament in the Light of Historical Research*, 101–671. Nashville, Tennessee: Broadman Press, 1934.

Robertson, Archibald Thomas. *Word Pictures in the New Testament.* 6 vols. Grand Rapids: Baker Book House, 1930.

Rods, Marcus. *The Expositor's Greek Testament*, vol. 1, 667 (Wm. B. Eerdmans Publishing Company, n.p.).

Ryle, J. C. *Expository Thoughts on the Gospels.* 2 vols, 156. New York: Robert Carter & Brothers, 1860.

Schaff, Philip, ed. *A Select Library of the Nicene and Post-Nicene Fathers of the Christian Church.* Vol. XIV: *St. Chrysostom: Homilies on the Gospel of St. John and the Epistle to the Hebrews.* New York: Charles Scribner's Sons, 1889.

Schauffler, A. F. *Training the Teacher*, 102. Philadelphia: The Heidelberg Press, 1908.

Septuaginta: *Id est Vetus Testamentum graece iuxta LXX interpretes edidit Alfred Ralfs.* Deutsche Bibelgesellschaft, 1935.

Skeat, Walter. *The Holy Gospels in Anglo-Saxon, Northumbrian, and Old Mercian Versions Synoptically Arranged with Collations Exhibiting All the Readings of All the MSS Together with the Early Latin Version as Contained in the Lindisfarne MS collated with the Latin Version in the Rushworth MS.* Vol. 4 *St. John.* Cambridge: Oxford University Press, 1878.

Smith, David. *The Gospel According to St. John*, vol. 3. In *The Disciple's Commentary on the Gospels in Three Volumes.* London: The Waverly Book company, Limited, in conjunction with Hodder and Stoughton, 1928.

Speer, John Elliott. *John's Gospel, the Greatest Book in the World: Suggestions for the Study of the Gospel by Individuals and in Groups.* N.p.: Kessinger Publishing, LLC, 1915.

Spinoza. As quoted in Charles Pettit M'Ilvaine's *The Evidences of Christianity: In Their External, or Historical, Division, Exhibited in a Course of Lectures.* Philadelphia: Smith & English, 1852.

Stroud, William. *A Treatise on the Physical Cause of the Death of Christ, and Its Relation to the Principles and Practice of Christianity.* London: Hamilton and Adams, 1847.

Swete, Henry Barclay. *The Gospel According to St. Mark: The Greek Text with Introduction and Notes and Indices.* London: MacMillan and Co., Limited, 1913.

Thayer, Joseph H., trans. *A Greek-English Lexicon of the New Testament: Bein Grimm's Wilke's Clavis Novi Testamenti.* Grand Rapids: Baker Book House, 1977.

Toy, Crawford H. *Proverbs.* In *The International Critical Commentary.* Edinburgh: T & T Clark, 1899.

Trench, Richard C. *Synonyms of the New Testament: Being the Substance of a Course of Lectures Addressed to the Theological Students, King's College, London,* 185. New York: Redfield, 1854.

Vincent, Marvin Richardson. *Word Studies in the New Testament,* New York: Charles Scribner's Sons, 1887.

Wesley, John. [No citation given.]

Westcott, B. F. and Fenton J. A. Hort. *New Testament in the Original Greek.* New York: Harper Publishing, 1881.

CPSIA information can be obtained
at www.ICGtesting.com
Printed in the USA
BVOW04*2232281217
503956BV00008B/41/P